SHAMBHALA

The Resplendent

Nicholas Roerich

Published 2018
Copyright © 2018 Aziloth Books

All Rights Reserved. No part of this publication may be reproduced, stored in a retrieval system or transmitted in any form or by any means, electronic, mechanical, photocopying, recording, scanning or otherwise, except under the terms of the Copyright Licensing Agency Ltd, 90 Tottenham Court Road, London, W1P 0LP, UK, without the permission in writing of the Publisher. Requests to the Publisher should be via email to: info@azilothbooks.com.

Every effort has been made to contact all copyright holders. The publisher will be glad to make good in future editions any errors or omissions brought to their attention.

This publication is designed to provide authoritative and accurate information in regard to the subject matter covered. It is sold on the understanding that the Publisher is not engaged in rendering professional services.

British Library Cataloguing in Publication Data

A catalogue record for this book is available from the British Library

ISBN-13: 978-1-911405-55-9

Cover Illustration: *Sanggye Lingpa*.
Tibetan painting (19th century)

CONTENTS

Note	4
SHAMBHALA, THE RESPLENDENT	6
TREASURE OF THE SNOWS	23
BUDDHISM IN TIBET	28
TIBETAN ART	39
THE VEILS OF DEATH	46
OBSESSION	51
CHINGIZ-KHAN	56
LAKSHMI, THE VICTORIOUS	58
THE BOUNDARIES OF THE KINGDOM	61
HIDDEN TREASURES	63
JALNIK, THE SITE OF COMPASSION	65
GAYATRI	70
DREAMS	74
THE DESERT CITIES	76
LYUT, THE GIANT	79
STAR OF THE MOTHER OF THE WORLD	81
PRAISE TO THE ENEMIES	86
A LETTER	89
URUSVATI	96
SON OF THE KING	107
SUBTERRANEAN DWELLERS	117
LIGHT IN THE DESERT	124
GODS OF KULUTA	142
KING SOLOMON	148
THE GREAT MOTHER	151
JOY OF CREATION	156
GURU - THE TEACHER	164

NOTE

The artist's eye and philosopher's spirit which are Roerich's, are as a magnet. Drawn by their power, there flows into Roerich's being a stream of experiences which he is able to transmute into beauty by that spiritual alchemy which is possessed by the teachers of men.

In *Shambhala the Resplendent*, Roerich has recorded the way of his journey through Central Asia and Tibet in the terms of spirit. It is a record of legends, of parables, of notes - the very substance of which the larger reality is composed, and all revealing different facets of the theme of Shambhala. In this book - as in his other books, *Altai-Himalaya* and *Heart of Asia*, one realizes that Roerich's vision is manifold. Traveling on his way, he discerns all the beauty of the natural spectacle through which he passes. And in his works - as in his paintings - he records this panorama in successive sparks which flow into a continuous pageantry. But in addition, Roerich perceives also that subtler manifestation of the countries and peoples through which he journeys. He discerns their thoughts; he perceives the pulsating, throbbing hopes and beliefs that sweep like winds across space. And it is this record - so little visible to the many of us - that becomes the vital force of Roerich's message.

One must remark the style of Roerich - it has the unrepeatable quality and synthesis of life. He transmits to us the essentials and we discern that these fragments of seeming fantasy are weaving themselves into a pattern of essential truth and essential beauty.

Roerich has named this book, *Shambhala, the Resplendent* advisedly. Reading it, one realizes that Roerich has woven a wreath which he has offered in full reverence to the great Principle which is Shambhala, the New Era; for truly it is the salutary wind of people's thought and faith which will aid the fires of Shambhala. And once again, as in all the deeds of his inexhaustible creative fervor, Roerich's *Shambhala, the Resplendent* pronounces the evocation of the fires of new human achievement and a new human destiny.

Kuluta. Nicholas Roerich (1936)

SHAMBHALA, THE RESPLENDENT

"Lama, tell me of Shambhala!" "But you Westerners know nothing about Shambhala - you wish to know nothing. Probably you ask only out of curiosity; and you pronounce this sacred word in vain."

"Lama, I do not ask about Shambhala aimlessly. Everywhere, people know of this great symbol under different names. Our scientists seek each spark concerning this remarkable realm. Csoma de Koros knew of Shambhala, when he made his prolonged visit to the Buddhist monasteries. Grunwedel translated the book of the famous Tashi Lama, Pal-den ye -she, about 'The Way to Shambhala.' We sense how, under secret symbols, a great truth is concealed. Truly, the ardent scientist desires to know all about Kalachakra."

"Can this be so, when some of your Western people desecrate our temples? They smoke within our holy sanctuaries; they neither understand nor wish to venerate our faith and our teaching. They mock and deride the symbols whose meaning they do not penetrate. Should we visit your temples, our conduct would be completely different, because your great Bodhisattva, Issa, is verily an exalted one. And none of us would defame the teaching of mercy and righteousness."

"Lama, only the very ignorant and stupid would ridicule your teaching. All the teachings of righteousness are as in one sacred place. And each one possessed of his senses, will not violate the sacred places. Lama, why do you think that the essential teaching of the Blessed One is unknown to the West? Why do you believe that in the West we do not know of Shambhala?

"Lama, upon my very table you may see the Kalachakra, the Teaching brought by the great Atticha from India. I know that if a high spirit, already prepared, hears a voice proclaiming *Kalagiya* it is the call to Shambhala. We know which Tashi Lama visited Shambhala. We know the book of the High Priest, T'aishan - 'The Red Path to Shambhala.' We even know the Mongolian song about Shambhala. Who knows - perhaps we even know many things new to you. We know that quite recently a young Mongolian lama issued a new book about Shambhala."

The Lama studies us with his piercing glance. Then he says:

"Great Shambhala is far beyond the ocean. It is the mighty heavenly domain. It has nothing to do with our earth. How and why do you earthly people take interest in it? Only in some places, in the Far North, can you discern the resplendent rays of Shambhala."

"Lama, we know the greatness of Shambhala. We know the reality of this indescribable realm. But we also know about the reality of the earthly Shambhala. We know how some high lamas went to Shambhala, how along their way they saw the customary physical things. We know the stories of the Buryat lama, of how he was accompanied through a very narrow secret passage. We know how another visitor saw a caravan of hill-people with salt from the lakes, on the very borders of Shambhala. Moreover, we ourselves have seen a white frontier post of one of the three outposts of Shambhala. So, do not speak to me about the heavenly Shambhala only, but also about the one on earth; because you know as well as I, that on earth Shambhala is connected with the heavenly one. And in this link, the two worlds are unified." The Lama becomes silent. With eyes half concealed by the lids, he examines our faces. And in the evening dusk, he commences his tale: "Verily, the time is coming when the Teaching of the Blessed One will once again come from the North to the South. The word of Truth, which started its great path from Bodhigaya, again shall return to the same sites. We must accept it simply, as it is: the fact that the true teaching shall leave Tibet, and shall again appear in the South. And in all countries, the covenants of Buddha shall be manifested. Really, great things are coming. You come from the West, yet you are bringing news of Shambhala. We must take it verily so. Probably the ray from the tower of Rigden-jyepo has reached all countries.

"Like a diamond glows the light on the Tower of Shambhala. He is there - Rigden-jyepo, indefatigable, ever vigilant in the cause of mankind. His eyes never close. And in his magic mirror he sees all events of earth.

And the might of his thought penetrates into far-off lands. Distance does not exist for him; he can instantaneously bring assistance to worthy ones. His powerful light can destroy all darkness. His immeasurable riches are ready to aid all needy ones who offer to serve the cause of righteousness. He may even change the karma of human beings…"

"Lama, it seems to me that you speak of Maitreya; is it not so?"

"We must not pronounce this mystery! There is much which may not be revealed. There is much which may not be crystallized into sound. In sound we reveal our thought. In sound we project our thought into space and the greatest harm may follow. Because everything divulged before the destined date, results in untold harm. Even the greatest catastrophes may be provoked by such light-minded acts. If Rigden-jyepo and the Blessed Maitreya are one and the same for you - let it be so. I have not so stated!

"Uncountable are the inhabitants of Shambhala. Numerous are the splendid new forces and achievements which are being prepared there for humanity…"

"Lama, the Vedanta tells us that very soon new energies shall be given to humanity. Is this true?"

"Innumerable are the great things predestined and prepared. Through the Holy Scriptures we know of the Teaching of the Blessed One about the inhabitants of the distant stars. From the same source we have heard of the flying steel bird . . . about iron serpents which devour space with fire and smoke. Tathagata, the Blessed One, predicted all for the future. He knew how the helpers of Rigden-jyepo would be reincarnated in due time; how the sacred army would purge Lhassa of all its nefarious enemies; and how the realm of righteousness would be established."

"Lama, if the great warriors are incarnated, will not the activities of Shambhala take place here on our earth?"

"Everywhere - here and in heaven. All benevolent forces shall come together to destroy the darkness. Each one who will help in this great task shall be rewarded a hundred-fold and upon this very earth, in this incarnation. All sinners against Shambhala will perish in this very incarnation, because they have exhausted mercy."

"Lama, you know the truth. Then tell me why there are so many unworthy priests."

"Certainly this is not an excuse: but if the Teaching must move to the South then it is not surprising that many learned lamas have left Tibet. In the West, do they know that Pan-chen-rinpoche (the Tashi Lama) is connected with Shambhala?"

"Lama, we certainly know that Pan-chen-rinpoche is greatly esteemed everywhere. In different countries we have heard how highly not only Buddhists, but the people of many nations, talk about His Holiness. It is even said that in his private apartments, long before his departure, the details of his coming travels were outlined in the frescoes. We know that Pan-chen-rinpoche follows the customs of all the great lamas. We have been told how during his flight he and his followers escaped many of the greatest dangers.

"We know how at one time his pursuers from Lhassa were already quite upon him, when a heavy snowfall cut off the pursuers' road. Another day, Pan-chen-rinpoche arrived at a lake in the mountains; a difficult problem confronted him. His enemies were close behind; but in order to escape, it would be necessary for him to make a long circuit around the lake. Thereupon, Pan-chen-rinpoche sat in deep meditation for some time. Arousing himself, he gave orders, that despite the danger, the entire caravan would have to spend the night on the shores of the lake. Then the unusual happened: During the night, a heavy frost arose, which covered the lake with ice and snow. Before sunrise, while it was still dark, Tashi Lama gave orders to his people to move on speedily, and he, with his three hundred followers, crossed the lake over the ice by the shortest way, thus escaping danger. When the enemies arrived at the same spot, the sun was already high and its rays had melted the ice. There remained for them only the roundabout way. Was it not so?"

"Verily, so it was. Pan-chen-rinpoche was helped by Holy Shambhala throughout his travels. He saw many wondrous signs when he crossed the uplands hastening to the North."

"Lama, not far from Ulan-Davan we saw a huge black vulture which flew low, close to our camp. He crossed the direction of something shining and beautiful, which was flying south over our camp, and which glistened in the rays of the sun."

The eyes of the Lama sparkled. Eagerly he asked:

"Did you also feel the perfumes of the temple-incenses in the desert?"

"Lama, you are quite right - in the stony desert, several days from any habitation, many of us became simultaneously aware of an exquisite breath of perfume. This happened several times. We never smelt such lovely perfume. It reminded me of certain incense which a friend of mine once gave me in India - from where he obtained it, I do not know."

"Ah - you are guarded by Shambhala. The huge black vulture is your enemy, who is eager to destroy your work, but the protecting force from Shambhala follows you in this Radiant form of Matter. This force is always near to you but you cannot always perceive it. Sometimes only, it is manifested for strengthening and directing you. Did you notice the direction in which this sphere moved? You must follow the same direction. You mentioned to me the sacred call - *Kalagiya*! When some one hears this imperative call, he must know that the way to Shambhala is open to him. He must remember the year when he was called, because from that time evermore, he is closely assisted by the Blessed Rigden-jyepo. Only you must know and realize the manner in which people are helped, because often people repel the help which is sent."

"Lama, tell me how are the simple people helped by Shambhala? We know of the adepts and of incarnate co-workers of Shambhala. But in what manner does the might of Shambhala manifest itself among the humble?"

"In untold and manifold ways. Each one who in previous incarnations followed the teaching of righteousness and was useful to the Common Cause, is helped by this Common Cause. Not many years ago during the war and unrest, one man asked a lama if he should change his dwelling. The lama answered that he could remain in the same place for about six months longer, but that afterwards he would be in great danger and would have to flee without delay. During the six months which followed, the man was most successful in his work; everything was peaceful and his possessions multiplied. When the six months had expired, he thought, 'Why should I risk my property by leaving this quiet spot? Everything seems so prosperous for me and there is apparently no danger. Probably the lama was mistaken.'

"But the cosmic flux was not arrested. And the predestined danger suddenly arose. The troops of the enemies approached the place at full speed from both directions. And the man realized that his best opportunity had been lost and his way was now cut off. He hurried to the same lama and told him of what had happened.

"The lama told him that for certain reasons it was necessary that he be saved - 'But,' he added, 'it is now more difficult to help you. The best opportunity is lost, but I still can do something for you. To-morrow, take your family with you and ride towards the North. On the road you will meet your enemies. This is inevitable. When you see them coming, go away from the road and remain quiet. Even though they may approach you, even though they speak to you, remain quiet and unmoving until they pass.'

"So it happened. The man, with his family and belongings, set out at early morning. Suddenly in the dusk of morning, they distinguished the outlines of soldiers rapidly approaching. They turned aside from the road and stood silent, tense.

"The soldiers hurriedly approached, and the poor man heard one of them shouting, 'Here they are. I see people here. Probably there is a nice booty for us.'

"Another one laughingly answered him, 'Friend, you probably slept poorly last night, since you cannot distinguish stones from humans. They are quite near us and you say that they are not stones!'

"The first one insisted, 'But I even see a horse!' The other one laughed.

" 'On such a stony horse, you will not ride far. Could you imagine that a horse, aware of all our horses, would remain immovable?'

"The soldiers all laughed heartily and, deriding the mistake of the first one, passed quite close to the immovable group. They then disappeared into the mist. Thus, even in the most difficult situation, the man was saved. For he had been useful to Shambhala just once.

"Shambhala knows all. But the secrets of Shambhala are well guarded."

"Lama, how are the secrets of Shambhala guarded? It is said that many co-workers of Shambhala, many messengers, are speeding through the world. How can they preserve the secrets entrusted to them?"

"The great keepers of mysteries are watching closely all those to whom they have entrusted their work and given high missions. If an unexpected evil confronts them they are helped immediately. And the entrusted treasure shall be guarded. About forty years ago, a great secret was entrusted to a man living in the Great Mongolian Gobi. It was told to him that he could use this secret for a special purpose, but that when he felt his departure from this world approaching, he should find some one worthy to whom to entrust this treasure. Many years passed. Finally this man became ill and during his illness, an evil force approached him and he became unconscious. In such a state he could, of course, not find any one worthy to whom to entrust his treasure. But the Great Keepers are ever vigilant and alert. One of them from the high Ashram hurriedly started through the mighty Gobi, remaining more than sixty hours without rest in the saddle. He reached the sick man in time to revive him and, though only for a short time, it permitted him to find some one to whom he might transmit the message. Perhaps you may wonder why the Keeper did not take the Treasure with him. And why the same succession had to take place. Because great Karma has its own ways and even the greatest Keepers of mysteries sometimes do not wish to touch the threads of Karma. Because each thread of Karma, if broken, results in the greatest harm."

"Lama, in Tourfan and in Turkestan they showed us caves with long, unexplored passages. Can one reach the Ashrams of Shambhala through these routes? They told us that on some occasions, strangers came out of these caves and went to the cities. They wished to pay for things with strange, ancient coins which are now no longer used."

"Verily, verily, the people of Shambhala at times emerge into the world. They meet the earthly co-workers of Shambhala. For the sake of humanity, they send out precious gifts, remarkable relics. I can tell you many stories of how wonderful gifts were received through the space. Even Rigden-jyepo himself appears at times in human body. Suddenly he shows himself in holy places, in monasteries, and at a time predestined, pronounces his prophecies.

"By night or at early morning before sunrise, the Ruler of the World arrives in the Temple. He enters. All the lamps at once kindle themselves. Some already recognize the Great Stranger. In deep reverence the lamas gather. They listen with the greatest attention to the prophecies of the future.

"A great epoch approaches. The Ruler of the World is ready to fight. Many things are being manifested. The cosmic fire is again approaching the earth. The planets are manifesting the new era. But many cataclysms will occur before the new era of prosperity. Again humanity will be tested, to see if the spirit has progressed sufficiently. The subterranean fire now seeks to find contact with the fiery element of the Akasa; if all good forces do not combine their power, the greatest cataclysms are inevitable. It is related how the blessed Rigden-jyepo manifests himself, to give commands to his messengers; how on the black rock, on the way to Ladak, the mighty ruler appears. And from all directions, the messenger-riders approach in deep reverence to listen; and in full speed they rush to fulfil what is ordained by the great wisdom."

"Lama, how does it happen that Shambhala on earth is still undiscovered by travelers? On maps you may see so many routes of expeditions. It appears that all heights are already marked and all valleys and rivers explored."

"Verily, there is much gold in the earth, and many diamonds and rubies in the mountains, and every one is so eager to possess them! And so many people try to find them! But as yet these people have not found all things - so, let a man try to reach Shambhala without a call! You have heard about the poisonous streams which encircle the uplands. Perhaps you have even seen people dying from these gases when they come near them. Perhaps you have seen how animals and people begin to tremble when they approach certain localities. Many people try to reach Shambhala, uncalled. Some of them have disappeared forever. Only few of them reach the holy place, and only if their karma is ready."

"Lama, you speak of an holy place on earth. Is there a rich vegetation there?

The mountains seem barren and the hurricanes and all-devastating frosts seem unusually severe."

"In the midst of high mountains there are unsuspected enclosed valleys. Many hot springs nourish the rich vegetation. Many rare plants and medicinal herbs are able to flourish on this unusual volcanic soil. Perhaps you have noticed hot geysers on the uplands. Perhaps you have heard that only two days away from Nagchu where there is not a tree or plant to be seen, there is one valley with trees and grass and warm water. But who may know the labyrinths of these mountains? Upon stony surfaces it is impossible to distinguish human traces. One cannot understand the thoughts of people - and he who can, is silent! Perhaps you have met numerous travelers during your wanderings - strangers, simply attired, walking silently through the desert, in heat or cold, toward their unknown goals. Do not believe, because the garment is simple, that the stranger is insignificant! If his eyes are half closed, do not presume that his glance is not keen. It is impossible to discern from which direction power approaches. In vain are all warnings, in vain are all prophecies - but only by the one path of Shambhala can you attain achievement. By addressing yourself directly to the Blessed Rigden-jyepo you can succeed."

"Lama, you said that the enemies of Shambhala would perish. How will they perish?"

"Verily, they perish in due time. They are destroyed by their own nefarious ambitions. Rigden-jyepo is merciful. But the sinners are their own assailants. Who can say when the merited wage is given? Who can discern when help is truly needed? And what shall be the nature of that help? Many upheavals are necessary and have their purposes. Just when our limited human understanding is convinced that all is destroyed, that all hope is perished, then the creative hand of the Ruler projects his powerful ray.

"How are sinners annihilated? One lama-painter had the exalted gift of painting with incomparable beauty, the sacred images. Superbly he painted the images of Rigden-jyepo and the Blessed Buddha and Dukhar, the All-seeing. But another painter became jealous and in his wrath determined to harm the righteous one. And when he started to slander the lama-painter, his house caught fire from some unknown cause. All his possessions were destroyed and the hands of the slanderer were seriously burnt so that for long he was unable to work.

"Another calumniator threatened to destroy all the labors of an honest man. And he himself was drowned shortly after, while crossing Tsampo. Another man, who performed many a beautiful deed for charity, was attacked by some one, who sought to destroy all the possessions which had been dedicated to the cause of humankind. But again the powerful ray of Rigden-jyepo reached the assailant and in a day his wealth was swept away and he became a beggar. Perhaps you may see him even now, begging at the Lhassa bazaar.

"In every city you may hear how those unworthy creatures who turned their venom against worthy ones, were punished. Only by the path of Shambhala may you walk safely. Each diversion from this road of glory will embroil you in the greatest dangers. Everything on earth may be searched and meted out. Not faith nor blind worship does the Blessed One ordain, but the knowledge of experience."

"It is so, Lama. I can also tell you how one of our near ones became a brother of Shambhala. We know how he came to India on a scientific mission, how he was suddenly lost from the caravan and how, long afterwards, an unexpected message revealed the news that he was in Shambhala.

"I can tell you how, from distant Altai, many Old Believers went to seek for the so-called 'Belavodye' (White waters) and never returned. I have heard the names of the mountains, rivers and lakes which lie on the way to the holy places. They are secret; some of the names are corrupted, but you discern their fundamental truth.

"I can tell you how a worthy student of this exalted teaching set out to reach Shambhala, before the time ordained for him. He was a pure and sincere spirit, but his karma had not been exhausted and his earthly task was still undone. It was premature for him, and one of the great Masters met him on horseback in the mountains and personally spoke to this aspiring traveler. Mercifully and compassionately he sent him back to complete his unfinished labors. I can tell you of Ashrams beyond Shigatse. I can tell you how the Brothers of Shambhala appeared in various cities and how they prevented the greatest human calamities, when humanity worthily understood them… Lama, have you met Azaras and Kuthumpas?"

"If you are familiar with so many incidents, you must be successful in your work. To know so much of Shambhala is in itself a stream of purification. Many of our people during their lives have encountered the Azaras and Kuthumpas and the snow people who serve them. Only recently have the Azaras ceased to be seen in cities. They are all gathered in the mountains. Very tall, with long hair and beards, they appear outwardly like Hindus. Once, walking along the Brahmaputra, I saw an Azara. I strove to reach him, but swiftly he turned beyond the rocks and disappeared. Yet I found no cave or cavern there - all I saw was a small Stupa. Probably he did not care to be disturbed.

"The Kuthumpas are no longer seen now. Previously they appeared quite openly in the Tsang district and at Manasarowar, when the pilgrims went to holy Kailasa. Even the snow people are rarely seen now. The ordinary person, in his ignorance, mistakes them for apparitions. There are profound reasons why, just now, the Great Ones do not appear so openly. My old teacher told me much of the wisdom of the Azaras. We know several places where these Great Ones dwelt, but for the moment these places are deserted. Some great reason, great mystery!"

"Lama, then it is true that the Ashrams have been moved from the vicinity of Shigatse?"

"This mystery must not be uttered. I already said that the Azaras may no longer be found in Tsang."

"Lama, why do your priests claim that Shambhala is far beyond the ocean, when the Shambhala of earth is far closer? Csoma de Koros even mentions, with justification, the place - the wondrous mountain-valley, where the initiation of Buddha was held."

"I have heard that Csoma de Koros reaped misfortune in life. And Grunwedel, whom you mentioned, became insane; because they touched the great name of Shambhala out of curiosity, without realizing its stupendous significance. It is dangerous to toy with fire - yet fire can be of the greatest use for humanity. You have probably heard how certain travelers attempted to penetrate into the forbidden territory and how guides refused to follow them. They said, 'Better to kill us.' Even these simple folk understood that such exalted matters may be touched only with utmost reverence.

"Do not outrage the laws! Await in ardent labor until the messenger of Shambhala shall come to you, amid constant achievement. Await until the Mighty-voiced shall utter, '*Kalagiya.*' Then you may safely proceed to expound this superb matter. Vain curiosity must be transformed into sincere learning, into application to the high principles of everyday life."

"Lama, you are a wanderer. Where shall I find you once again?"

"I beg you, do not ask my name. Moreover, should you meet me in some city, or in any other inhabited place, do not recognize me. I shall approach you."

"And if I should approach you, would you merely depart or would you in some way hypnotize me?"

"Do not force me to utilize these natural forces. Among certain Red Sects, it is permitted to apply certain powers. But we may only utilize them in exceptional cases. We must not break the laws of nature. The essential Teaching of our Blessed One bids us be cautious in revealing our inner possibilities."

"Lama, tell me further, if you have personally seen Rigden-jyepo."

"No, I have not yet seen the Ruler in the flesh. But I have heard His Voice. And during the winter, while the frost lay over the mountains, a rose - a flower from the far-off valley - was His gift to me. You ask me so much that I can see you are grounded in many matters. What would you do, should I begin to examine you?"

"Lama, I should be silent."

The Lama smiled: "So, you do know much. Perhaps you even know how to use the forces of nature, and how in the West during the last few years, many signs were witnessed, especially during the war, which you, or one of you, started."

"Lama, certainly such unprecedented slaughter of human beings must have precipitated an unexpected flow of reincarnations. So many people died before the predestined hour and through such occurrences, so much was distorted and upheaved."

"Probably you did not know the prophecies by which these calamities were foretold long since. If only you would have known, you could never have begun this horrible holocaust."

"If you know of Shambhala, if you know how to utilize your latent natural forces, you also must know of Namig, the Heavenly Letters. And you will know how to accept the prophecies of the future."

"Lama, we have heard that all the journeys of Tashi Lama and the Dalai Lama were foretold in the prophecies, long before they occurred."

"I repeat, that in the private apartments of the Tashi Lama, at his order, were painted all the events of his future travels. Often unknown strangers report these prophecies, and you can see and hear evident signs of approaching events.

"You know, that near to the entrance of the great temple of Geser Khan, there are two horses - a white and a red one. And when Geser Khan is approaching, those horses neigh. Have you heard that recently this great sign occurred, and many people heard the neighing of the sacred horses?"

"Lama, you mentioned the third great name of Asia…"

"Mystery, mystery, you must not speak too much. Sometime we shall speak to one very learned Geshe of Moru-ling. This monastery was founded by our Dalai Lama the Great, and the sound of the Great Name is part of the name of the monastery. It is said that before leaving Lhassa forever, the great Dalai Lama had a mysterious communion in this monastery. Verily, from this monastery, several lamas disappeared for great new tasks.

"There you could find something familiar to yourself."

"Lama, can you tell me something of the three greatest monasteries near Lhassa - Sera, Ganden and Depung?"

The Lama smiled. "Oh, they are great official monasteries. At Sera, among the three thousand lamas, you can find many real fighters. Many lamas of foreign countries, such as Mongolia, are in Ganden. There is the chair of our great Teacher, Tsong-kha pa. No one can touch this great seat without trembling. Depung has also some learned lamas."

"Lama, are there some hidden passages under the Potala? And is there a subterranean lake under the chief temple?"

The Lama again smiled. "You know so many things that it seems to me you have been at Lhassa. I do not know when you have been there. It makes little difference if you were there now or in other garments. But if you have seen this subterranean lake, you must have been either a very great lama, or a servant bearing a torch. But as a servant you could not know the many things which you have told me. Probably you know also that in many places of Lhassa there are hot springs and in some houses, people use this water for their household."

"Lama, I have heard how some animals - deer and squirrels and jackals - approach the meditating lamas in the caves of the Himalayan forests; and how apes and monkeys sometimes bring them their food."

"On my part, I shall ask you, what is impossible? But one thing is evident, that a deer would not approach a human being in a city because only rarely do you find well-intentioned people in these crowded places. Humanity does not know the significance and the definite effect of auras; they do not realize that not only human beings, but even inanimate objects, have their significant and effectual auras."

"Lama, we know about it and we have even begun to photograph auras. And as for inanimate objects, Lama, we know also something about the Chair of the Master, and how this Chair must not be touched by any one. In this way the presence of the Great One is always near."

"If you know the value of such a venerated armchair, then you know the meaning of Guruship. Guruship is the highest relation we can attain in our earthly garb. We are guarded by Guruship and we ascend to perfection in our esteem to the Guru. He who knows the essential meaning of the Guru will not speak against relics. In the West you have also some portraits of dear ones and you have great esteem for symbols and the objects used by your forefathers and great leaders. So do not take it as idolatry, but only as a deep veneration and remembrance of the work performed by some one great. And it is not alone this external veneration, but if you know something of psychical emanation from objects, then you also know about natural magic. What do you think of the magic scepter which indicates the subterranean riches of earth?"

"Lama, we know many stories everywhere about the strange power of this moving stick, through which many mines, springs and wells are located."

"And who do you think is working in these experiments, the stick or the man?"

"Lama, I think that the stick is a dead thing, whereas man is full of vibration and magnetic power. So that the stick is only as a pen in a hand."

"Yes, in our body everything is concentrated. Only know how to use it, and how not to misuse it. Do you in the West know something about the Great Stone in which magic powers are concentrated? And do you know from which planet came this stone? And who possessed this treasure?"

"Lama, about the Great Stone we have as many legends as you have images of Chintamani. From the old Druidic times many nations remember these legends of truth about the natural energies concealed in this strange visitor to our planet. Very often in such fallen stones are hidden diamonds, but these are nothing in comparison with some other unknown metals and energies which are found every day in the stones and in the numerous currents and rays.

"*Lapis Exilis*, thus is named the stone, which is mentioned by the old Meistersingers. One sees that the West and East are working together on many principles. We do not need to go to the deserts to hear of the Stone. In our cities, in our scientific laboratories, we have other legends and proofs. Would any one have thought that the fairy tales regarding the flying man would ever be fulfilled? Yet now, each day's mail, each day's visitors, may come flying."

"Certainly the Blessed One said long ago that steel birds would fly in mid-air. But at the same time, without the necessity of lifting such heavy masses, we are able to soar in our subtler bodies. You Westerners always dream of ascending Mount Everest in heavy boots; but we reach the same heights and far higher summits without trouble. It is necessary only to think, to study, to remember and to know how to grasp consciously all one's experiences in the finer bodies. Everything has been indicated in the Kalachakra, but only few have grasped it. You in the West, with your limited apparati, can hear sounds at long distances. You can catch even the cosmic sounds. But long ago Milaraspa, without any apparati, could hear all the supreme voices."

"Lama, is it true that Milaraspa in his young days was not a man of spirit? Somewhere we have read that he even killed the entire family of his uncle. How, then, can such a man become a spiritually developed being after such excesses of wrath and even murder?"

"You are right. In his youth, Milaraspa not only killed this family but probably committed many other heinous crimes. But the ways of the spirit are inexplicable. From one of your missionaries, we have heard of your Saint, named Francis. Yet in his youth he also committed many offenses, and his life was not so pure. Then how could he in one lifetime attain such perfection as to make him esteemed in the West as one of the most exalted of saints? From your missionaries, who visited Lhassa in former centuries, we have learned many tales; and some of your books are in our libraries. It is said that books of your gospel may be found sealed in some of our Stupas. Perhaps we know better than yourselves how to venerate foreign religions."

"Lama, it is so difficult for us Westerners to venerate your religion, because many things are so confused, many things are corrupted. For instance, how could a stranger, on seeing two monasteries completely alike in exterior, understand that in one, Buddhism is preached, while the other is the bitterest enemy of Buddhism. Even if one enters these monasteries, one sees almost the same images superficially. Thus, for a stranger to distinguish whether a Swastika is turned in an inverse direction or not, is as difficult, as to understand why the same iconography can act for and against Buddha. It is difficult for an outsider to understand why people who are completely illiterate and given to drink are called by the same title of lama as yourself, who know many things and are so deeply cultured."

"You are right. Many lamas wear the lamaistic garment, but their inner life is far worse than that of a layman. Often among many thousands of lamas, you can find only a few isolated individuals, with whom you can converse about exalted matters and expect a worthy response. But is it not thus in your own religion?

"We have seen many missionaries - probably they speak of the one Christ, but they assail one another. Each one calls his teaching superior. It is my belief that Issa gave one teaching - then how can this great Symbol have divisions which declare themselves hostile to the other? Do not think that we are so ignorant. We have heard that rites celebrated by one sect of Christian priests are not recognized by another Christian priest. Therefore you must have many opposing Christs.

"In our deserts, many Christian crosses have been found. Once I asked a Christian missionary if these crosses were authentic, and he told me that they were spurious crosses; that during all ages false Christianity had penetrated Asia, and that we should not regard these crosses as exalted symbols. Then, tell me, how shall we distinguish the authentic cross from the false one? We also have a cross in the Great Sign of Ak-Dorje. But with us, this is the great sign of life, of the fiery element - the eternal sign. Against this sign, none would speak!"

"Lama, we know that only through the knowledge of spirit can we perceive what is authentic."

"Again, you show your knowledge of great things. Again you speak as though from our mighty Kalachakra. But how shall we develop our great understanding? Verily, we are wise in spirit; we know everything - but how shall we evoke this knowledge from the depths of our consciousness and transmit it to our minds? How shall one recognize the needed frontiers between the ascetic life and the plain life? How shall we know for how long we may be hermits and how long we must work among men? How shall we know what knowledge can be revealed without harm, and what - perhaps the most exalted - may be divulged but to a few. This is the knowledge of Kalachakra."

"Lama, the great Kalachakra is practically unknown, because its teaching is confused with low Tantrik teaching. Just as you have real Buddhists, and their opposites, Bon-Po, so you have also the lowest Tantra of sorcery and necromancy. And did not the Blessed One denounce sorcery? Tell me frankly, if a lama should be a sorcerer?"

"You are right. Not only sorcery, but an undue display of super-normal forces were forbidden by our great Teachers. But if one's spirit is so advanced that he can perform many things and utilize any of his energies in a natural way and for the purpose of the Common Good, then this is no longer sorcery, but a great achievement, a great labor for humanity.

"By our symbols, by our images and tankas, you may see how the great Teachers functioned; among the many great Teachers, you see only few in complete meditation. Usually they are performing an active part of the great labor. Either they teach the people or they tame the dark forces and elements;

they do not fear to confront the most powerful forces and to ally themselves with them, if only it be for the common well-being. Sometimes you are able to see the Teachers in actual conflict, dispersing the evil forces of spirit. Earthly war is not sanctioned by us, but Buddhists throughout all history, have been attacked; they have never been the aggressors. We have heard that during your recent Great War, the Christian priests on either side claimed that Issa and God were with them. If God is one, we must understand by this that he was in conflict with himself. How can you explain a contradiction which was so inexplicable to all Buddhists?"

"Lama, this war is over. The most disastrous of mistakes may happen, but now all nations are thinking of how to abolish not only the idea but the veritable material and implements of war."

"And do you think that all guns and warships should be abolished? Let them rather be transformed into the implements of peace and of a loftier teaching. I would like to see the great warships become traveling schools of high learning. Is that possible? During my journey to China, I saw so many guns and warships that I thought, if only these ghastly creations might be the symbols of lofty teaching, rather than the symbols of murder, what a tremendous flow of cosmic energy the world would see!"

"Lama, the serpent stings, yet he is considered the symbol of wisdom."

"Probably you have heard the old parable of how the snake was cautioned not to bite, but only to hiss. Each one must be powerful - but which protection do you regard as the most powerful?"

"Lama, certainly it is the protection afforded by the power of the spirit. Because only in spirit are we fortified mentally, and physically. A man, spiritually concentrated, is as strong as a dozen of the brawniest athletes. The man who knows how to use his mental powers is stronger than the mob."

"Ah, now we once again approach our great Kalachakra: Who can exist without food? Who can exist without sleep? Who is immune against heat and cold? Who can heal wounds? Verily, only he who studies the Kalachakra.

"The great Azaras who know the Teachings of India, know the origin of Kalachakra. They know vast things which, when they will be revealed to help humanity, will completely regenerate life! Many of the Teachings of Kalachakra are unknowingly used both in East and West, and even in such unconscious utilization, much that is wonderful results. It is therefore comprehensible how incomparably great would be the possibilities made manifest by a conscious achievement, and how wisely could be used the great eternal energy, this fine imponderable matter which is scattered everywhere and which is within our use at any moment. This Teaching of Kalachakra, this utilization of the primary energy, has been called the Teaching of Fire. The Hindu people know the great Agni - ancient teaching though it be, it shall be the new teaching for the New Era. We must think of the future; and in the Teaching of Kalachakra we know there lies all the material which may be applied for the greatest use. Now there are so many teachers - so different and so hostile to each other. And yet so many of them speak of the one thing and this very thing is expressed in the Kalachakra. One of your priests once asked me, 'Are not the Kabala and Shambhala parts of the one teaching?' He asked, 'Is not the great Moses an initiate of the same teaching and a follower of its very laws?' We may assert one thing only - Each teaching of truth, each teaching of the high principle of life, issues from the one source. Many ancient Buddhist Stupas have been converted into Linga temples and many mosques bear the walls and foundations of ancient Buddhist viharas. But what harm is there, if those buildings have been dedicated to the one lofty principle of life? Many Buddhist images upon the rocks find their origins in teachings which long antedated the Blessed One. Yet they also symbolize the same high Essence.

"What is revealed in the Kalachakra? Are there any forbiddances? No, the lofty teaching sets forth only the constructive. So it is. The same high forces are proposed for humanity. And it is revealed most scientifically how the natural forces of the elements can be used by humanity. When you are told that the shortest way is through Shambhala, through Kalachakra, it means that achievement is not an unattainable ideal, but that it is something which may be attained through sincere and industrious aspiration here, upon this very earth and in this very incarnation. This is the Teaching of Shambhala. Verily, each one may attain it. Verily, each one may hear the pronunciation of the word, *Kalagiya*!

"But to attain this, a man must dedicate himself entirely to creative labor. Those who work with Shambhala, the initiates and the messengers of Shambhala, do not sit in seclusion - they travel everywhere. Very often people do not recognize them and sometimes they do not even recognize each other. But they perform their works, not for themselves, but for the great Shambhala; and all of them know the great symbol of anonymity. They sometimes seem wealthy, yet they are without possessions. Everything is for them, but they take nothing for themselves. Thus, when you dedicate yourselves to Shambhala, everything is taken and everything is given to you. If you have regrets, you yourself become the loser; if you give joyously, you are enriched. Essentially, the Teaching of Shambhala lies in this - that we do not speak of something distant and secreted. Therefore, if you know that Shambhala is here on earth; if you know that everything may be achieved here on earth, then everything must be rewarded here on earth. You have heard that the reward of Shambhala is verily here and that it is manifold in its returns. This is not because the Teaching of Shambhala is unique from others, but because the Teaching of Shambhala is vital, is given for earthly incarnations and can be applied under all human conditions. In what way can we study how to work? How to be ready for all manner of attainments; how to be open and all-accepting? Only in the practical study of Shambhala.

When you read many books about Shambhala, partially translated in other languages and partially veiled, do not be confused with the great symbols. Even in the West, when you speak of great discoveries, you use technical language, and the layman does not understand them and takes the expressions literally, judging only on the surface. The same may be said of the great scriptures, and of scientific documents. Some take the great Puranas in their literal aspect. What conclusion may they draw? Only that which may be gathered from the surface of language, from its philology, but not from the significance of the signs which are used. The harmony of exterior and interior can be attained only through the study of Kalachakra. Probably you have seen the signs of Kalachakra on the rocks, in quite deserted places.

"Some unknown hand has set a design upon the stones or has chiseled the letters of the Kalachakra upon the rocks. Verily, verily, only through Shambhala, only through the Teaching of the Kalachakra can you attain the perfection of the shortest path.

"*Kalagiya, kalagiya, kalagiya.* Come to Shambhala!"

Then our conversation became still more beautiful and sacred. Therein entered that note which exalts all human strivings. We spoke of the mountain Kailasa, of the hermits which until now live in the caves of this wondrous mountain, filling the space with their evoking calls of righteousness.

And then we spoke of That Place which lies to the north of Kailasa…

The twilight fell and the whole room seemed enveloped in new significance. The image of Chenrezi, superbly embroidered upon the lustrous silk, which hung above the head of the Lama, seemed to glance down at us in a significant way. Such images are no longer to be found in Tibet.

On either side of this image was another, also of rare luster. One of them was Amitayus; the other the Lord Buddha, ever-steadfast with the unconquerable sign of lightning, the dorje, in his hand. From the shrine in the room benignly smiled Dolma, the White Tara.

From a bunch of fresh fuchsias and violet dahlias, emanated a refreshing vitality. From there, also, shone the image of the Mighty, the Invincible Rigden-jyepo, and His Presence again reminded us of the mysterious Place to the north of Kailasa. In the corners of this banner were four most significant images. Below, was the successor of Rigden-jyepo with a Hindu pundit, one of the first exponents of the Kalachakra. In the top corners were two images of the Tashi Lama - that on the left being the Third Tashi Lama, Pan-chen Pal-den ye-she, who gave intimations of Shambhala. And in the right was a corresponding figure of the present Tashi Lama, Pan-chen Cho-kyi nyi-ma ge-leg nam-jyal pal-zang-po, who has recently issued another prayer to Shambhala the Resplendent. In the center of the banner was Rigden-jyepo himself and from the base of his throne there radiated the crossed Ak-ojir-Ak-dorje - the Cross of Life. A legion of people were gathered before the throne of Rigden: who was not among them! There was a Ladaki, in his high black hat; Chinese, in their round headgear with the red ball on top; here, in his white garments, was a Hindu; there, a Moslem in a white turban. Here, Kirghiz, Bur-yats, Kalmuks; and there, Mongolians, in their characteristic dress.

Each one offered to the Ruler the best gifts of his lands: Fruits and grains; textures and armor and precious stones. No one coerced these nations; they came voluntarily from all parts of Asia, surrounding the Great Warrior. Perhaps they were conquered? No, there was no humility in their approach to Him. The nations approached Him as their own, their sole ruler. His hand pointed toward the earth as in the majestic gesture of the great Lion-Sange; upon the stronghold of earth he gave his oath always to build steadfastly.

From the aromatic incense before the image, bluish streams ascended, floating before the image, inscribing numerous signs in the mysterious Senzar language. Then lest those who do not know the Great Truth should desecrate it, the fragrant signs floated together and faded on, out into space.

Talai-Pho-Brang, 1928.

TREASURE OF THE SNOWS

Throughout Sikhim again thunder the huge trumpets! For all it is a great, a solemn day. Let us go to the temple to see the Dances on the Great Day of Homage to Kinchenjunga!

From all parts of Sikhim many peoples gather in their strange and varied attire. Here are the Sikhimese, in their short red garments, with their conical, feathered hats; here are the sober Bhutanese, startlingly like the Basques or Hungarians; here stand the red-turbaned people from Kham; you can see the small round caps of the valiant Nepalese Gurkhas; the people of Lhassa, in their Chinese-like long garments; the timid, quiet Lepchas, and many Sharpa people; all types of Hill-men from all parts come to pay homage to the Five Treasures of Kinchenjunga, which points the way to the Sacred City of Shambhala.

Trumpets are roaring. The drums beat. The crowd shouts and whistles. Enters the Protector of Sikhim, in a huge red and gold mask, with a short spear in his hand. Around the fountain, from which the sacred water is drawn each morning, the impressive Protector of Sikhim turns about in a slow benevolent dance, completing his magic circles. Perhaps he is peering into the religious situation of Sikhim. In each monastery in Sikhim, at the same hour, the same sacred dance of the Protector is being performed. Finishing his role, the Protector joins the picturesque file of musicians.

Again sound the trumpets and the roar of the crowd. Then the Protectress emerges from the temple. As a Kali or Dakini, with skulls adorning her head, in dark garment, the deity outlines the same circle; after performing her invocation, she also seats herself beside the Protector.

Again the crowd shouts and cries. One by one the Protectors of the five Treasures of Kinchenjunga emerge. They are ready to fight for the Holy Mountain, because in its caves, all treasures are guarded for centuries. They are ready to guard the religion, which is supported by the hermits, who send their benevolent blessings from mountain depths. Radiant are the streamers on the garments of these Guardians. They glisten as snows glowing in the rays of the sun. They are ready to fight. They are armed with swords and protected with round shields. Begins the Dance of the Warriors - reminiscent of the dances of the Comanchis of Arizona - the swords are brandished in the air; guns are fired. The population of Sikhim may rejoice - beholding how the treasures of Kinchenjunga are guarded! They may be proud - never yet has the rocky summit of this White Mountain been conquered! Only exalted keepers of the Mysteries, high Devas, know the path to its summit. The Guardians finish their dance; they divide into two parties. In slow tread they march, intoning a long song; they boast and bet. Each tells of his prowess: "I can catch fish without nets" - "I can ride over the world without a horse" - "None can resist my sword" - "My shield is strong." And again follows the short dance of the warriors. They pass into the temple. Both Protectors rise and again, after several encircling dances, enter the low door. The performance is over.

Now is the power of Kinchenjunga disclosed in another way. One sees bows and arrows in the hands of the people. The old joy of Sikhim - the ancient art of archery, - is to be demonstrated. Far off are the targets. But the hill-men still know the noble art and the arrows shall reach the heart of the mark, as they shall reach the hearts of Kinchenjunga's enemies. The festival is over. The long giant trumpets once again are carried into the temple; drums, gongs, clarinets and cymbals are silent. The doors of the temple are closed. This is not Buddhism; this is an Homage to Kinchenjunga.

And when we see the beautiful snowy peak, we understand the spirit of the festival, because veneration of beauty is the basis of this exalted feeling. The hill-people feel beauty. They feel a sincere pride in possessing these unrepeatable snowy peaks - the world giants, the clouds, the mist of the monsoon. Are these not merely a superb curtain before the great Mystery beyond Kinchenjunga? Many beautiful legends are connected with this mountain.

Beyond Kinchenjunga are old menhirs of the great sun cult. Beyond Kinchenjunga is the birthplace of the sacred Swastika, sign of fire. Now in the day of Agni Yoga, the element of fire is again entering the spirit and all the treasures of earth are revered. For the legends of heroes are dedicated not so much to the plains as to the mountains! All Teachers journeyed to the mountains. The highest knowledge, the most inspired songs, the most superb sounds and colors, are created on the mountains. On the highest mountains there is the Supreme. The highest mountains stand as witnesses of the Great Reality. The spirit of prehistoric man already enjoyed and understood the greatness of the mountains.

Whoever beholds the Himalayas recalls the great meaning of Mount Meru. The Blessed Buddha journeyed to the Himalayas for enlightenment. There, near the legendary sacred Stupa, in the presence of all the gods, the Blessed One received his Illumination. In truth, everything connected with the Himalayas reveals the great symbol of Mount Meru, standing at the center of the world.

The ancient people of wise India discerned in the splendor of the Himalayas the smile of mighty Vishnu, who stands as an heroic, indefatigable warrior, armed with discus, mace, war-trumpet and sword. All ten Avatars of Vishnu were consummated near the Himavat. The most remote and oldest of them is the Avatar Dagon, the man-fish, who saved the forefathers of the earthly race, Manu. As far back as the time of the first cataclysm, the flood, Burma remembers Dagon, and claims that the Dagoba dedicated to him is more than three thousand years old. Then came the Tortoise - the pillar of heaven - which in the depths of the ocean of space, assisted the great upheaval which endowed the earth with the radiant goddess Lakshmi. Then came the ponderous earthly Boar; then the inconquerable Narasimha, the man-lion, who saved Prahlada from the wrath of his sinning father. The fifth Avatar, the dwarf Vamana, triumphed over another king, Bally, who like Prahlada's father tried to possess the throne of Vishnu. The sixth Avatar, bearing the name of Brahman, is the great warrior of Parasu Rama, said in ancient scriptures to have annihilated the race of Kshatri-yas. The seventh Avatar appeared as Rama, the mighty beneficent king of India, extolled in the Ramayana. The eighth Avatar is Krishna, the sacred shepherd, whose teaching is glorified in the all-embracing Bhagavad Gita. The ninth Avatar, the Blessed Buddha, is the great Avatar predicted by Vishnu, as the triumph of wisdom and the destruction of demons and sinners by their own karma. Vishnu's tenth Avatar, not yet manifest, is the future Maitreya. A great horseman, saviour of humanity, the Kalki Avatar, shall appear riding upon a white horse; resplendent, with his triumphant sword in hand - he will restore the pure law of righteousness and wise rule on earth.

The advent of the resplendent day-goddess, Lakshmi, Vishnu's bride, has ever rejoiced the Indian heart, even as do the Himalayan summits. Vishnu's second Avatar, the blue Tortoise, aided in stirring up the great ocean of space, indicated in the Mahabharata, the Ramayana and the Vishnu Purana. To restore to the three regions of earth, air and heaven, their lost treasures, Vishnu commanded the Devas, sons of heaven, sons of fire, to join the dark demoniac Asuras in stirring the cosmic ocean, in order to create the sea of milk, or Amrita, the heavenly nectar of life. The Devas, in glowing sheen, came to the edge of the sea, which moved as the shining clouds of autumn. And with the help of the Great One, they uprooted the holy mountain to serve as a churning-pole. The great serpent Ananpa offered himself as a pole, and the mighty Vishnu, assuming the form of an immense Tortoise, made a pivot for the pole. The Devas held the tail of the serpent and the Asuras approached the head; and the great creative churning began. The first creation of this tumultuous labor was the divine cow, the fountain of milk, shown in the Vedas as the rain-cloud, which conquered the drought. Then was manifested Varuni. Vishnu's crystallized radiance. After came the Purijara, source of all-heavenly fruits. Afterward rose the moon and was possessed by Siva. At this moment conflagration, destructive fumes, emitted by this process, engulfed the earth and threatened the whole universe. Then Brahma, the creator, arose and bid Siva manifest his power. Siva, for the sake of all existing beings, swallowed the poison self-sacrificingly and became Nilakanta the blue-throated. Then appeared Dhanivantari bearing the precious cup of Amrita. Hark and rejoice! After him came Lakshmi the effulgent, herself. Radiant, surrounded by her celestial attendants, glowing as a lustrous chain of clouds. At the same time, the gray rain clouds, the powerful elephants of heaven, poured water over her from golden vessels. Amrita was manifested and the eternal battle over the treasure of the universe began. The Devas and Asuras clashed in battle but the Asuras were vanquished and driven to Batala, the gloomy recesses of earth. Again came joy and happiness to the three worlds - the festival of gods and men.

As you ascend the peaks of the Himalaya and look out over the cosmic ocean of clouds below, you see the ramparts of endless rocky chains and the pearly strings of cloudlets. Behind them march the gray elephants of heaven, the heavy monsoon clouds. Is this not a cosmic picture which fills you with understanding of some great creative manifestation? The mighty serpent in endless coils sustains the milky way. The blue tortoise of heaven, and stars without number, are as diamond treasures of a coming victory. You recall the huge mendangs in the Sikhimese range, with their stone seats used by the great hermits for meditation before sunrise; the great poet Milaraspa knew the strength of the hour before dawn, and in this awesome moment his spirit merged with the great spirit of the world, in conscious unity.

Before sunrise there comes a breeze, and the milky sea undulates. The shining Devas have approached the tail of the serpent and the great stirring has begun! The clouds collapse as the shattered walls of a prison. Verily, the luminous god approaches! But what has occurred? The snows are red as blood. But the clouds collect in an ominous mist and all which was erstwhile resplendent and beauteous becomes dense, dark, shrouding the gore of the battle. Asuras and Devas struggle; the poisonous fumes creep everywhere. Creation must perish! But Siva, self-sacrificingly, has consumed the poison, which threatened the world's destruction - he, the great blue-throated. Lakshmi arises from darkness, bearing the chalice of nectar. And before her radiant beauty all the evil spirits of night disperse. A new cosmic energy is manifest in the world!

Where can one have such joy as when the sun is upon the Himalayas; when the blue is more intense than sapphires; when from the far distance, the glaciers glitter as incomparable gems. All religions, all teachings, are synthesized in the Himalayas. The virgin of dawn, the Ushas of the ancient Vedas, is possessed of the same lofty virtues as the joyful Lakshmi. There can also be distinguished the all-vanquishing power of Vishnu! Formerly he was Narayana, the cosmic being in the depths of creation. Finally he is seen as the god of the sun and, at his smile, out of the darkness, arises the great goddess of happiness.

And may we not also notice this link between Lakshmi and Maya, mother of Buddha? All great symbols, all heroes, seem to be brought close to the Himalayas as if to the highest altar, where the human spirit comes closest to divinity. Are the shining stars not nearer, when you are in the Himalayas? Are not the treasures of earth evident in the Himalayas? A simple sardar in your caravan asks you, "But what is hidden beneath the mighty mountains? Why are the greatest plateaux just in the Himalayas? Some treasures must be there!"

In the foothills of the Himalayas are many caves and it is said that from these caves, subterranean passages proceed far below Kinchenjunga. Some have even seen the stone door which has never been opened, because the date has not arrived. The deep passages proceed to the Splendid Valley. You can realize the origin and reality of such legends, when you are acquainted with the unsuspected formations in Himalayan nature, when you personally perceive how closely together are glaciers and rich vegetation. The homage to Kinchenjunga from the simple people does not surprise you, because in it you see not superstition, but a real page of poetic folk-lore. This folk-reverence of natural beauties has its counterpart in the lofty heart of the sensitive traveler who, enticed by the inexpressible beauties here, is ever-ready to barter his city-life for the mountain peaks. For him, this exalted feeling has much the same meaning as has the conquering dance of the Guardian of the Mountains, and the bevy of archers who stand vigilant, ready to guard the beauties of Kinchenjunga.

Hail to unconquered Kinchenjunga!

Talai-Pho-Brang, 1928.

BUDDHISM IN TIBET

The waves of human intelligence, human faith and religion, are a true ocean of enlightenment, as you mark their ebb and flow. It is not discouraging to see recessions of the human spirit because at the same time in another part of the world you may see the spirit ascending still higher and attaining new summits of knowledge. Hence if something shows retrogression somewhere, we know that at the same time elsewhere the same substance has conquered new spaces. This is the true spiral of evolution.

During the last four-and-a-half years we visited an entire chain of Buddhist countries: we admired India with its sacred sites, which commemorate the personal travels of the Blessed Buddha, where the loftiest thoughts and the most inspired art creations have been spread. We visited Ceylon. We heard the many beautiful reminiscences of Java and Bali. We sensed how many new discoveries could still be made in these memorable sites. If Anuradhapura is but slightly explored, then Sarnath - so central a site - is still concealing numerous relics under its untouched hill. And the scenes of the birth and departure of Buddha are still unexplored, in the jungles where the mighty roots carefully envelop the treasures.

We have seen Sikhim, land of heroes, land of the most beautiful snows, where so many aspiring spirits have been exalted, where so many caves and rocks are enveloped in sacred memories.

We passed Kashmir where the soil conceals numerous monuments of the labors of Ashoka's followers. We rejoiced in Ladak with its remarkable legends, with its sacred pride at being the patrimony of Geser Khan, so often identified with the Ruler of Shambhala. We studied the magnificent images of Maitreya which bestow upon Ladak their benediction for a happy future. In Khotan, the sands cover the remains of Buddhism and yet, in this place, is the great ancient Suburgan, the hope of all Buddhists; because on this spot the Age of Maitreya shall be acclaimed by a mysterious light over the ancient Stupa.

When we approached Yarkent and Kashgar it seemed that we had traveled far from the path of Buddhism. But it is just in Kashgar that you can see the old Stupa, which is comparable in grandeur to that built by Ashoka in Sar-nath. And in the same district, surrounded by the Mosques and Moslem cemeteries, you can see the entrances of the Buddhist caves, unapproachable as eyries. We enjoyed visiting the remarkable cave-monasteries in the Kuchar district, the former capital of the Tokhars. Although all the relics are removed and scattered, the charm of these constructions remain, and one feels that in the subterranean caves are hidden many more relics covered by the care of time. Karashahr, the Black City, capital of the Kalmuks, where the chalice of Buddha was preserved after it left Peshawar, has many evidences of Buddhism. Although it is Lamaism - not pure Buddhism - you can feel the traces of religion. The Kalmuks dream to find once again the chalice of the Blessed One. One may hear the same faith expressed in their nomad monasteries, made up of movable yurtas, in the foothills of the "Celestial Mountains," T'ien Shan. The Altai Mountains have identified themselves with the name of Buddha. It is said that the Blessed One, after visiting Khotan, visited the great Altai, where stands sacred Belukha. In Oirot, where the nomadic Oirots await the Coming of Buddha, the White Burkhan, they know that the Blessed Oirot is already traveling throughout the world, announcing the great Advent.

Buryatia and both Mongolias offer the most remarkable material for study. We verified the legends about the Ruler of Shambhala having visited in Erdeni-dzu on the Orkhon, and the Narabanchi monastery. Everywhere, these legends about the visitations of the past and the coming Advent, have the utmost significance for the population. In Ulan Bator Khoto they plan to erect a Dukhang, dedicated to Shambhala, where an image of the Ruler of Shambhala is to be placed. The Province of Kansu, with its cave temples, suggestive of Tun Huang, recalls the flourishing days of Buddhism. Some unexpected images and inscriptions are to be found on the rocks in the environs of Nanshan. Although Tsaidam has not many Buddhist monuments, yet the lamas of Tsaidam, under the influence of the great Kumbum monastery, are learned, and revere the name of Tsong kha pa. In Bhutan, as we have heard, Buddhism - or rather Lama-ism - is in the hands of a few learned lamas. The high standing of the scholars of Buddhism in Burma, China and especially Japan, is well known.

Details of the conditions of Buddhism in the above-mentioned countries may be outlined separately as the material is vast. For the moment it is most important to outline the conditions of Buddhism in Tibet because Tibet has been regarded by many as a citadel of living Buddhism. And many Europeans dream of finding in modern Tibet, possibilities for unearthing the true teaching of Buddha. We entered Tibet with the best hopes and the highest expectations.

In the year 1923, as is known, the Tashi Lama was compelled to depart from Tibet. The reasons for this unprecedented departure are unclear. One hears of misunderstandings between him and his fellow-ruler, the Dalai Lama. One hears that the Tashi Lama was arraigned by Lhassa, for his attentions to the West. One hears that Shigatse and Tashi Lhunpo, by order of Lhassa, were oppressed by heavy taxes. One hears that in the old prophecies, this unusual departure of the Tashi Lama was prophesied. And before his departure the Tashi Lama ordered frescoes to be painted in his personal apartment, in symbolical subjects, revealing the entire itinerary of his approaching departure. This unprecedented exodus suggests much which one can only surmise. In any case the spiritual leader of Tibet could not longer endure the reality of the present situation of his country. With three hundred riders the revered Tashi Lama escaped through wild and impenetrable Chantang, pursued by several military detachments. Quite a host of cultured abbots and lamas of the monasteries followed the exalted refugee. The details of the flight of these worthy ones do not lack in heroism. The once celebrated Tashi Ihunpo, monastery residence of the Tashi Lama, has now become deserted beyond recognition. And, bereft of its spiritual leader, Tibet became a prey to the intrigues of the retrograding lamaistic parties. By his departure the Tashi Lama revealed a strong spirit and deep penetration into the current moment of Tibet. In different parts of Tibet the people tremulously ask, "Will the Tashi Lama return?" It is difficult for them to be without their spiritual leader, whose name is veiled with sincere reverence.

During our stay in Tibet, crossing several of the provinces of this country from the extreme north to the south, we met people of various ranks, beginning with the high officials, favorites of the Dalai Lama, and ending with the dark savage nomads. I will not give my personal conclusions here. I will only repeat the outspoken statements of the Tibetans or mention what I have seen personally. The reader may draw from it his personal conclusions about the state of religion in Tibet.

Tibet has been wrapped in the reputation of being a country of high religious covenants, a country where everything is based on religious foundation. Let us examine if Buddhism actually exists within Tibet or whether we find rather complex conceptions there instead. In Tibet there are devout followers of the true spiritual San-gha established by the Blessed Buddha. As in its former days Tibet still is the scene of serious research into the literature and the knowledge of natural forces.

We are receptive to lofty legends and fairy tales, but life is life, and we must take it in its full reality, recognizing the high and the base. If we find that the superstitious people are being terrorized with crude manifestations, we must expose this, because a high teaching has nothing to do with terrorization and superstition. From what the Tibetans themselves reveal, you understand that the high teachings of Buddha, of his enlightened followers, of Mahatmas, take place in general outside the walls of Lhassa.

Let us observe several pictures from contemporary Tibetan reality among the low-class lamas. I shall be the photographer and you shall be judge:

Here are some lamas, who on their sacred rosaries, calculate their commercial accounts, completely concerned with the thoughts of profit. Did Buddha ordain such usage of sacred objects? This custom suggests the low Shamanistic conventions. The prayer wheels are turned by water. Windmills and clock-works are used for the same mechanical process. In this way indolent pilgrims are freed from all expenditure of energy. They enjoy themselves and everything must work for them! Can it be possible to relate this to the covenant of Buddha?

Some lamas denounce the killing of animals; but the monastery store rooms are piled high with the carcases of muttons and yaks, killed for the use of the monks. But how to cause the death of the animals without sinning? Again the law of Buddha is circumvented. The animals chosen as victims are driven to the edge of the rocks so that, falling, they kill themselves.

It is noticed that in the monasteries, the Mongol lamas are often regarded with greatest importance. We asked a Tibetan lama of considerable rank to discuss with us a high metaphysical subject, a subject which should have been very close to him. The lama avoided it by saying: "But a man cannot have read everything!" It is strange to notice that the Mongols even now make pilgrimages to Tibet, not realizing that their spiritual potentialities are equal to those of the Tibetans. Even the number of commercial caravans traveling to Tibet has become insignificant. During five months on the main trade route we saw only three such caravans.

Many strange offers are brought to us! A lama offers to arrest the snow clouds and melt the snow. This meteorological phenomenon is offered at a very reasonable fee - altogether, for two American dollars. We consent. The lama pipes on a bone flute, crying out his conjurations. But he is a business man and he gives us an ostentatious receipt for our two dollars. We keep it as a unique curiosity. It is of no consequence that the snow continues to fall and it becomes still more bitterly cold. The Tantrik is not discouraged. He places some sort of paper wind-mills above his black tent and through the entire night he howls into the horn made of human bones…

In a corner of a shop, sits the owner, a lama, laboriously turning his prayer wheel. Many sacred objects are piled together with his goods. On the walls, hang images of Shambhala and Tsong kha pa. And in the opposite corner of an adjoining room stand great kegs, filled with the local wine made by the same lama, to intoxicate his people. The lay people as well as the lamas drink viciously. And even small children demand money for whiskey, so that one might think intemperance was ordained by Buddhism.

Certain lamas, who agree to carry loads by caravan, throw them away on the road, saying they are not responsible because they are lamas. The same lamas affirm that Buddha forbade labor, agriculture and uncovering the depths of the earth. This is an invented slander against Buddha himself, who sent his pupils to work in the fields, in order to help the villagers. As was indicated in old scriptures, even a Bodhisattva must have some type of craftsmanship at hand. Thus was labor extolled by the Teacher and thus are labor and knowledge slandered by some uncultured lamas. Another typical picture: An honored officer of the Tibetan army which pursued the Tashi Lama in 1923, assured foreigners that Eastern Buddhists drink and smoke. He repeated constantly that he is a religious man, and expressed his willingness to transmit to a monastery our donation of thirty-five dollars. Afterwards we had proofs from this monastery that this true lamaist transmitted only ten dollars to the monastery, retaining for himself the remaining twenty-five. When he was exposed, he simply refused to send the twenty-five dollars to the monastery, again repeating that he was a religious man.

A lama-diplomat in the special confidence of the Dalai Lama goes into a rage when he learns that we have contributed one hundred narsangs to a monastery for oil for the image lamps. He says: "You must know that our monks will appropriate your money for themselves and never will light the image lamps. If you wish that the holy images should be honored with lights you must buy this oil only from me."

A lama ranking as an abbot, says: "Our monks are savages. You have seen some lamas in Sikhim or Ladak but do not think that our Tibetan lamas are like them." The same lama warned us that the monks would beat us with stones.

A lama approaches your tent and into your very car beats a drum until you give him a handful of *sho* (Tibetan money). But in ten minutes, probably believing that you have already forgotten his face, he removes a part of his attire and with the same shamelessness he gives you no rest, just as your *sho* do not give rest to his piety.

In Central Tibet, in the district of Shekar, you are approached by several lamas, without prayers, but with a word familiar to everybody who visits the bazaars. To your astonishment, you can quite clearly distinguish the word of the bazaar beggar - "Bakshish." This "Bakshish" on the lips of the lamas depresses one. From where comes this multitude of wasters and idlers?

Lamas, even of the yellow sect, sometimes marry. But they claim that if their services for the Dalai Lama are valuable then His Holiness consents to annul the marriage and even gives them high posts. We were shocked to hear that the people call their ruler the "pocked monk." The temples most often are ill-smelling and dirty, and quite close to their walls, all sorts of bargaining and bribery go on. How isolated are the few dignified individuals, in this market of ignorance! How many monasteries lie in ruins; how many walls are already crumbling! You feel that these ancient monasteries and castles were built by a people quite unlike the present Tibetans. The former kings of Tibet and the great Dalai Lama the Fifth were distinguished by their vast energy, to which the Potala bears witness, the only imposing and significant structure of all Tibet.

Some more pictures from reality! The pious servant of the Dalai Lama, became sick on the road, and out of compassion we took him into our caravan. With great care and with our unreplaceable medicines, we brought him as far as Tibet. But here at once he left us and with "piety" devoted himself to betraying us. What covenant of Lamaism has ordained treason?

A general of a princely line, invites you to his own camp, sends his special officers for you, accepts your gift, bows in reverence before the sacred objects and zealously tells his rosary. But afterwards his entrusted officer communicates that the general has announced to the government that you came to him of your own accord, imposing yourself without an invitation.

A chieftain of a large settlement asks permission to pull out three hairs from the beard of your camel; they possess great magic power! And he will sew them into the "lamaistic" amulet on his breast. A head of a dead camel is a very precious matter in Tibet. They pay up to twenty narsangs for one - to such an extent is this object needed for fortune-telling.

A lama, with an air of deep mystery, offers to sell you miracle-working pills. They are of great power and cure all diseases. When you appear unconvinced of the need of this purchase, the lama, as the highest recommendation, informs you that the formula for these pills includes the excrement of His Holiness or of some high lamas.

Then comes a pious-looking Lhassan, attendant of a high personage, bringing an amulet for sale. This amulet completely guarantees safety against bullets. The amulet is of such power that the cost is no less than three hundred rupees! He explains that the amulet is guaranteed and blessed by a very high lama. Since there is so complete a guarantee of safety you suggest that he perform a test on himself. But the religious man prefers to confine his test to a goat, meanwhile continuing to assure you of the complete power of the amulet. But when you do not agree to permit the goat "to be the goat" the Lhassan departs very indignantly.

We saw many monasteries. And we also saw numerous lamas coal black with dirt. When you see these faces and arms, black and shining as if polished, issuing from dirty red rags, you may associate them with many things, but never with Buddhism. It seems impossible that they can affirm that Buddha and Tsong kha pa ordained this unmitigated dirt.

Near a sacred mendang, half covered with slabs of sacred inscriptions, is stretched the decaying carcass of a dog and the same sacred inscriptions are covered with human excretions. Never have we seen such pollution of stupas or mendangs. In Sikhim or in Ladak even the oldest monuments of religion, though no longer used, are never so desecrated. No foreigners or strangers are near Tibetan monasteries so you may be sure that some religious Tibetans alone are responsible for such sacrilege. The sacred stone inscriptions are thrown on the fields discarded. Many stupas and mendangs have fallen into ruins.

Near Lhassa exists a huge flat site of stone where corpses are hacked and thrown to the birds of prey, dogs and pigs. It is a custom to roll oneself naked on these remnants of corpses for the preservation of one's health. No one can explain from where comes such a strange belief. But the Buryat, Tsibikoff, in his book on a pilgrimage to Tibet, assures his readers that His Holiness the Dalai Lama has fulfilled this absurd ritual, in imitation of certain animals. I quote Tsibikoff for this information because I cannot presume on my own responsibility to accuse the Dalai Lama of such non-Buddhistic action! What has this to do with Buddhism?

Among the many things related by the local populace, one remembers that the custom of polyandry is still practised, and not only among the followers of the "black faith," Bon po, but also among the orthodox followers, Geluk-pa. If you ask them whether the old books indicate such customs, the people only smile.

It is also said that the house built by the Dalai Lama in European style at his summer residence at Norbuling, has been demolished by order of His Holiness and that in its place a palace is now being constructed, Potang, in Chinese character. It is rumored that during the erection of the European house black rites were performed and that since then, fortune has forsaken Tibet. One often hears of fortune having left Tibet also in connection with the peculiar behavior of the Lhassa officials.

But let us not forget that a considerable part of the population belongs to the sect of Bon po, to the "black faith" which rejects Buddha altogether, and claims a completely unique protector and guide. They openly consider all Buddhists as enemies and recognize the Dalai Lama only as a civil ruler without religious power. These people are very assertive and do not permit Buddhists and lamaists to enter their temples. In their rituals everything is reversed. They revere some mysterious gods of Swastika. They perform their lamaistic rituals invertedly, not considering themselves Tibetans and completely isolating themselves from Lhassa. Among them, the lowest type of Shamanism, sorcery, and dark-incantations are practised. One might imagine oneself in the Middle Ages. But the name of Buddha is not protected by Lhassa. And the Lhassa officials do not protest against the anti-Buddhistic incantations. Outside of this multitudinous sect, there exists a great number of savage tribes with special dialects, at times so different they cannot understand each other. Nomads and forest-dwellers practising the lowest grade of fetichism, smear the sacrificial stones with grease, with the full sanction of the Lhassan government. They worship stone arrows and revere the most absurd amulets. To my astonishment, I saw an amulet around the neck of such an individual, and he told me that it was given to him by the Dalai Lama himself. I will not draw any conclusion from this. The ignorance of this savage people is simply appalling.

So, eliminating all the harmful and ignorant conditions, we see that conscious reverence for the higher Teachings in Tibet is maintained by small numbers of people, of whom many are in far-off hermitages. Tibetans themselves say that the enlightened teaching of Buddha needs to be purified in Tibet; it is necessary to make the lamas subject to far more serious State examinations, ejecting the ignorant and idlers from the monasteries. Only then can the lamas be reestablished as high teachers of the people.

Did the Dalai Lama, during his unusually long rule, make any attempts to purify the teaching, clogged by ignorance? Did he try to reestablish the original austere monastery Vinaya-discipline, in order to raise the understanding of labor and to eject superstition? We have not heard of such attempts. Not in secrecy, not in fear, can religion be purified, but in solemn dignified actions. Of course, we must not forget that it is not simple for the Dalai Lama to do anything for religion. If you think that a command of the Dalai Lama beyond the walls of Lhassa is worth much, you are mistaken. We had an ostentatious, broadly inclusive passport of the Dalai Lama's government; yet under our very eyes, the people refused to fulfil the commands of their ruler. "We do not know Devachung (the government)," said the Elder. And the officials in different dzongs only invent methods, each in his own way, to interpret the text of the document in proportion to the generosity of the gift for which they shamelessly hint. We have heard how delegated messengers to the Dalai Lama disappear on their way. We have seen how the letters addressed to His Holiness are thrown torn on the road. Very recently the Lhassan government put on the market sacred objects which belonged to the Tashi Lama. Into the hands of traders passed the rare ancient Tankas and other sacred images blessed by high priests. Thus was this Blessing regarded by the government which claims to be religious! The Maharajah of Sikhim told us with great pain of this act of barbarism. The principles of life are distorted. Not we, but Tibetans themselves, remarked this. They understand that without intercourse with other countries, lacking a strong spirit of its own, Tibet is excluded from contemporary evolution.

It is inconceivable to imagine how often the given commands of Buddha and his closest followers in Tibet have degenerated. We recall the remarkable works, full of vital wisdom, of Asvaghosha and Nagarjuna, the hymns of the hermit Milaraspa and the canon of Atisha and the great Amdosian, Tsong kha pa. Would these Guardians of the teaching have permitted impious demonstrations here? Could they have reconciled themselves to these lies, betrayals and superstitions, which have penetrated to many classes of people, especially the ruling class. During the British Expedition to Lhassa in 1904, Dr. Waddell relates in his book how the Tibetan government intimidated the British by pretending that forty thousand men from Kham were impatient for battle and the government was unable to restrain them. But not a single warrior revealed himself. This boasting appears very characteristic in the mouth of some Tibetan officials. Sir Charles Bell, in his Tibetan dictionary, gives such phrases as "Do not lie" and a second, "Again do not lie," and "Do not lie or otherwise you will be whipped."

Exaggeration sometimes reaches such a point that a pitiful clay-beaten hut, in a document of Tibetan officials is termed, "a majestic snowy palace." The title of the Lhassa government, stamped even on the sho, the poor copper coins, boastfully proclaims the blessed government to be "victorious in all directions."

At the root of such boasting lies ignorance, through isolation from the entire world. The Buddhists of Ladak, Sikhim and Mongolia, who have come close to the outer world, manifest far more enlightened thought. Ignorance gives birth to boasting; and self-praise to the unlimited lie.

Near such sacred places as Kapilavastu, Kushinagara, Bodhigaya and Sarnath, where passed the life of the Blessed One himself, near India, with its great Vedic wisdom, only uplifting signs should exist.

Those venerable lamas who, in an enlightened life of labor, follow the covenants of the Blessed One, will not take for themselves what has here been said. This pertains to the ignorant and harmful falsifiers. The best lamas will say with us in the name of true teaching, "Depart, Shaman! You have not taken part in evolution. The Blessed Buddha denounced thee, Shaman! Arise, enlightened pupil of the true covenants, because you alone can call yourself a lama-teacher of the people. Only through learning and labor shall you realize what is knowledge, truth, fearlessness and compassion."

We shall not draw any general conclusions. In fact, we shall always recall with special joy those happy manifestations which we saw on the way. We know many fine things about the Tashi Lama. I am glad to state what reverence surrounds his name in Mongolia, China and everywhere. I recollect some fine personalities among the High Lamas who followed the spiritual leader of Tibet in his flight. One recalls the sympathetic face of the abbot of Spitug; the old abbot of Tashi-ding in Sikhim, a carved medieval image; the Mongolian lama who busied himself with the translation of algebra; the sincere and industrious abbot of Ghum; the gelongs and skilful artists of Tashi Lhunpo. With pleasure and satisfaction we shall always remember the exalted spirit of Geshe-rinpoche of Chumbi. But all these good people are far from Lhassa. With them we would, as several years ago, meet in trust and friendship, and would speak, in the peace of the evening twilight of the mountains, about the highest subjects.

The guarding of the covenants of Buddha, imposes a high responsibility. In the prediction of the approaching advent of the illumined Maitreya, you can see the steps to the creative evolution. The great conception of Shambhala obliges one to incessant accumulation of knowledge, obliges one to enlightened labor, and broad understanding. Is there a place, together with this exalted understanding, for the lowest Shamanism, and fetichisms? The fearless Lion-Sanghe incessantly fought against superstition and ignorance. He would have ejected all hypocrites from their self-appropriated possessions. Mme. David-Neel, who spent several years in Tibet, near the Tibetan boundaries, quotes a Tibetan prophecy about the purification, soon to come, of Lhassa from its poisonous elements. We had occasion to become convinced that such belief is held among the folk masses, who in a peculiar but quite decisive way, isolate themselves from the Lhassa government. The Hor, the tribes of the Tibetan uplands, asked us not to confuse them with the Lhassa Tibetans. The people from Amdos and the inhabitants of Kham always emphasize their distinction from the Lhassans. And of course the Mishimi and all kinds of forest and savage tribes believe themselves to be quite free from any influence from Lhassa. All these peoples, outside of Lhassa, speak quite openly against the Lhassa officials. They quote the prophecy that a new ruler from Shambhala, with numberless warriors, shall come to vanquish and to establish righteousness in the citadel of Lhassa. From the same people we also learned that, according to the prophecy which has originated from the monastery Tanjyeling, the ruling Dalai Lama is called the thirteenth and the last. From some monasteries also originated the prophecies that the true teaching shall depart from Tibet and return again to Bodhigaya, whence it originated.

Tibet calls itself the heritage of Buddha and the guardian of the true teaching. Thus, the accepted responsibility is great. Isolation and ignorance have created misconception - some of the Tibetans hate the Chinese; they look from on high on Ladakis, Sikhimese and Bhutanese. Tibetans are afraid of the English and Russians. They do not trust the Japanese and do not allow the learned Japanese Buddhists to enter their country. They turn away from Moslems; they call the Buryats oxen; they treat the Kalmuks arrogantly. They consider the Mongols as their serfs. They hate the Hinayana of Burma and Ceylon. Thus, one perceives a strange mixture of human hatreds, which have nothing in common with the peaceful, all-comprehending teaching of Buddha. This ignorance forces these Tibetans into apparent hypocrisy, for although they despise all neighbors and every one in the world, they are not averse to using for profit every one of the enumerated nationalities. Electric light and Western machinery are temporarily forbidden now in Lhassa but some Tibetans like very much to receive as gifts all Western products.

Under such circumstances, the populations can no longer forbear. Rebellions are rising. Litang and Batang, the most fertile parts of Eastern Tibet, are again occupied by the Chinese. In the fall of 1927, there were misunderstandings with the Northerners of Horpa. At present there is an uprising in Eastern Tibet. It is said that the governor and five hundred soldiers were killed. Some Tibetans told us that several lamas are leading the rebellion. The arrow of war - this peculiar sign of mobilization - wrapped in red silk, followed our caravan for several days. Even in such a special case the population would not come to the aid of the Lhassa government alertly. Instead of sending a specially despatched rider they preferred to send out this urgent message on the yaks of a stranger's caravan going ten or fifteen miles a day. The powerful garrison of Shigatse was moved, and at the Nepalese frontier, from Tingri, half the garrisons have been taken.

Obtaining evidence of the actual conditions in Tibet, of course depended on a personal knowledge of the language. Through local interpreters it is not possible to approach the sensitive, complex apparatus of religious strata. But we were fortunate in this circumstance and therefore we can speak about the reality of Tibet: my son, George, has so mastered the Tibetan language, that, according to the Tibetans themselves, he is regarded second only to Sir Charles Bell whom they consider the authority in their language. In this manner of personal intercourse with the people, in true contact with the life, we became acquainted with the unadorned truth.

It is my custom to look on all circumstances with a tolerant eye. I gathered sympathetically everything that I could find in Sikhim, Ladak, Mongolia which was worthy. When the great teachings are demeaned and a pure philosophy is defiled, one should affirm it with full justice and frankness. I do not speak in order to attack the Tibetans. I know that the best Tibetans will agree that all that is related here is the truth, and is useful in the approaching rejuvenation of Tibet.

Certainly as in every country, in Tibet live two consciousnesses - one illumined, evolving; the other, dark, prejudiced, hostile to light. But we as friends, certainly wish that the first should prevail and that this light should lead this country towards the steps of beautiful commandments for the betterment of spiritual life. Before me is an exquisite image of the Dalai Lama the Fifth. Again remember that this builder could uplift the country to high pages of history and progress. He was so needed for the State, that even his death was temporarily concealed.

A similarly illumined and constructive consciousness just now is so needed for Tibet to strengthen the high traditions of the past for the happiness of the future. We can affirm that inwardly, Tibetans are open to Spiritual rejuvenation.

Forseeing the future, Buddha said: "The teaching is like a flame of the torch which lights up numerous fires; these may be used to prepare food or dispel darkness. But the flame of the torch remains unchangingly aglow" (Sutra 42).

Now in Ladak and Sikhim, the enlightened lamas erect great images of Maitreya as a symbol of the approach of the new era; they - the solitary ones - understand how much purification and resurrection must be achieved without delay. These can still adorn the words, "Let the light be firm as adamant; victorious as the banner of the Teacher; powerful as an eagle, and let it endure eternally."

Kampa Dzong, May 19, 1928.

TIBETAN ART

The red door, aglow with the gold of ornament, slowly opens. In the twilight of Dukhang, the gigantic image of Maitreya majestically rises into the height. Through the velvety patina of time, one begins to discern upon the walls the delicate silhouettes of images - a whole series of stern Bodhisattvas, guardians and keepers... Powerfully they stand, outlined by a firm hand. Time has enriched the colors and mellowed the sparks of gold. They transmit an unforgettable impression of exalting joy!

The entrance is blue-white, like old Chinese porcelain. There is a tiny door and a high threshold. Like old banners of the great spiritual battles, rows of Tankas hang from the carved balustrade. Numerous paintings glow with a multi-form variety of themes. Golden and purple riders gallop against a black background. The golden filaments of clouds and edifices are interwoven into a scroll of inexhaustible imagination. Upon them are depicted hermits taming the elements. Teachers are ascending the perilous paths. The dark forces are humbled. Hosts of the righteous as well as sinners are thronging around the thrones of the Blessed Ones. On white hatiks - ceremonial scarfs - travelers cross the abysses of life. And the Blessed Tathagata, in the circle of chosen Arhats, sends His Blessings to the approaching ones who are un-fearful of the Great Way. We shall not forget this shrine of precious banners. It shall always fill us with a strength as for battle.

There is another carved entrance. Above the broad steps, in full power, stand the Dharmaraja - the Rulers of all lands. They guard the gates to the great Mother of All Being. The multiple-eyed, omniscient Dukhar, surrounded by resplendent Taras - these are the self-sacrificing guardians of mankind. The gold surface has not yet been completely subdued by the noble covering of time. But dampness already weaves its pattern on the walls. High above the Taras is the Mandala of Shambhala. The indefatigable ruler Rigden-jyepo keeps vigilance on the tower, in the sacred circle of the snowy mountains. The warriors are gathered together. We shall not forget this great symbol.

Now we are on remote mountain passes. The snows are already nearby. On this pathway of antiquity appears a gigantic image of Maitreya carved on a rock, bestowing blessings upon the travelers. Not by an average hand was the surface of the rock transformed into this mighty, monumental image. The fire of achievement, a strength of touch, and an indefatigability of labor summoned human forces to the creation of this image upon the now-deserted path. Verily, this is great and significant in thought and in expression, and impelling in masterly craftsmanship. A great art!

The black and gold banners are of Chinese origin. The character of the design and composition is apparently reminiscent of China. Dukhar and Taras - they are the Mother Kali of Great India and the Blessed Kwan Yin of hoary China; they have come from afar to this Tibetan Dukhang. Maitreya recalls the Bodhigaya of India. The Image of the Blessed One directs your thought to Sar-nath; the Hindu origin of the image is even pointed out to you. The mighty Maitreya on the rock was carved by some hand in the Sixth or Seventh Centuries - one which knew of great India. You recall the technique of the Trimurti of Elephanta. You are transported to the sculptures of Mathura, to the frescoes of Ajanta, to the fairy tale of Ellora, to the majestic ruins of Anuradhapura, to the picturesque masses of Rangoon and Mandalay.

Everything that we see in Tibetan temples inevitably evokes reminiscences of India and China. The flow of the water-fall recalls its source!

Four years of wanderings through all the Buddhist countries have permitted the accumulation of many impressions. From the unforgettable fairy-tale of the cave temples of Central Asia to the Ten Thousand Buddhas recently ordered by Buddhists of Mongolia from Polish factories (as if the East had become depleted to such an extent!); from the impoverished monastery comprising a transportable yurta of the steppe, to the painting of Shambhala carried by the wandering lama - we have seen all.

Of course, everywhere we have been astonished by the distinction between the old and modern images. The powerful conception of ancient temples, their grandeur and proportions, their discriminately chosen sites and the lavishness of their construction, speak to us of quite a different spiritual condition in their creators. The meager proportions, indifferent choice of sites, instability of construction and ornamentation make some of the new Tibetan temples unconvincing. Those who lived as eagles upon the heroic rocks, have passed away. The Tibetans themselves stress the advantages of the ancient work, and the importance of the site in view of its antiquity. And this is not the mirage of antiquity; it is simply reality, and an evident difference in the quality of the creation.

Certainly, time with its inimitable accumulations adorns all things. We know how ennobled by time are the Primitives of Italy, Spain and the Netherlands. The Persian merchants spread their carpets under the feet of the bazaar crowds in order to obtain the precious patina. So we may attribute a great deal of the attractiveness of old Tibet to the lure of time.

Besides, it is entirely evident that the mastery of old artists of Tibet was finer and keener. Their spiritual striving gave them an inspiration which passed beyond the boundaries of the conventional mechanical canon.

Dalai Lama the Fifth, called the Great, who was responsible for the Potala, the only significant structure of Tibet, knew how to strengthen the nerve of spirit. Several of the Tashi Lamas knew how to encourage talent.

It is significant to note how everywhere the inner stimulus establishes the quality of production. It lights or extinguishes the fire of creation, of all the productions of a nation. The true history of a nation could be written by the monuments of its creation and production. Now, after the departure of the Tashi Lama, Tibet is somewhat lowered spiritually and in the expressions of its art.

The entire literature of the Buddhist teaching emanated from India and China. It is pointed out that Tibetan translations from the Sanskrit are stereotyped because of the paucity of expression in the Tibetan language and fail to express many of the subtleties which evolved from the wisdom of India.

Of course, in addition to India and China, Tibet has more ancient heritages. On the rocks we found old drawings. Out of the vastness of antiquity, the Swastika summons us - this sign of the fiery cross of life. Since the periods of ancient migrations there remain in Tibet some typical forms of handicraft. But the art of the great wanderers is entirely forgotten by modern Tibetans. True, that up to now, the swords of Tibet remind you of the Gothic tombs. Fibulae and buckles reveal to you the Goths and Alans. One recalls the unexpected information from the chronicles of Catholic missionaries, that the site of Lhassa is somewhere called Gotha. In the Doring district, in the Trans-Himalayas, we found an old buckle with the double-headed eagle, so much like our discoveries in the South Russian steppes and northern Caucasus. In the same locality we discovered ancient tombs entirely like the tombs in Altai where the Goths passed.

The women of this district wear a head-dress of the form of the Kokoshnik - so typical of the Slavonic countries of Europe. At an altitude of fifteen thousand feet, we also found ancient stone sanctuaries like those of the Druidic sun-cult - but of this we shall speak later in detail. Hence, when we, freezing in Chunargen, called Tibet jestingly the Land of the Niebelungen, we were closer to the truth than we could have foreseen. Recalling all the assimilations and imitations of Tibet, it is really impossible to speak about Tibetan art. Really it is difficult to recall architectural, sculptural or pictorial monuments which do not find their source in the refined treasures of India and China.

Let us also not forget the technical influence on Tibet on the side of Nepal. Nepal itself has not created original forms and was nurtured by the influence of India. In paintings, Nepal is without distinction, but good Nepalese metal workers and goldsmiths from time immemorial, carried into Tibet a specific form of technique.

Just before me I have two excellent images of old Tibet: the image of Buddha in which you immediately discern the Hindu type and Hindu influence. Another of very fine work, is an image of Dalai Lama the Fifth, justly called the Great. This image recalls the fine Chinese work and probably came from Derge. Now Tibet does not make images of such perfection.

Authorities say that the best Sino-Tibetan objects are to be found through

China. And that is so. Again, the Nepalo-Tibetan images can easily and justly be attributed to Nepal and India.

A collector once hearing my opinion that an original Tibetan Art did not exist, became worried, and asked me whether it was at all worth while to collect this art. To this I replied: "Of course it is worth while. Surely you do not love and value these images for the sake of Tibet as such. Be it a Chinese or Nepalese hand that made them, is this not immaterial to you? You are interested in the results of craftsmanship. And whether you place the object in the Chinese section of your collection or whether in the Indian-Nepalese one, does not influence the characteristics of craftsmanship nor does it diminish the value of iconographical symbology."

One consequently observes the very curious fact, that east of Lhassa, China, in certain respects, begins at once; whereas to the west there is the influence of Nepal, although even in some monasteries of Ladak we noticed Tankas of a comparatively recent date and of decidedly Chinese meaning and expression. There is also much Chinese influence in Sikhim. Visiting monasteries, one often meets typical Chinese images in gold on black backgrounds, and statues of Chinese dragons and lions. In the Sikhim monasteries one observes incidentally, a custom which certainly merits praise. None of their sacred objects are for sale, and they are all entered into special inventory lists; which indicates already a certain degree of cultural self-consciousness. In Tibet and in the western provinces of China this rule unfortunately does not yet apply.

An interesting instance of western influence, we saw in Tibet where we found a peculiar coin minted in Unan, representing Queen Victoria in Chinese garments. The popular appreciation of silver Indian rupees produced this strange imitation in which is seen the unique spell that the name of Queen Victoria cast throughout the expanses of Asia.

After mentioning the interpretive arts, such as painting, sculpture, wood and metal work, one cannot omit also to refer to the condition of Tibetan architecture. Of architecture in Tibet one may say about the same as of the other arts: It is based on the Chinese. In the old constructions one may notice a considerable solidity and a certain sweep of fantasy. Looking at them, there involuntarily comes to mind that it would not be difficult to furnish these monumental many-storied structures and their effective balconies, terraces and cornices with the latest innovations of the American skyscrapers. But this strikingly decorative quality is to be found only in ancient constructions, where the large architectural planes are set into beautiful proportions by elaborate multicolored ornaments. All the new houses, however, having lost in constructive grandeur, also lose the sharpness of accurate craftsmanship. As often happens, a misguided emulation of "civilization" destroys the most characteristic parts and the Tibetan house of to-day resembles rather a clumsy badly built box in its construction.

As regards temples, one must say that voluntary contributions have apparently become rare and, whereas in old temples one sees work of wrought-gold and finely carved ornaments, in the more recent temples only shoddy gilt clay images, cheap tin and poorly carved wood-work are to be found.

One still sees the curious Tanagra-like pottery, which in its proportions reminds one so much of the antique amphoras. The appearance of the clumsy, heavy Tibetans of to-day seems to have little in common with these fine and elaborate lines. These forms were certainly created in the past under the effect of a different psychology.

The same thing is apparent, also, when you compare the new swords with the ancient ones, or when comparing the present-day headwear with the family heirlooms inherited from their grandmothers.

Among the artistic handwork and ornaments, the so-called "dzi" beads have quite a special place. They are considered as sacred objects and many legends and beliefs have gathered about them. Some say that these stones are of natural origin, like the onyx. Others say that they are found in the excrements of cranes and also in the dung of yaks. Others say that they are found during the field work and that they spring out of the grass with a special cracking sound. And the people add that if one dzi springs out, others may usually be found near that place.

In view of the sacred and guarded peculiarities of the dzi, the price for them has risen to fifteen hundred rupees, depending on their properties. An oblong bead with one white eye is high in price, but still higher is the dzi with nine eyes. For some strange reason the seven-eyed dzi is completely unknown.

Naturally in view of the great value of the dzi, which brings health, wealth and good fortune, there have appeared many imitations in China. But the Tibetans and the Sikhimese easily discern them from the old ones. Incidentally, this is not very difficult, for the present day dzi is much coarser and sharper in line, and is devoid of that special transparency, which is so typical of the old dzi.

In view of the definitely outlined designs, the possibility of a natural mineral origin of the dzi must be absolutely rejected. Of course, they are the handiwork of very old times. The story that dzi are found when working the fields and usually several dzi together, would lead to the same conclusion. Only one question remains unsolved: From where did the dzi originally come into Tibet, and to what people did they belong?

As is usual in many countries, objects brought into a country by foreign travelers are considered to be of heavenly origin and a sacred meaning is attached to them... Maybe the excavation of ancient burial places in Tibet could afford a solution to this question, which is almost unmentioned in literature, but to which such importance is attached in Tibet itself. Already the unprecedented high prices and the specially designed imitations indicate what attention the local population gives to the dzi beads.

In the technical tradition it is very interesting to trace the same methods which are characteristic of the medieval Ikon paintings which were used until recent times by the professional Russian rustic Ikon painters. Watching the work of lama Ikon painters, I recognized a method of work completely like the work of the Russian provincial Ikon painters. In the same way the wood or canvas is prepared. In the same manner the "levkas" - that is chalk and glue - is prepared for the background. Similarly is the prepared wood and canvas polished by a shell or horn. In the same way is the stencil transferred and colored with very fine brushes. The only difference is that the Russian Ikon painters cover the Ikon with oil varnish. They carefully preserve the formula of this varnish and are proud of the durability of the work. Russian Ikon painters often have manuscripts in script about the technique of Ikons and these are sometimes written in a secret symbolical code. Such manuscripts are preserved in families and only handed down from father to son. Of such manuals I have never heard in Tibet. One more resemblance between Tibetan and Russian Ikon painters: Both chant during their work and often the Russian Ikon painters intone the old chants about Yosephat Tzare-vitch, not suspecting that they sing of the Blessed Buddha. Yosephat is the altered pronunciation of Bodhisattva.

Another circumstance indicated the close influence of China on the art of Tibet. The best Tibetan Ikon painters come from Kham. The best images are molded in Derge, and there also the printing is best. Tibetans themselves say that they cannot imitate the perfection of the Chinese work. The Maharajah of Sikhim possesses a group of very colorful Tankas of apparent Chinese quality. Certainly the series must be from Kham. Some good works are also to be found in Tashi Lhunpo as befitted the residence of the spiritual head of Tibet.

One may find, however, many touching details of ikonographic work. There still is left to us the interest in ikonography and the symbolism of images! To study it is highly instructive. You may find many forgotten occult laws. Pay attention to how the auras are depicted. Look on the magic mirrors. Study the meaning of the magic circle of Mandala of Norbu-rinpoche. But the contemporary artists know less of these laws. The Kalachakra, brought from India by Atticha, is repeated without application to life. But "will everything which has fallen - not rise again?" In the future there will be a new Tibetan people ... and a Tibetan art. But when and how?

"With fire is the space filled. Already the lightning of Kalki Avatar - predestined Maitreya - flashes upon the horizon."

The regeneration of Tibet will come. There were moments when after cataclysms the consciousness was awakened in full vigor by these explosions of spiritual accumulations. Entire vivid epochs were created. Some people may still remain immovable, devouring raw meat, losing their teeth from scurvy, from an unhealthy life and rotting in unchanged germ-ridden skins. In Lhassa it is temporarily forbidden to have electric lights on the streets. Moving pictures are forbidden. In all Tibet the laity is forbidden to shave its hair and has again been ordered to garb itself in long khalats, and in Tibetan-Chinese shoes. All these symptoms are not ordained by the Blessed One. Because each teaching foresees the possession of possibilities and the evolutionary movement. These Tibetan forbiddances are revealing mechanical superstitious worship of the past. But we shall ask: "Which past do you worship? To which of your grandfathers do you wish to pay homage?" In retrogression one can go back even to the inarticulate sounds of his forefathers. The past is good as long as it does not impede the future. We love and value all the beauty and charm of the past. We confirm that "from the stones of the past may be erected the steps of the future." But from the stones, let us lay out the complete majestic steps of new beauty and knowledge. And what can evolve, if the death of the past has occurred and the future is forbidden?

* * *

But from where shall Tibet now accept the teachings? Yet in the midnight, into the tent a lama comes and cautiously peering about, speaks of the purification of the entire teaching. Such lamas do not live in Lhassa but on the heights.

Out of the desert distances a rider rushes from unknown friends. He whispers friendly advice - arranges his gold-woven kaftan and disappears into the twilight of the desert.

Whence art thou, messenger? Whence is thy smile?

Shekar Dzong, 1928.

THE VEILS OF DEATH

Many are the veils which dim the pages of history. The dust of life covers much...

"Where is our old *aya*, the wife of the Red Lama, she who so zealously executed her tasks, who so quietly entered the room and as quietly departed? She who was so discreet, knowing only what it was her duty to know?"

"She is dead."

"But she always seemed healthy! Apparently she never drank and was never loose in her ways."

"No - she was poisoned!"

"But how can you speak so indifferently of such a violent crime? How did it happen?"

"Many are poisoned here. This no longer surprises us. There may have been many reasons. Perhaps she knew more than she should have known. Perhaps she aroused some one's vengeance through an unintentional act. Or perhaps she was too often among her relatives."

Thus lightly, is poison regarded, as a cause of death in the East.

Ts'ai-han-chen, our old Chinese, becomes very worried when we are invited to the Amban for dinner. He offers us much advice and finally ends with, "Altogether, it is better not to eat there. The Dao-tai is a wicked man. He is not an official - his acts are those of an assassin!"

"So, you think he will poison us?" we inquire.

"I did not say so - but all precautions must be taken. You know that when the Governor of the Province, the mighty Yan D'u-t'u, wanted to rid himself of some undesirable relatives, he invited them to dinner. Behind each guest was stationed an honorary guard. But when the dinner was almost finished, the D'u-t'u himself shot his closest relative and the guards cut off the heads of the others.

"It was the same D'u-t'u who, wishing to free himself of an undesirable official, gave him a mission of honor. When the official had set out on his way, the D'u-t'u's people waylaid him in a remote spot and strangled him in a unique way; they pasted him over completely with paper.

"You know," continues Ts'ai-han-chen smiling, "D'u-t'u is most ingenious. He can get a man to confess to anything. One of his most effective methods is to pass a horsehair from one corner of the eye through to the other - then they start drawing it back and forth. So, you had better avoid eating during the dinner; better tell them that your constitution does not permit you to eat food to which you are unaccustomed."

Our Kalmuk lama also bids us farewell with, "I shall pray for you - because one never knows what may happen in the course of a dinner."

These local people know so many stories of the treachery of the officials; to support their statements they will show you secretly a photograph of the crucified Ti-tai, the high commander of Kashgar, who was treacherously trapped by the cruel Dao-tai of Khotan. Innumerable tales of treason and poison envelop the old cities.

The Tibetans have learned much about the Chinese Ambans. A high Tibetan official says, "When they offer you tea - be careful. In one notable family, I was offered tea, but I am experienced and I noticed that odd bubbles were rising to the surface of the cup. I happen to know the poison which gives this effect - so I avoided drinking."

Another Tibetan relates how one of the high and worthy lamas was almost poisoned by food given to him with the appearance of utmost reverence. But immediately on tasting it, he noticed a strange taste and did not swallow it. Although he became ill, he thus escaped death. Numerous legends are related about high lamas who have been poisoned, and even in the history of the Dalai lamas this practise is mentioned more than once. It is striking to hear what strange practises are attributed to lamas. It is said that some lamas became wandering spirits after death, using a type of magic dagger to kill even the innocent. The famous "Rollang" of Tibet, the resurrection of corpses is often linked with the names of lamas.

You may still see the ruins of a monastery and hear how during the funeral rites a corpse revived and in a fury killed eight monks. Since that time the monastery was deserted. It is said that a corpse may be brought back to a living condition, if a heavy blow is struck against it and if a large amount of blood is permitted to flow from the body.

One may find various explanations for these stories but they are recorded and related with great frequency.

Not only in Tibet but also in Nepal, strange stories are told. For instance, it is said that even up to the present time, during the burial of the Maharajah, the senior high priest must eat a piece of the flesh of the dead ruler. And as a reward he receives the great privilege of admission to the most exalted spheres of heaven.

Parallel with these strange customs one may see various objects skilfully adapted for poisoning. For instance, there are daggers and arrows with special secret appliances for poison. A favorite object employed in this practise is, of course, a ring containing a poison compartment. One should also mention poisoned fabrics.

Probably the strangest belief encountered here is that he who poisons a man of high standing is said to receive all the luck and privileges of his victim. Where and how such a corrupt idea could have originated is even impossible to imagine. Along this same trend of thought, it is said that there are certain families who collect secret formula of special poisons and have the special privilege of being poisoners. When you hear of cases of certain people perishing from unknown sicknesses, you wonder whether these strange customs have been exercised upon the victims.

Friendly Tibetans advise you to be cautious of food in strange houses. Sometimes, in token of special reverence, food is sent to your home. You must take the greatest care. In fact at all times in these lands it is best to be careful with food, because outside of poison deliberately sent, you might easily receive spoilt food. The dried meat is often not fresh. The corn and barley may be mixed with small stones and all kinds of dirt. The bread may not be properly baked. Some of the Chinese canned foods may be spoilt, either because of the long journey or because of poor packing. Naturally it is understood that the same dish is used for every possible and every unexpected purpose. Ignorance and cleanliness are not good companions.

I remember that several officials did not take one particle of food throughout an entire official dinner and visit. They gave poor health as a reason. Perhaps they desired to prolong their lives, or. perhaps they recalled various precedents - and even their own practises. I also remember how when certain honorary offerings were brought to us in the form of various dishes, even the simplest asked dubiously: "Are you going to eat it?"

But all this physical poison is perhaps nothing in comparison with "spiritual" poisoning. Every one has heard of the effects of hypnotic influence. It is impossible to control the acts of an evil will-power; all kinds of "sunniums" are based on this power of incantation. The ancient tales of the "terraphim" are corroborated even in modern times, and the "murderous" eye is given credence in stories of revenge and curse.

This "psychic" murder and injury is far more ancient and more widely distributed than actual poisoning itself. For instance, I remember one conversation to which I was a witness, when one person thus tried to convince his fellow-conversationalist: "Why don't you use a hypnotist in your scheme? Imagine what possibilities you could have to smooth and direct everything!"

The other one replied, "If I invite a hypnotist, he will hypnotize me, first of all. And then I will not do what I wish but what he wishes himself."

How many unconscious hypnotists are at work over all the earth sending their thoughts out along the streams of space!

History has also known many self-hypnotized crowds working enthusiastically for some true movement for the common good. But there have also been many more occasions when a self-hypnotized mob worked unconsciously for destruction. Only a real unfoldment of the Spirit can guarantee that the psychic force will be directed toward a high constructive purpose.

In the Westerner whose eyes more often glide over the surface in haste and rush, the fixation of the eye does not attain tremendous intensity. But when you examine the glances of people in various countries of Asia you notice quite a different force in the effect of this look. ... It is not the result of conscious study but is rather a racial characteristic. As one physician said to me, "It seems that the crystal of the eye of an Easterner is placed somewhat differently than ours." Incidentally one may notice that an Easterner, after long lapses of time, will recall your face much more quickly than do many people in the West. I recall how, after many years, quite simple people in the East recognized and placed us at once, although our meeting took place under completely unrelated circumstances. When, added to this natural ability, you add special training and special refining of the inner human forces, one may realize with what a powerful apparatus one has to deal.

Some time ago, I spoke of the story about the Tashi Lama during his visit to India. He was asked whether he possessed any "supernatural" powers, but he only smiled and was silent. In a few moments, however, to the utter atonishment of every one present, he completely disappeared. But at that moment, a new guest entered and saw a strange sight - the Tashi Lama was sitting on the very place where he had been, but every one was rushing about in commotion searching for him! Almost identical incidents are told about many high lamas and Hindu Yogi. And in the extension of this power of suggestion, we approach the example of the charming of animals and one recalls the greatest evidences of suggestion in the stories of the murderous eye, which could smite even tigers.

In widely scattered stories of sorcery on the Malabar coast, one may hear of the invoking of disease and even of death upon enemies. Even more often than disease, are depression and the lowering of the psychic energy, the results of the invocation on a weak will power. One involuntarily recalls the desert saying: "If your companion is cross-eyed you should also squint."

This folk-saying expresses the belief about the need of using caution with one's fellow traveler.

Of course after the natural fund of psychic energy became exhausted and to a certain extent lost, there appeared that ally of evil minds, poison. Side by side with stories of recent fatal effects of suggestions, one may hear some convincing story of how one person was poisoned by fast poison, another by a slow poison. At the same time, as one descends the slopes of the Himalayas, he is astonished by the great amount of curative herbs and fruits. When one sees how nature itself offers of its best for healing and for humanity's happiness, all these tales of poison and murder seem but a gloomy specter in the dark passages of ruins. And one feels that the psychic energy prophesied in ancient wisdom will once again be directed toward life and not death.

We are told about the new era of the fire of space which is approaching. What new constructions will it bring into our reality? The might of fire may destroy certain rocks and islands, truly, but what a benevolent force will be attracted by this purifying element!

Within our own recollection, the flames of pyres consumed unhappy widows. On the walls of China we read inscriptions that "on this site it is forbidden to drown girls." Out of these facts of the quite recent past and even of the present, one may draw a most depressing picture. But in recollecting the worst, we often erect the strongest walls dividing the undesirable past and the blessed future. One knows how enemies, in their exaggeration, carry matters to absurdity. He, who knows the characteristics of his enemies, has never poisoned them, because life itself - like the blessed plants on the Himalayan slopes - has brought forth the healing fruit and herbs and called humanity to enlightened study and incessant research.

And we shall not fear to call by their proper terms acts of the greatest frailty. This is not a pitiless condemnation; it is an act impelled by cosmic justice. Each frailty, when recognized, is already ripe for improvement. The dark melts away into darkness, but each shaft of light is already a ray of resurrection.

Nagchu, 1927.

OBSESSION

"I still cannot believe what you tell me about obsessions. They may be simply a reflection of the subconscious mind. For do we not all hear and read and see all kinds of things during our lifetime? Then we forget them; but the fissures of our brain somehow retain these facts and then later, unexpectedly disclose them. Then they seem entirely foreign to us."

Thus spoke a friend in Urga to me. He, being an official, regards skepticism as the supreme mark of dignity.

One must never insist, nor even try to convince. Often, it is only necessary to draw another's attention to a slight incident, and at this sign of the semaphor, the entire trend of life may change its course. Hence, without insistence, our friend was informed of a few other events, which had obsession as their underlying theme. He was told about the Tibetan "Rollang" - the resurrection of the dead. But of course the skeptic only shrugged his shoulders; he disdained to speak of it.

We told him of an incident in the United States, where a person of high intelligence maintained that her deceased bridegroom had taken possession of her and was controlling her entire life, offering advice and giving her orders. In fact, her obsessor demonstrated such distinction from her own consciousness, that he caused her not only spiritual indisposition but even physical pain.

Our skeptic answered that such "obsessed" people could probably be found by the scores in our lunatic asylums and that in the practise of the law, such incidents of irresponsible consciousness were well known. However, this did not convince him in the least. We then told him how, according to the Chinese, the Tao-tai of Khotan had become obsessed by the Thai whom he himself had killed. And how the Chinese now point out that the murderer has adopted certain characteristic habits of the dead man and that even the face of the murderer has changed most characteristically within a short time.

The skeptic again only shrugged his shoulders.

Several days passed. Then one evening our skeptic came to visit us, looking somewhat strange. Apparently something perplexed him and he seemed to search for an opportunity to blurt it out. Finally he exclaimed:

"One listens to your tales - and then all kinds of strange things begin to happen. After the last conversation we had concerning the 'obsessed' people, as you call them, I dropped in to the Chinese photographer. He is married to a very simple Buryat woman, quite illiterate. I've known them for a long time. I noticed that the Chinese was somewhat sad, quite changed, so I asked him if he was ill.

" 'No,' he answered me. 'I'm all right - but it's my wife. It's bad. I don't know how to cure her. Recently she began to talk of the strangest things! She says that some one has taken possession of her - not one person but two simultaneously. God knows where she gets the strange words from. It seems that one of them was drowned. The other died from over-drink. I know that things like that happen, because we used to have many cases like that at home in China."

"I asked him to call his wife. In she came. She always was small and slight, but now she looked far thinner. You know, she is quite a simple Buryat woman, entirely illiterate. When she entered, her husband left the room. I asked her, 'Won't you have tea with me, too?'

" 'No,' she answered, 'he forbids me to drink tea with you because you do not believe and you wish me harm.' - 'Who forbids you?' I asked her. 'Oh, it's always he - the German.' - 'What German? Tell me where he comes from.'

"'Well,' she continued, 'one is Adolph; the other is Felix. They are in me for three weeks already!' - 'And where are they from?', I asked.

" 'Some time ago,' she began, 'a man came to see my husband, to have his picture taken. He was a fat German - maybe you have seen him in the street; he has some kind of business. These two were with him. He went away, but the two remained and they became tied up to me. One of them, Adolph, became a coolie after the war in Vladivostok. He was drowned when he went out boating. They had a fight. The other, Felix, is also a German, and he is always drunk and swears terribly!'

"And so she continued to tell me what they made her do, how they compelled her to eat much meat, especially uncooked, because they liked it with blood. They also suggested to her to drink wine because they liked it very much. One of them, the drunkard, continuously whispers to her to hang herself or to cut her throat and that then they could help her to accomplish anything.

"The Buryat woman told me the kind of things the men tell her. They seem to have traveled a great deal on ship, especially one of them. He must have been a sailor. Why, think of it, she gave me the names and descriptions of towns of which she couldn't have had the slightest notion. Then she spoke of ships, and used such technical terms that only a person completely at home on sailing craft would know them. Many of the terms she was unable to explain, when I questioned her further, but she insisted she heard them from the men. I must confess that I left the Chinaman rather puzzled. This is the first time I ever heard such things with my own ears, and it all correlates with the things you have been telling me.

"I must confess I had an insatiable desire to go and see the people again, so I went to-day for the second time. When I asked the Chinese about his wife, he just waved his hands in despair and said that things had become worse. As I asked him whether I could see his wife again, she herself entered the room. - 'I cannot stay here with you,' she said to me. 'They forbid me; they say you want to harm me. They want me to be happy and you can spoil it all. Because you know some people who can drive them away.' Then she left the room and her husband, waving his hands once again, muttered, 'Bad, very bad indeed. Our home will be destroyed.'

"You see, I am a man of the law and I therefore like everything to be authentic. I confess that I did not believe the tales you told me last time, because nothing like it had ever occurred previously in my life. But since I have heard and have seen this thing myself, I can no longer doubt it, because I have known the woman for a long time and she now impresses me quite differently.

"She does not just talk, or talk nonsense as happens in cases of paralysis or pathological cases such as I have often had in my practise. No, in this case I can clearly see something foreign, not her own, with a decided and characteristic psychology. For when she repeats the sentences told to her by the sailor, one can distinctly feel the speech of a seaman, and a seaman of recent, prewar days. Thus also in the speech of the other man, the drunkard; it is precisely that of one of the derelicts whom the war cast into the far-off lands of Siberia.

"By the way," suddenly the confused skeptic asked, "how does one proceed to drive away such obsessions? Because, when she hinted at people I know, I felt at once that she spoke of you."

I laughingly remarked to the skeptic that it appeared as though we had changed roles, and that he would probably laugh if I told him that in such cases of obsession one puts pieces of bloody raw meat on the table and then pours strong-smelling intoxicants all around the room. Then every one must leave the house and the person obsessed must never return to it again. Of course, other methods may be used.

This reminded me of a curious episode which happened in America, when I had a serious disagreement with the spirits. I was asked to view some paintings which were alleged to have been done by an obsessed woman. Up to that time, the woman knew nothing about art and had never touched a brush. I saw a series of strange paintings, obviously painted in various technics and by different hands.

On one and the same canvas, one could see the characteristic technic of a French impressionist, and besides it an equally clear Japanese technic. Here also were Egyptian temples with a decidedly German romantic turn. Thereupon, I remarked to the artist that it seemed peculiar to me that such varied styles should be painted together and on one canvas without any coordination whatsoever. But the artist stated that the painting had been done thus not accidentally, because the spirits who guided her were indeed of various nationalities. Thereupon I observed that this technical medley did not contribute to a completeness of painting. Upon this the artist reflected for a long time and then said sharply, "They find it very good so!" I continued to persist in my opinion and the spirits in a very brusk and rough manner persisted in their own wish that the painting remain as it was. Thus proceeded a quarrel with the spirits which continued with some vigor... "I do not know anything of your American incident," interrupted the skeptic. "But after all I have seen and heard, I now consider it entirely possible. But I would not like to leave the Buryat woman in her present situation. I think that I ought to go there again and try to take some measures."

I attempted to explain to the skeptic that with his complete ignorance of the subject he would only bring harm to the woman, and that he might easily cause her to commit suicide or take other extreme measures. Finally we exchanged roles completely. I tried to dissuade my friend from all further visits to the Chinese, while he, like a drunkard who smells wine, began ingeniously to invent all kinds of excuses to continue this adventure ... It was strange to see how the old lawyer, recently so staid, was trying to find every invention decently possible to justify himself and to show his need of continuing his visits to the Chinese. Naturally, he did not overlook poor science: he had to continue his excursions in the name of science! And again, it was in the name of science that humanity had to be warned. But behind all these important considerations, there was clearly revealed an instinct suddenly aroused to the knowledge of invisible worlds.

The wife of the skeptic, who was also present and who had previously upheld me, now insisted by every measure that I should dissuade her husband from his excursion, for during the last days he had been talking only about the Buryat woman and the Germans. Finally the recent skeptic gave his promise to drop the matter, after I assured him that if he would but look around him, he would see many far more significant things.

On leaving, he suddenly suggested to me that I accompany him just once to a Mongolian witch - "You know, it is the same woman who foretold to Ungarn the day of his death and all his immediate future, which was exactly fulfilled. She lives near here now."

I declined to visit the sorceress but I wonder whether the skeptic did not go to see her himself!

As always happens, an unusual conversation does not cease at once. Hardly had the skeptic left our house, when two other visitors came. One of them, a local Mongol, was highly educated and had lived abroad. The other, an ex-officer, had served throughout the war. The conversation began with some entirely unrelated matters The Mongol was telling of the natural wealth of Mongolia, where mineral oil flows in streams through the desert and where the rivers carry inexhaustible gold. Then describing the gold districts, he added in the same calm narrative tone, "And those murdered Chinamen allowed us no sleep all the time we were staying at the mines."

"But how could the dead disturb your sleep?"

"Those were the dead Chinamen who were killed during the riots, after the war and the revolution."

"But look here, how could people, killed long since, prevent you from sleeping?"

"Exactly by walking around, talking, knocking the ashes out of their pipes and rattling the crockery."

"You are certainly joking."

"No," was the serious reply. "We could not see them but all through the night we could hear them. A lot of them had been killed there and, as people say, they were killed unawares. They went to bed quite calmly that night, not suspecting an attack. It is always so; people who are unexpectedly killed cannot give up their daily habits. The Chinese are especially like that. They love their ground and their houses. And when people are attached to their earthly possessions, it is always difficult for them to leave them behind." So seriously spoke the Mongol.

The officer who had thus far been silent, then added, "Yes, with the Chinese this often happens. In Mukden there is an old house in which no one wants to live. A Chinaman was killed there and he gives no one any peace. Each night he screams out as if he was being killed again. We wanted to verify this rumor once, and we went there and stopped overnight. But about one o'clock we noticed a bright blue sphere descending from the top floor along the railing of the staircase. That was enough for us, I admit, and we packed off.

"But now I remember another case that happened during the war near the Prussian border. The whole staff had stopped over night in a small hut. At midnight we all suddenly awoke together, each one shouting something about horses. One man shouted, 'Who brought the horses in here!' Another roared, 'Look at the horses running away!' I also awoke and in the darkness near me, I saw some horses pass me by in a flash neighing as though in fright. The guards stationed outside had heard nothing. But in the morning we discovered that our drove of horses had been blown up by a shell."

The Mongol became lively thereupon and confirmed this, "I also have heard about invisible animals. It was in the Yurta of our Shaman-sorcerer. The Shaman invoked the lower elementary powers and we all could hear the galloping and neighing of whole droves of horses; we could hear the flight of entire flocks of eagles and the hissing of innumerable snakes right inside the yurta . . . you should speak to our minister of war. He is a fortune teller and he could tell you numberless unsuspected things."

"But why do you think they are unsuspected?"

"Well, I have become accustomed to think that all foreigners regard our customary occurrences as most strange…"

Ulan Bator Khoto, 1927.

CHINGIZ-KHAN

A Song

When Chingiz-Khan was born his mother was no longer a favorite of the Khan and therefore the child found no love in the heart of his father, who sent him to a far-off estate. There, when he had grown into manhood, Chingiz-Khan gathered round him others who were unloved and began to lead an aimless life. He seized arms and bond-maids, went hunting and sent no reports about his life to his father, the Khan.

One day, when perhaps drunk with kumiss, Chingiz-Khan made a pact with his friends that they should follow him in all things till death parted them. Then he ordered a whizzing arrow to be made, and commanded his servants to lead out the horses. They mounted - and this is how Chingiz-Khan began his work.

He rode into the steppes and approached his droves of horses. Suddenly he sped his whizzing arrow, striking his best and fleetest horse. A horse is valued as a treasure among Tartars. Some of his friends hesitated to kill their horses and they were beheaded.

Once more Chingiz-Khan went to the steppes and again let fly his whizzing arrow. This time he struck one of his wives. Not all would follow his example. Then those who were afraid were immediately beheaded. The friends were frightened. But he had bound them by an oath to follow him till death. Truly clever, was Chingiz-Khan.

Then rode Chingiz-Khan toward his father's droves of horses. He sent his whizzing arrow into his father's horse and all his friends did the same. Thus Chingiz-Khan prepared his friends to work with him and tried his men. Not loved, but feared was Chingiz-Khan. Truly clever was Chingiz-Khan!

One day Chingiz-Khan planned great doings. He rode to his father's camp and sent a whizzing arrow into his father's heart. All the friends of Chingiz-Khan followed his example. The old Khan was killed by all the people! And Chingiz-Khan became the Khan of the Great Horde. Truly clever was Chingiz-Khan!

The khans of the Neighboring Empire were not pleased with Chingiz-Khan. They looked disdainfully on the young man and sent an arrogant messenger demanding all his best horses, all the arms set with precious stones and adorned with gold - all the treasures of the Khan. Hearing these demands Chingiz-Khan bowed to the messenger.

Then Chingiz-Khan summoned all his men to a council. His counselors argued together loudly: it was impossible to fight over horses. And all that was demanded of him Chingiz-Khan sent to the neighboring khans. Truly cunning was Chingiz-Khan!

Swollen with pride, the khans of the Neighboring Empire now demanded that all Chingiz' wives should be sent to them. The counselors protested loudly, they pitied the wives of the Khan and threatened to start war. Again Chingiz-Khan dismissed these counselors and sent all his wives to the Neighboring Empire. Truly cunning was Chingiz-Khan!

The khans of the Neighboring Empire were proud beyond measure. They considered the men of Chingiz-Khan cowards; they insulted and abused the people of the Great Horde; and in their pride they took the guards away from the frontier. The khans amused themselves with Chingiz' wives and rode his horses while wrath against them grew stronger and stronger in the Great Horde.

Suddenly, Chingiz-Khan rose up by night, ordered his men to follow him on horseback, and attacked the khans of the Neighboring Empire, taking captive all their people. He took all the treasures, the arms and the horses back again; back he took all his wives.

The victory of Chingiz-Khan was praised by his counselors. And Chingiz-Khan said to his eldest son Otokay: "Know how to make people proud, and pride will make them stupid. Then wilt thou master them!" Throughout the Great Horde the Khan was praised. Truly clever was Chingiz-Khan!

And Chingiz-Khan enjoined the Great Horde eternally to keep these precepts: "He who covets a wife - shall be beheaded. He who blasphemes - shall be beheaded. He who takes others' property - shall be beheaded. He who kills a peaceful man - shall be beheaded. He who passes over to the enemy - shall be beheaded." Thus, for every one Chingiz-Khan appointed a punishment.

Soon the name of Chingiz-Khan was honored everywhere. All the princes feared Chingiz-Khan. As never before the wealth of the Great Horde grew. Each man had many wives. They dressed in silk cloth, and ate and drank exceeding well. Truly, always clever was Chingiz-Khan!

Chingiz-Khan saw far ahead. He ordered his friends to tear the silken cloth, to feign that they were ailing from good eating. Let the people, as of old, drink milk; let them dress in skins as of old; so that the Great Horde might not weaken! Truly clever was our Chingiz-Khan!

The Great Horde was always ready for battle. And Chingiz-Khan would suddenly lead it into the steppes. He conquered all the steppes of Taourmen. He took possession of all the deserts of Mongolia. He vanquished all China and Tibet. He seized all land from the Red Sea to the Caspian. Such was Chingiz-Khan!

LAKSHMI, THE VICTORIOUS

To the east of the mountain Zent-Lhamo, in a resplendent garden, lives the Blessed Lakshmi, Goddess of Happiness. By unending toil she beautifies her seven veils of peace. This is known to all men. All men pay reverence to the Goddess Lakshmi!

But all fear her sister, Siva Tandava. She, the Goddess of Destruction, is full of malice, terrible and destructive.

From behind the mountains came Siva Tandava herself. The terrible one went straight toward the dwelling of Lakshmi. Cautiously the terrible goddess approached the palace of Light and lowering her voice, called out to Lakshmi.

Lakshmi laid aside her precious veils and came forth to meet her. And behind her walked her maidens, full-breasted and round of hip.

Lakshmi, walking, disclosed her body. Large were her eyes, her hair was dark. Her armlets were golden. Her many necklaces were of pearls. The nails of Lakshmi were of the color of amber. Over her breasts and shoulders, and on her abdomen and down to her feet were poured unguents of special sacred herbs. Lakshmi and her maidens are as sparklingly pure as the images of the Temple of Mathura after the storm.

But all righteousness became stricken at sight of the dreaded Siva Tandava, so terrifying was she even in her apparent humility. From out her canine jaw were thrust threatening fangs. So red was her body and so shamelessly hirsute, that it was indecent to look upon. Even the armlets of blood-red rubies could not beautify Siva Tandava. One might even imagine her a man.

The Terrible one spoke:

"Hail to you, Lakshmi, righteous one, my near one! Much happiness and welfare hast thou created. Even too zealously didst thou perform thy work. Thou adornest temples with gold. Thou enrichest the earth with gardens. Thou Protectress of Beauty!

"Thou hast created the rich and the generous. Thou hast created the poor, unreceiving yet rejoicing. Thou hast ordained peaceful trade. Thou hast planted among men all ties called benevolent. Thou hast conceived of joyous frail distinctions for man. Thou hast filled the hearts of people with the joyous realization of their superiority and pride. Thou art generous!

"Thy maidens are tender and caressing. Thy youths are strong and aspiring. Joyously, people create according to their own likeness. People forget about change and destruction. Hail to Thee!

"Calmly you observe the human procession. And there is little left for Thee to do! I worry over thee, my near one! Without labor, without worries, thy body will become heavy. And the precious pearls will fade upon it. Thy face shall shine and thy lovely eyes shall become bovine.

"Then will the people forget to bring pleasant offerings for Thee. They will bring sacred flowers no longer. And you will no longer find any excellent workers for Thyself. All the sacred designs will become entangled. People cannot remain inactive. Here I am, full worrisome about thee, Lakshmi, my near one!

"During long nights I have conceived a labor for Thee. We are akin to each other. Do not pay attention to the exterior. Hard is it for me to await the lengthy destruction of time. Let us unite and let us annihilate all human structures. Let us demolish all human joys. Let us eject all the foundations accumulated by men. Do not be so assured that people follow Thee. People dimly perceive the boundaries.

"Tear down Thy seven veils of peace. And then I shall rejoice and at once accomplish my tasks, so that you may be aflame with zeal and creation. And again you shall shed benevolent tears over men and again you may weave still more ornamental veils for Thyself. You shall create still richer ornaments. You, the inexhaustible Giver! Again people will search for Thee.

"In humiliation once more they will accept with gratitude Thy gifts. Thou shalt conceive for men so many small new conditions and petty inventions that even the most foolish will think himself clever and important. I do not fear the human curse and already perceive the joyous tears offered to Thee by men!

"Ponder deeply, Lakshmi, my near one! My thoughts are useful to Thee and to me, Thy sister, they are full of joy."

A cunning power has Siva Tandava. Only think! She recalled the past wars and human miseries. Only think! Again she wished to evoke upon earth the destruction through evil. Only think! What evil notions re-awoke in this malicious brain.

But not one word did Lakshmi say in response. Silently, only by a gesture, she rejected the evil project of Siva Tandava.

Then once again the evil Goddess, ready with threats and grinding her fangs, and forgetful of all her previous benevolent approaches began:

"Foolish Lakshmi! You surround yourself with these peaceful female embroiderers. They cherish the small walls of their miserable homes. Bent over their earthly designs they forget to look at the stars. They forget the threatening conjunction of stars. People cannot grasp that which comes in peace. They revere the thunder and lightning.

"Thy old altars are covered with fetid grease. Thy beauty cannot dwell in the dust of old houses. The best designs are destroyed by time and the best pattern is covered with mold. Follow me! I will show Thee such chorus of conceit that Thy wisdom shall be confounded!"

Such fearful things did Siva Tandava utter. And earthquakes pierced the earth with their convulsions. And islands sank into the oceans. And new mountains rose. But Lakshmi rejected all the offers of Siva Tandava.

The Blessed Goddess answered: "To give you alone joy, and to cause men sorrow, I shall not tear my veils. With a delicate web shall I extol mankind. I shall gather from among all noble hearts, excellent workers. I shall embroider new signs on my veils! The most beautiful, the most precious, the most powerful. And in these signs, in the images of the noblest beasts and birds, in the outlines of flaming flowers and healing herbs, I shall send to the hearts of people my most benevolent invocations. I will evoke from the abyss the greatest creative fire. And with a rampart of flame will I safeguard the luminous strivings of the Spirit."

Thus ordained Lakshmi.

Out from the resplendent Garden in defeat walked Siva Tandava. Rejoice, people!

Now shall Siva Tandava, in violent wrath await the long destruction of time. With incalculable ire, at times she crushes the earth and then hordes of people perish. But Lakshmi, ever in time, casts her blessed veils. And over the ashes of those who have perished, again men will gather.

They will meet in solemn procession.

The righteous Lakshmi adorns her veils with the new sacred signs. And from out the space she kindles a new Fire.

THE BOUNDARIES OF THE KINGDOM

This so happened in India. A son was born to a King. All-powerful fairy witches, as is the custom, brought their gifts to the Prince.

The most benevolent of them pronounced the conjuration:

"The Prince will never see the boundaries of his kingdom."

All thought that this prophecy foretold a kingdom limitless in boundaries.

But years passed, the Prince grew up, good and wise, but did not increase his kingdom.

The Prince began to rule. But he did not lead his armies to destroy his neighbors and thus did not enlarge the boundaries. And every time when he wished to inspect the boundaries of his kingdom, the mist covered the mountains of the borderlands.

In the waves of clouds new distances were created. And the clouds whirled up like high castles and structures.

But each time, the King returned to his palace full of new power, wise in all earthly decisions.

Jubilant were the people, glorifying their King, who without war could raise his kingdom and make it famed even in distant countries.

But when all is benevolent on earth, then the black serpent cannot rest under the ground.

Thus three old haters of mankind began to whisper:

"We are full of fright. Our King is obsessed by strange powers. Not a human mind has our King. Who knows, maybe such a mind is destructive of the current of earthly forces! A man should not be above human conception.

"We are marked by earthly wisdom and we know the limits. We know all charms and temptations.

"Let us save our King, let us make an end to the magic charms. Let our King know his boundaries. Let the fire of his mind be lessened. Let his wisdom become restricted within good human limits. When he shall see his boundaries, he will no longer ascend the mountain. And then he shall remain with us."

And the three haters of mankind came together to the King - the three old ones - pointing to their gray beards, and for wisdom's sake inviting him to ascend with them a high mountain. And there on the summit all three of them pronounced a conjuration. A conjuration to subdue the King's power within human limits:

"Lord, thou who guardest the limits of men!

"Thou, who alone canst measure the mind. Thou fillest the flow of mind in the limits of the current of the earth!

"Upon a turtle, upon a dragon, upon a serpent I shall swim. But I shall learn my limits. On a unicorn, on a tiger, on an elephant I shall swim. But I shall learn my limits.

"On a leaf of a tree, on the blade of a grass, on a flower of the lotus I shall swim. But I shall learn my limits.

"Thou, Lord, shalt reveal my shore. Thou shalt indicate my limits.

"Every one knows and thou knowest. No one is greater. Thou art greater. Deliver us from charms."

Such was the conjuration the haters of mankind pronounced.

And at once as a purple chain, the summits of the limiting mountains became aglow.

The haters of mankind turned away their faces. Bowed low.

"Here, King, are thy boundaries."

But the best of the fairy witches was already hurrying from the Goddess of the benevolent earthly wanderings.

The King did not have time to follow the advice of the three old haters of mankind, and to look. Over the peaks there suddenly rose a purple city. And behind it, veiled in mists, lay hitherto unseen regions. Over the city flew a fiery host. And the signs of highest wisdom began to glow in the heavens.

"I do not see my boundaries," exclaimed the King.

And he returned exalted in spirit. He filled his reign with most wise decisions.

HIDDEN TREASURES

Through the immense spaces of Siberia, many ancient wanderers scattered their treasures. Many tribes, in an unceasing procession, filled the soil of Mongolia, Minusinsk and Altai. In Altai they remembered the call of other remote mountains, and again strove onward, counting nor the days, nor years, nor centuries of their wandering.

The memory of the people preserves the sacred stories about the relics of these great wanderers. And fantasy adorns them with most beautiful garlands.

Oh, these hidden treasures! What aspiration is directed towards them!

This is not merely anxiety to become possessor of riches. It is the eternal striving toward the mystery of the earth.

Many manuscripts flow through the people's hands. Wandering singers, minstrels, monks and beggars carry wonderful tales inscribed in a peculiar secret language. And why do these not acquire the treasures themselves? They have always some excuses; the hidden language must be understood...

At times you can see these curious writings on yellow leaves, their corners ragged from long usage. Through many villages and camps these scriptures went their ways. They were written in old script, sometimes like old prayer books, with strange flourishes and ornamentations. Really it is not easy to decipher these rudimentary signs. Many people try to follow these indications. It is true, that some places are indicated correctly. Some typical details are marked down. But it is not known that precisely in these places treasures were found. Either an exact indication was veiled, or fortunate discoverers had reason for maintaining silence. From most ancient times, old graves and tumuli have been pillaged. It appears that people who lived shortly after their erection carried on the sacrilege. It seems that the desecrators knew well all approaches and passages to the places of burial. The old custom to kill all who performed the burial had its special reason. But we do not speak now of burials, but of treasures; about the treasures, whose origin and destiny are so mysterious. We are speaking of treasures.

One remembers the majestic burial sites in the tumuli, under huge golden plaques. How many of them have been pillaged! I remember how in the steppes a boy shepherd noticed on a slope of a hill a spark of gold. His attention was attracted and he was rightly rewarded. He found two hundred pounds of gold in ancient vessels.

Let us see how treasures are indicated in the books of treasure seekers:

"From the Red Field thou shalt go in the direction of the winter's sunrise. Follow this trail until thou shalt see a tombhill. Ascend this hill and turn to the left and proceed to the rusty stream. And then go up the stream until thou shalt see a huge gray stone. Upon this stone find a trace of a horse's hoof. Leave behind thee the stone and proceed from this imprint of a hoof until thou comest to a small swamp. Thou must know that some strange unknown people buried in there five huge pieces of gold..."

"In the elkforest on the crosspath, is a huge horny fir-tree. This fir-tree remains here not without reason. He who searches can find some signs cut into it. Stand with your back to these signs and walk straight from them across a moss swamp. And having passed, there will be a stony place. Two stones will be larger than the others. Stand between them in the center and count forty steps towards the spring sunset. There is a large barrel of gold buried there during the time of Tzar the Terrible..."

Here is a still better treasure:

"On the river Peresnya find a fording. And it will be called the Prince's fording. From this fording walk again toward the spring sunset. And when you will have walked three hundred steps turn half sideways. And walk across thirty steps to the right. And there will be something like an old pit. And behind this pit you will see a stump of a large tree. And there is buried a great treasure. All gold krestovics (big golden coins) and all kinds of golden armor. And one cannot count all the golden treasures. And this treasure was buried during the Mongol invasion..."

Another good big treasure:

"On the very shore of the Irtysh you will find an old site. And on this site is an ancient chapel. And behind it you may see an old cemetery. Amidst the tombs you behold a small kurgan. Under this kurgan, as told by old men, is a deep subterranean passage. And this passage leads into a small cave and in there are to be found untold riches. An old writing about this treasure is in the cathedral of Sophia. And the high one himself, the Metropolite, once a year gives this writing to read to those who come from afar." Now I shall tell you the most difficult one: "This treasure was buried with a deathly conjuration. Should you decide to go after it, you will have headaches and great anxiety of the soul. And at midnight you will hear horrifying voices. And a bell will ring over you, as for a funeral service. But if you will succeed in conquering all deadly terrors, if your heart will decide to go against all fear, then yours is the great fortune.

"There is a place called Great Mane. From the mountain there flows a golden stream and into this stream robbers have sunk innumerable quantities of gold. And over this place tiny birds are always fluttering. It is said that the souls of the former masters of this gold turned into these birds. And when you hear the chirping of the birds and behold this place, close your ears and look into the stream. If you see that you are not looking in alone do not be disturbed by this. You will see on the bottom of the stream a large slab. And into this slab is screwed an iron ring. And above it, from the mountains flows the water, and it will seem to you in the ripples that this slab is shaking and the ring is disappearing. Do not be disturbed by this either, but begin to read the sacred prayer to the Holy Virgin Mary. And after this prayer say: 'Omnipotent! On Thy Vestment are woven all healing herbs. Be merciful! Send me from out of these herbs an herb of power!'

"And here know how to show your luck. If you succeed in deflecting the water from the ground and if you succeed in unearthing the conjured slabs, and if you catch hold of the ring in time - then your luck is untold and inexpressible!

"Many treasures are buried everywhere. I do not speak in vain. Our grandfathers wrote much about them. Even recently in our forge a passing traveler repaired a wheel. He spoke and I overheard: 'In subterranean Siberia,' said he, 'many riches are buried. Guard Siberia!'

"He was of great appearance, this man.

"From grandfather I know this. Sometimes on the eve of a great holiday he spoke to us, lighting the candles before old ikons.

"Thus he spoke: 'For every man a treasure is buried. Only one must know how to take these treasures. To a traitor, a treasure is not given. A drunkard does not know how to approach it. Do not harken to the treasure with evil thoughts. The treasure knows its worth. Do not dare to harm the treasure. One should cherish the treasures. Many treasures fell from the stars. Angels guard many treasures. Treasures are not buried with a foolish word, but with prayers and conjurations. And the conjurations are awe-inspiring. And wherever there is blood on a treasure it is better not to approach it.'

"Satan himself and with him all devils guard the bloody gold.

"And if your heart has decided to go for a treasure, then go cautiously. Long before approaching, do not talk in vain, do not show yourself too open; think your thoughts. There will be terrors before you, but you should not fear. Something will appear to you, but do not look. Do not harken to cries. Go in great caution. Do not stumble. Because to go for a treasure is a great thing.

"Over the treasure hasten thy efforts.

"Do not look around and chiefly do not rest. Because to every one the rest is ordained later on earth. And if you should want to raise your voice, sing prayers to the Virgin. Remember, never take with you any companions in the quest for the treasure.

"If your luck comes and you take the treasure, do not prattle to any one about it. Let people think that misfortune silences you. But be you silent, because of fortune. In no way reveal at once to people your treasure. Because the human eye is heavy. Treasures are unaccustomed to people. Treasures lay long in the honest earth. If you reveal them to people, they will again depart into the earth. And you will not have the treasure nor shall any one else. Many treasures were spoilt by people because of their pettiness."

" - And where is your treasure, blacksmith? Why did you not take your treasure?"

" - And for me there lies buried a treasure. I, alone, know when to go after it."

And the blacksmith spoke no more about treasures.

JALNIK, THE SITE OF COMPASSION

On the high hills of Altai, the tops of old pines and fir-trees engage in peaceful communion. They know much - these mountain forests! They stand in wonder before the snowy ranges of the mountains. Their roots know what riches, what innumerable mineral treasures, are guarded in the stony depths of the mountains, for the future prosperity of humanity.

And the roots of these giant trees tenderly embrace the gray stones. These are the stones of the "site of compassion."

Who knows who placed these stones here? And who saw these men transfixed in awe beneath the stone stronghold?

Had these people heard of the future wealth of this country? Did they know of Zvenigorod, the City of the Bells? Was it they, who conceived the saga of the river Katum, of all the events which passed on the shores of this river, as it rolled down the great stones from the White Mountain, Belukha?

Were these people settlers or wanderers?

Old grandmother Anisya knows something about this place.

She comes here to perform her invocations and conjurations. Do not be afraid! She is not a witch, she is not a Shaman sorceress. No one would speak ill of grandmother Anisya. But she knows many precious things. She knows the healing herbs; she knows conjurations which serve as prayers; she learned them from her grandmother. And a century ago the same stones and the same forest stood here as now.

Grandmother Anisya knows conjurations against all evils. No one besides herself knows that the kirik stone from the nest of a hoopoe is the best protection against treason. No one besides herself knows the best time to find this nest and how to obtain the stone.

She can tell you how hard are the present times and that you can be saved only by conjurations. At the present time three conjurations need be remembered:

The first of them is against enemies, against thieves and evil men. The second - do not forget it! against mortal weapons. The third - remember sharply! against lightning, against all thunder of heaven or earth! The thunder of earth resounds and heavenly forces rise.

Remember the first one:

"On the sea, on the ocean, on the Buyan Island, there is an iron chest and in this iron chest there are steel swords. Ho, steel swords! Approach our enemy! Cut his body in pieces! Pierce his heart! Until he renounces all evil; until he returns the stolen booty; until he will surrender all, without concealing anything. Thou enemy, adversary, be cursed by my powerful conjurations!

"Be damned in the depths of hell! Beyond the Arrarat mountains, into the boiling tar! Into the burning ashes! Into the scum of swamps! Into the bottomless abyss!

"Be you, enemy, pierced by the spike of an aspen tree!

"And be dried even more than the hay!

"And be frozen even more than the ice!

"Become cross-eyed, lame, mad, armless, impoverished, hungry, outcast; and perish by another's hand!" . . .

You see, what strong powers grandmother Anisya possesses! Who can withstand such conjurations!

And not only does she speak in a strident voice, but she also holds in her hand a tiny stick, and as she speaks of the death of an enemy, she breaks this stick, just as the life of her evil adversary shall be broken. And never shall he know from what hill, from what mountain, came this unconquerable power.

The second conjuration is against weapons. Each warrior must know this conjuration. Hear and remember!

"Beyond the far-off mountains is the sea of iron. In the sea stands a pillar of bronze. And on that bronze pillar there stands a shepherd of cast iron. And this pillar rises from earth into heaven. From the East to the West.

"And the shepherd commands his children; he commands the iron, the steel, red and blue, the copper, the lead, the silver, and the gold. He speaks to guns and to arrows. He gives to the fighters and warriors the great command:

" 'You iron, copper, lead, go back into your mother-earth, away from the warrior; return, tree, to the far-off shore, and you, arrow-feathers, return to the birds! And you birds - disappear in the sky!'

"And he commands swords, axes, boar-spears, knives, arquebuses, arrows and all warriors - to be calm and peaceful!

"And he orders every warrior not to shoot at me from a gun!

"But he orders the arbalest and stringbows to bend and cast all arrows deep down into the earth!

"Let my body be stronger than stone. Firmer than steel. Let my armor be stronger than helmets and ring-armor.

"I seal my words with all locks. I cast the keys under the white Flaming Stone, Alatyr!

"And as locks are strong, so strong are my words." . . .

No one would care to be in the position of this conjured adversary. What weapons could avail against this powerful incantation! The White Flaming Stone itself, Great Alatyr, bears witness to this immutable might! And again, not only words are projected into the space, but grandmother Anisya has four stones in her hands and she throws them to the four ends of the earth.

But the third conjuration is the most awe-inspiring one. This one is against lightning, against the thunders of heaven and earth:

"Holy! Holy! Holy! Thou, who dwellest in the thunder! Thou who subduest the lightning! Thou who floodest the earth with rain! Thou, mightiest Ruler! Thou alone adjudge the cursed Satan with all the devils! But save us, sinners!

"Thy wisdom is incomparable, all-powerful! All honor from God! From him comes liberation to the motherland! Be it so now, eternally and forever! Thou, Lord of Terror! Thou, Lord of all miracles! Thou, who dwellest on the most high! Thou, who movest in the thunder! Mastering fire! Lord of all miracles! Thyself destroy the enemy, the Satan! Be it so now, eternally and forever. Amen!" . . .

This is most powerful. The highest, heavenly power is summoned. From the mountain stream, grandmother Anisya takes a handful of clear water and dashes it into space. And glistening drops, as heavenly lightnings, surround the conjuror.

The conjurations are ended. And the power departs from grandmother. She becomes small and bent. And the small old woman walks away beyond the hill. From Jalnik - site of compassion - to the lake at the foot of the mountain, through fields of spring wheat, into a distant village, she goes. Not for her own ends, did Granny come from afar to invoke the high forces. Grandmother sent out conjurations for all people, for distant warriors, for a new life. But she also prayed for the unknown silent ones, who are buried under the stones and roots of the pine-trees. She brought holy oil for the saints. Because on the highest pine-tree, in the bark, an old ikon is carved out and it is said that the ikon appeared of itself.

On the summits of Altai, on the ranges of Ural, far off up to the very hills of Novgorod, fir and cedar groves tower high. From the far, far distance one may behold their dark caps. Under the roots of firs, many stones are gathered together with great labor. Beautiful sites! Ancient sites! How did they come to be here? Was it the unknown pilgrims who built them? Was it the Mongols? Was it the Tzar, the terrible? Or are they from times of unrest? Or from wars and foreign invasions? All these at one time were here.

And the silent ones lie buried here. Lie in rest, unknown to all grandfathers. And thus one prays for them!

For the known and unknown, for the sung and unsung, for the storied and unstoried…

"Jalniks," the sites of compassion, so are called these beautiful sites of silence. They are also called "divinets," sites of wonder.

Divinet, site of wonder, resounds with exultation. But "Jalnik" - site of compassion - is still nearer to the heart. In this expression lies so much of love and gentle pity, so much of rest and words of eternity. The giant fir-trees guard this place with their mighty branches. Only the tops rustle. Below is silence and shade. The gray juniper. Only two or three dry blades of grass. Everywhere, blackberries and dried evergreen needles. High on the fir tree sits an old raven. He is so old that he has claws, not only on his feet but even on his wings. As we regarded this raven with awe, as a prehistoric relic, he fell down dead. The stones are set in rows and in circles. All of them must remember the moraines of the glacier period. White, grayish, violet, bluish and almost black. From the East to the West these stones may be observed, adorned by a white moss. Everywhere, too, is gray moss. Everywhere there is ancient grayness. In grayness, sleep the "calm ones." In white garments, repose the "resting ones." Oh, through what sufferings they passed! Many things they witnessed! Wise and without doubts is their wisdom!

"As in heaven, so upon earth. As above, so below. That which was, shall come again!"

GAYATRI
"Ye Birds, Homas, ye beautiful!

You You do not love the earth - Never will you descend to earth! Your birdlings are born in heavenly nests. You are nearer the Sun. Let us ponder about the sun, the Resplendent!
But the Devas of Earth are also miraculous.
Upon the Summits of Mountains, in the depths of seas, seek patiently.
Thou shalt find a glorious Stone of Lore,
In Thy heart search for Brindavan, abode of Love.
Seek patiently and you will find. Let the Ray of Wisdom pierce us. Then all which moves will become affixed. The shadow will become the body. The spirit of air will return to land. The dream will be transformed into thought.
We will not be moved by the storm.
We shall rein the winged steeds of morning.
We will guide the currents of the evening wind.
Thy Word is the Ocean of Truth. Who turns our ships to the shore? Do not fear Maya. Her untold might and power we shall conquer.
Harken! Harken! Have done with dissension and fights."
Surendra Gayatri prayed.
From the stones of the city he went to the shades of
Aranyani. And in the blissful stillness he rested.
But the battle began.
Kings of the ancient lands set plans to shatter the sacred vessels!
Let the wisdom of Nilgiri perish!
Let the Ghat and Khunda ranges droop!
Let Gaya be destroyed.
The river Falgu shall over-flow! Naught can break the terror - Fire and arrows, Poison and deadly thunders rain from above and below. Black birds are flying.
The people found Gayatri.
The people approached him.
The people besought his help.
The people, in despair, compelled Gayatri to change
his good prayers.
"Forget your righteous prayers, Gayatri. Search the mortal word. Find the deadly eye. Pray for oath of victory.
"Farewell, Aranyani!
Farewell, celestial silver and gold!
Farewell, thou most quiet forest!" Gayatri hears the calls. Gayatri departs from the forest. Gayatri ascends the summit. Gayatri is alone.

Gayatri encircles himself with a Ray. Gayatri prays with all his being:
"Lion and Swan!
Eagle and deer!
Bull, lion, eagle!
Ruler of the World!
Ruler of the Stars and the Moon!
Ruler of Light and of the Sun!
Indra!
"Do not invoke the Black Age! Our strength is exhausted. Asleep is the sacred jewel! No longer it defeats the wandering spirits. No longer it stays our enemies.
"Sound the command for hostilities.
Sound the command of strength!
A conjuration for victory!
Let us defeat the enemy. Say the words of Nagaima. Bestow the strength of Exola. Bestow the deadly word. Open the deadly eye. Rakshasi conquered the people.
Samyasa, Leader of the Sons of Heaven, Ruler of the
Serpents, also taught Power. Azaciel also taught the forging of arms. Amazaraka also revealed the mysterious powers of herbs and roots.
They are dark, evil, insignificant. But You are able. You have Power. Allelu! Allelu! Allelu!"
The Supreme hears Gayatri.
The Supreme shall fulfil Gayatri's request.
The Supreme does not admit the destruction of Nilgiri.
Dear to the Supreme is the wisdom of the summits.
The Supreme shall set a test: "I will not give thee Exola, nor Nagaima. Neither against the hosts, nor for success. I will not give thee Zaadotota, nor Addivata, Neither against enmity, nor for revenge. I will not give thee Kaalbeba, nor Alsibena, Neither against animus, nor for harm and rupture. I will not give thee the deadly word. The deadly eye, I will not open.
All conjurations I will gather.
Alshill! Alzelal! Alama! Ashmekh!
Kaaldalbala! Kaalda! Kaldebda!
I will leave them, will forget them!
Anax! Aluxer! Ataiya! Atars!
I will end, will part from them! I will bestow another thing - That which shall have the power of repulsion -
It will open the Power to none. Hear!
There walks one,
Walks peacefully.
In a white garment he walks.

Swordless he walks.

All that has been done against thee will turn against them. All that they wished against you, they will themselves receive. Good and evil.

Who desired evil - will receive it. Who desired good - he may accept it. All will receive. Go. Do not hesitate. I will make an end to the trial.

Alm! Alm! Algarfelmukor!"

What passed?

Gayatri passed on -

In white and calmly.

Without arrow nor sword

Without hatred nor threat. What passed? The enemies shot their arrows against Gayatri, poisoned arrows.

The arrows turned and struck those who sent them. Others threw spears at Gayatri and fell, transfixed. Poison they spilt for him and died themselves terrified.

What passed?

Hosts of enemies died by their own hand.

With hatred their spirit overflowed.

Their hearts swelled with revenge. What passed?

They destroyed and burned. They poisoned rivers and lakes. They sped a shower of flames. They shrieked their curses. They burned and drowned. They turned black, convulsed. They gashed and strangled - Themselves.

What passed?

They forgot the good.

They lost the good meeting.

The good eye darkened.

The word of caress they deadened. Thus it passed! The foolhardy perished. By the strength of enemies, Gayatri went through the

kingdom of the old lands.

Passed through gates and palaces, bridges and villages. Quiet was the old kingdom. Destroyed were the foolhardy. Gayatri stood still. To stay the power, he knew not. He could not lay bare the strength. He could not dare to turn toward his own.

Gayatri kindled a fire.

He bestowed the Power upon the fire.

He sowed the Power to the winds! "Sacred ashes! Light veil of Bliss! Thou coverest! Thou cleanest! And liberate!"

But the Supreme does not pause:

"Do not ponder over ashes.

Turn toward your own people.

Meet the child.

Carry it before you.

Teach. In the name of the Highest, two cannot fight.
One of them is a dark one -
Conquer the dark.
I made a test -
Into the whirlpool I submerged the old land.
I will overthrow the useless.
I will again raise the summits.
I will uplift. I will test. In heaven and on earth
I fulfil the Law." Gayatri found the child. Gayatri raised the child. And returned to Nilgiri. Gayatri forgot Aranyani. He left the forest behind.

Gayatri prayed for the opening of the righteous eye. And to find the righteous word.

Harken, people!

DREAMS

Such were the dreams before the war: We were traveling through a field. Behind the hill the clouds rose. A storm. Through a cloud, head downwards, a fiery serpent pierced the earth. The serpent was double-headed.

Or another dream: Again we travel over a gray plain. No sign of life. Before us, a high hill glimmers dark. We look, but it is not a hill; it is a huge, coiled gray serpent.

And long before were conjurations. The evil ones were conjured. The untruth was conjured. Bird and beast were conjured. Earth and water were conjured. But to no avail. The monsters crept out.

Later were signs. They did not perceive them. They did not trust them. They did not grasp them. The crowds stamped upon them.

And the serpent awoke. The enemy of mankind rose. Attempted by slander to conquer the world. To destroy cities. To defame temples. Turn to ashes human strivings.

He rose to his own destruction.

There were conjurations. There were signs.

Dreams remained. Those dreams that are fulfilled.

He laid himself to rest for the night.

He thought - I shall see great Magi.

There was desire to see - how they look.

There was desire to hear - what names they bear.

He wished to see what is bound to their saddles. What road they take. They should reveal. Whence and whither.

But they did not appear, the Magi.

Possibly it was too soon.

Did not start out yet.

Instead of the Magi two others appeared.

One middle aged in an old blue shirt. In an old dark kaftan. Long hair. In the right hand three staffs.

He holds them to-day with points upwards. Mark, upwards. All has its meaning. But this is Saint Prokopyi, himself.

He who saved Ustyng the Great.

He, who took away the stony cloud from the city. He, who upon high shores prayed for the unknown travelers.

Marvelous tidings! Himself came Prokopyi the Righteous.

And another one with Him - white and old. In one hand a sword and in another the city.

Certainly he is Saint Nicholas.

Instead of the Magi with the star, these came.

Prokopyi speaks:

"Do not depart from the earth. The earth is red, red hot with evil. But the heat of evil nurtures the roots of the Tree. And upon this Tree the good creates its Benevolent nest. Attain the labor on earth. Ascend to the heavenly ocean, the resplendent, but dark only for us. Guard the Benevolent Tree. Good lives on it. The earth is the source of sorrow, but out of sorrow grow joys. He who is the highest knows the predestined date of your joy.

"Do not depart from the earth. Let us sit down and ponder about far-off wanderers."

The other, the white one, lifted the sword.

And people came closer to him. Many came forward.

"Nicholas, the Gracious! Thou Miracle Maker! Thou, All-powerful! Thou, Holy Warrior! Thou, Conqueror of Hearts! Thou, Leader of true thoughts! Thou, Knowing heavenly and earthly forces!

"Thou, Guardian of the Sword! Thou, Protector of Cities! Thou knowing the Truth! Do you hear the prayers, Mighty One?

"Evil forces are battling against us.

"Protect, Thou Mighty One, the Holy City! The resplendent city calls wrath in the enemy. Accept, Thou Mighty One, the beautiful city. Raise, Father, the Sacred Sword!

"Invoke, Father, all saintly warriors. Miracle-maker, manifest a stern face! Cover the cities with the holy sword! Thou canst, to Thee is given Power!

"We stand without fear and tremor..."

THE DESERT CITIES

The world is described as an old man...
The people answer for their striving.
Thoughts grow through striving.
Thought gives birth to desire.
Desire has stirred up the command.
The human structure quivers with desires.
Do not fear, ancient man!
Joy and sorrow are as a river.
Waves are passing, purifying.

The Czar rejoiced: "My land is vast. My forests are mighty. My rivers are teeming. My mountains are precious. My people are merry. Beautiful is my wife."

The Czarina rejoiced:

"Many forests and fields have we. Many song birds have we. Many varied flowers have we."

An old man entered the palace. A newcomer. He greeted the Czar and Czarina. And he sat down exhausted.

The Czar asked:

"Why art thou weary, old man? Hast thou been wandering long?"

The old man became sorrowful.

"Vast is thy land. Mighty, thy forests. Teeming are thy rivers. Thy mountains are unsurpassable. During my wanderings I nearly perished. Yet I could not reach a city where I could find rest. Few cities hast thou, O Czar! We old ones love city structures. We love the trusty walls. We love the watchful towers and the gates, which are obedient to command. Few cities hast thou, O Czar. Thy neighboring rulers surround themselves more strongly with walls."

The Czar became sorrowful.

"Few cities have I. Few trusty walls. Few towers have I. Few gates to encircle all my people."

The Czar commenced to mourn.

"Old man! Wise in years! Teach me how to cover my vast domain with cities. How shall I set within walls all my people?"

The old man rejoiced.

"Thou shalt set all thy people within walls. Two lands beyond thine lives a giant Czar. Give him a great prize. The giants shall bring thee from the Indian Czar, countless cities. They shall bring them with walls and gates and towers. Do not spare in rewarding the giant Czar. Give him a great prize. Even if he shall demand the Czarina, thy wife."

The old man got up and departed - as though the passer-by had never been there. The Czar sent his request into the land of the giants.

The giant, woolly Czar was laughing.

"He sent his people to the Indian Czar to steal away the cities with walls and gates and towers."

And the giant, woolly Czar did not take a small reward. He took a precious mountain. He took a teeming river. He took an entire mighty forest. He took into the bargain the Czarina, the wife of the Czar. Everything was promised to him. Everything was ceded to him.

The Czarina sorrowed.

"O, the woolly Czar will take me to please a strange man, an old one! All the people will be enclosed by heavy gates. O, they will trample all my flowers with cities. And they will cover with towers the whole starry canopy. Aid me, my blooms - the underground secrets are known to you. The giants bear the Indian cities, with walls and gates and towers!"

The blossoms heard the complaint. They began to wave their flowery heads. From beneath the world rose their thought. The great thought began to stir beneath the earth. The forests began to waver with thought. The mountains were devastated by thought: they crumbled even into small stones. The earth was fissured with thought. Fissured also became the heavens.

The thought came flowing across the desert sands. The thought stirred the free sand. It rose as undulating ramparts. The sands rose against the giant people.

The giants stole the Indian cities with walls, gates and towers. They drove the Indian people from their huts. They lifted the cities upon their shoulders. Swiftly they returned. They went to earn their great prize for the woolly Czar.

The giants approached the desert sands. The desert sands lifted into masses. The sands rose like dark whirlwinds. The sands veiled the beautiful sun. The sands raised themselves into the heavens. And how the sands smote the giant people!

The sands crept into the broad jaws. The sands flowed into the woolly ears. The sands obscured the eyes of the giants. The sands conquered the giant-people. The giants abandoned the cities to desert sands. Scarcely did they escape, without eyes or ears.

The desert sands buried the Indian cities. They buried them with walls, gates and towers. The people know of these cities, even up to the present time. But who brought the cities to the desert sands, the people do not know. The flowers bloom as never before. From the flowers the Czarina understood that the cities were razed. And the Czarina sang a merry song - for honest people to hear, to the glory of the Saviors!

The Czar heard the song and rejoiced, exulting. And the Czar laughed at the giant's misfortune. And the Czar smiled at the cities, hidden in the desert sands. No longer yearned the Czar for foreign cities.

The teeming river remained with the Czar. His was the precious mountain. His was the mighty forest. His, the flowers and singing birds, and all his people. His, the beautiful Czarina. His, the merry song. Greatly rejoiced the Czar. Not so soon shall the old man again enter the Palace.

LYUT, THE GIANT

On the echoing cape, near the sacred grove, On the lake, lived the Giant, Lyut. A mighty one, great and good. And a mighty hunter was he. The beard of Lyut had seven tips. An hundred foxes made his head-gear. The garments of Lyut were of gray wolf. The ax of Lyut was of red flint. The spear of Lyut was of white flint. The arrows of Lyut were black, never-failing. Beyond the lake lived the brethren of Lyut. And on the mountain site Lyut built his dwelling. From the echoing cape he called his brothers - Even in a whisper.

To his brother beyond the lake, he handed his ax. With his brother, beyond the lake, Lyut hunted. With his brother beyond the lake, Lyut cast his nets. With his brother beyond the lake, he brewed his ale. He boiled his tar and fetched his forage. He lit his bonfires and danced merrily with his sister.

Then Lyut went strolling beyond the lake.

Ill-starred was his stride - he sank.

Lyut, the Giant, sank even up to his chest. Badly he fared.

His dog followed him and sank.

Who can call the brethren of Lyut?

For a day's distance, there is no one in sight.

The lake splashes. The wind murmurs.

Death itself walks over the ridge.

Lyut raised his eyes to the clouds -

Cargoose flew by. The giant called,

"Do you see me in the lake?"

"I see-ee," came the answer.

"Tell my brethren - I drow-w-w-n! I drow-w-wn!"

Far flies the cargoose.

Resoundingly echoes its call: "I drow-w-w-n! I drow-w-wn!"

The cargoose knows not that it proclaims misfortune -

The lake holds no evil for it.

The lake is kind.

Only in the wood the cargoose fares badly, and in the fields.

The brethren are laughing.

They do not hear the cargoose.

They have caught an elk in the marshes.

Finally the brethren of Lyut arrive

But Lyut has perished.

A long mound is built - and a round one for his dog.

Of sorrow dies the sister of Lyut.

The giants throw bars into the lake.

They bury their axes beneath the roots of trees.
The giants abandon our land.
But the cargoose lives on the lake since those ancient days.
A foolish bird. But a prophet bird. It confuses the call of the giant
In fair weather it calls, "I drow-w-w-n! I drow-w-w-n!" As if drowning, it flutters its wings. In foul weather, it calls - "Ho, ho - ho, ho!" Over the water, it flies and screams, "See-ee-ee! I see-ee-ee-"
People remember the lake of Lyut.
People remember the long mounds.
The long mounds of giants.
And the length of the mounds is nine scores of cubits.
The shores of the lake remember the giants.
The trunks of the oaks remember the giants.
The giants carried the stones to the mounds.
The people remember how the giants departed.
From ancient time it was even so. I so affirm!

STAR OF THE MOTHER OF THE WORLD

Toward that seven-starred constellation known as the Seven Sisters, the Seven Elders or the Great Bear, the consciousness of humanity has at all times been directed. The Scriptures extol this celestial sign and Buddhism's sacred Trepitaka dedicates an imposing hymn to it. Ancient Magi and Egyptians carved it upon the stones. And the black faith of Shaman of the wild taiga paid their obeisance to it.

To another of heaven's miracles, the constellation of Orion, which the wisdom of astronomers has named the "Three Magi," were dedicated the ancient temples of mystery in Central Asia.

As a pair of iridescent wings, these two constellations are spread out across the firmament. Between them, darting headlong toward earth, is the Star of the Morning, resplendent abode of the Mother of the World. By its dominating light, by its unprecedented approach, it foretells the new era of humanity.

The dates, recorded eons since, are being fulfilled in the starry runes. The predictions of the Egyptian Hierophants are being invested with reality before our eyes. Verily, this is a time of wonder for its witnesses. Likewise predestined and also descending over humanity is that satellite of the Mother of the World - Beauty, the living raiment. As a garment of purification must the sign of Beauty glorify each hearth.

Simplicity - Beauty - Fearlessness: so it is ordained! Fearlessness is our guide. Beauty is the ray of comprehension and upliftment. Simplicity is the sesame to the gates of the coming mystery. And not the menial simplicity of hypocrisy, but the great simplicity of attainment encircled in the folds of love. Simplicity which unlocks the most sacred and mysterious gates to him who brings his torch of sincerity and incessant labor. Not the Beauty of conventionality and deceit, which harbors the worm of decadence, but that Beauty of the spirit of truth which annihilates all prejudices. Beauty alight with the true freedom and attainment and glorious with the miracle of flowers and of sounds. Not the Fearlessness of artifice, but the Fearlessness which knows the unsounded depths of creation and discriminates between self-confidence in action and the presumption of conceit. Fearlessness which possesses the sword of courage and which smites down vulgarity in all its forms even though it be adorned in riches.

The understanding of these three covenants creates faith and support of the spirit. For within the last decade everything has been endowed with motion. The most massed clods have become mobile and the greatest dullards have comprehended that without simplicity, beauty and fearlessness, no construction of the new life is conceivable. Nor is the regeneration of religion, politics, science or the revaluation of labor possible. Without Beauty the closely inscribed pages, like withered and fallen leaves, will be whirled away by the winds of life and the wail of spiritual famine shall shake the foundations of the cities, deserted in their populousness.

We saw revolutions. We saw crowds. We passed through the mobs of insurrection. But only there did we behold the banner of peace waving overhead, where beauty was aglow and by the light of its wondrous power evoked united understanding. We saw in Russia how the apostles of beauty and the collectors - the true collectors, not those who were the incidental possessors of some inheritance - were singled out for honor by the crowd. We saw how the most ardent youth stood in breathless vigilance, in prayer, under the wings of beauty. And the remains of religion were revivified there where beauty did not perish and where the shield of Beauty was most firm.

By practical experience we can affirm that these words are not the Utopia of a visionary. No, these are the essence of experience gathered on fields of peace and of battle. And this manifold experience did not bring disillusion. On the contrary, it strengthened faith in the destined and in the near, in the resplendence of the possibilities. Verily, it was experience which constructed confidence in the new ones who hastened to help in the erection of the Temple and whose joyous voices resounded over the hill. The same experience directed our eyes toward the children, who, untaught, but already permitted to approach, began to unfold like the flowers of a beautiful garden. And their thoughts became crystal; and their eyes became enlightened and their spirits strove to proclaim the message of achievement. And all this was not in nebulous temples but here upon earth - here where we have forgotten so much that was beautiful.

It would seem incredible that people could want to forget the best possibilities - but this happens oftener than one can imagine. Man lost his key to the symbols of the Rig-Vedas. Man forgot the meaning of the Kabala. Man mutilated the glorious word of Buddha. Man, with gold, defiled the divine word of Christ and forgot, forgot, forgot the keys to the finest gates. Men lose easily, but how to regain again? The path to recovery permits every one to have hope. Why not, if a soldier of Napoleon discovered the Rosetta Stone in a trench, key to the understanding of the complete heiroglyphs of Egypt? Now, verily when the last hour strikes, men - still too few - begin hurriedly to recall the treasures which were theirs long since, and again the keys begin to clink on the girdle of faith. And dreams clearly and vividly recall the abandoned but ever-existing beauty. Only accept! Only receive! You shall discern how transformed shall be your inner life; how the spirit shall quiver in its realization of unbounded possibilities. And how simply beauty will envelop the temple, the palace and the hearth, where a human heart is throbbing. Often one does not know how to approach beauty - where are the worthy chambers, the worthy raiments, for the festival of color and of sound? "We are so poor," is the reply. But beware lest you screen yourselves behind the specter of poverty. For wherever desire is implanted, there shall bloom decision.

And how shall we start to build the Museum? Simply. Because all must be simple. Any room may be a museum - and if the wish that conceived it is worthy, it shall grow in the shortest time into its own building and into a temple. And from far will come the new ones and knock - only do not outsleep the knocking.

How shall we commence our collecting? Again, simply - and without riches, only with unconquerable desire. We have known many very poor persons who were very remarkable collectors, and who although limited by each penny, gathered art collections full of great inner meaning.

How can we publish? We know also that great art publications began with almost negligible means. For instance, such an idealized work as that tremendous publishing project of art postcards, Saint Eugenie, began with five thousand dollars, and in ten years afforded hundreds of thousands of profit yearly. But the value of this work was not measured by its financial profits. Rather was it gaged by the quantity of widely-spread art publications which attracted a multitude of new, young hearts to the path of beauty. The colored post-cards which were artistically published, and in a definite method penetrated into new strata of the people and created young enthusiasts. How many new collectors were born! And measuring their approach to new hearts, the publishers sent into the world, reproductions of the most progressive creations. Thus, through fearlessness, in the simplicity of clearness, were created new works of beauty.

How can we open schools and teach? Also simply. Let us not expect great buildings or sigh over the primitive conditions and lack of material. The smallest room - not larger than the cell of Fra Beato Angelico in Florence - can contain the most valuable possibilities for art. The smallest assembly of colors will not diminish the artistic substance of creation. And the poorest canvas may be the receiver of the most sacred image.

If there comes the realization of the imminent importance of teaching beauty, it must be begun without delay. One must know that the means will come, if there be manifest the enduring enthusiasm. Give knowledge and you will receive possibilities. And the more liberal the giving, the richer the receiving.

Let us see what Serge Ernst, director of the Hermitage in Petrograd, writes about the school which was started by private initiative in one room and which later grew to an annual enrolment of two thousand:

"On a bright May day, the great hall in Marskaya conveys to the eye a bright festival. What can be lacking! A whole wall is covered with austere and shining ikons; whole tables are dazzling with polychrome rows of majolica vases and figures; finally, here are painted ornaments for the tea table and further off, luxuriantly embroidered in silk and gold and wool, lie rugs and pillows and towels and writing pads. Furniture, cozy and ornamented with intricate handcraft, stands here. And show-cases are filled with lovely trifles. Upon walls hang the plans for the most various objects of home decoration, beginning with architectural plans and ending with the plans for the composition of a porcelain statue. Architectural measurements and drawings of the monuments of ancient art are the interesting illustrations from the class of graphics; on the windows in colorful and brilliant spots are exhibited the creations of the class in stained glass. Further off, in front of the spectator, stands a white company of the productions of the class of sculptors, of the class of drawings of animals; and on the top awaits a whole gallery filled with paintings in oil and still life. And all this variety of creation lives, is vital with full young enthusiasm. All the happy field of art of our day receives here its due consideration, in close relation with the artistic questions of the present. And what is finer, what can recommend more highly the art school, than this precious and rare contact?"

In these contacts of enthusiasm and in the economy of all precious achievements, the school work quickly progresses and yearly new forces are gathered as the most worthy guardians of the future culture of the spirit. How to recruit these new ones? This is most simple. If over the work shall glow the sign of simplicity, beauty and fearlessness, new forces will readily assemble. Young heads, long deprived and long expecting the wonderful miracle, will come. Only, let us not permit these seekers to pass us by! Only, not to let one of them pass by in the twilight!

And how to approach beauty ourselves? This is the most difficult. We can reproduce paintings; we can make exhibitions; we can open a studio; but where will the paintings of the exhibitions find an outlet? To what parts shall the products of the studio penetrate? It is easy to discourse, but more difficult to admit beauty into life's household. But while we ourselves deny entrance to beauty in our life, what value will all these affirmations possess? They shall be meaningless banners at an empty hearth. Admitting beauty into our home, we must determine the unquestionable rejection of vulgarity and pompousness, and all which opposes beautiful simplicity. Verily, the hour of the affirming of beauty in life is come! It came in the travail of the spirits of the peoples. It came in storm and in the lightning. Came that hour before the coming of Him Whose steps already are sounding.

Each man bears "a balance within his breast"; each weighs for himself his karma. And so now liberally, the living raiment of beauty is offered to all. And each living rational being, may receive from it a garment, and cast away from him that ridiculous fear which whispers, "This is not for you." One must be rid of that gray fear, mediocrity. Because all is for you if you manifest the wish from a pure source. But remember, flowers do not blossom on ice. Yet how many icicles do we strew, benumbing our worthiest striving through menial cowardice.

Some coward hearts inwardly determine that beauty cannot be reconciled with the gray dross of our day. But only faint-heartedness has whispered to them, the faint-heartedness of stagnation. Still among us are those who repeat that electricity is blinding us; that the telephone is enfeebling our hearing; that automobiles are not practical for our roads. Just so timorous and ignorant is the fear of the non-reconciliation of beauty. Expel at once from our household this absurd unsounding "no" and transform it, by the gift of friendship and by the jewel of spirit, into "Yes." How much turbid stagnation there is in "No" and how much of openness to attainment in "Yes"! One has but to pronounce "Yes" and the stone is withdrawn and what yesterday still seemed unattainable, to-day comes nearer and within reach. We remember a touching incident: a little fellow not knowing how to help his dying mother, wrote a letter as best he could to St. Nicholas, the Miracle Maker. He went to put it in the letter box, when a "Casual Passer-by" approached to help him reach it, and perceived the unusual address. And verily the aid of Nicholas the Miracle Maker came to this poor heart.

Thus through the work of heaven and earth, consciously and in living practise, will the raiment of beauty again be enfolded about humanity.

Those who have met the Teachers in life, know how simple and harmonious and beautiful They are. The same atmosphere of beauty must pervade all that approaches Their region. The sparks of Their Flame must penetrate into the lives of those who await the Soon-Coming! How to meet Them? Only with the worthiest. How to await? Merging into Beauty. How to embrace and to retain? By being filled with that Fearlessness bestowed by the consciousness of beauty. How to worship? As in the presence of beauty which enchants even its enemies.

In the deep twilight, bright with a glory unequaled, shines the Star of the Mother of the World. From below, is reborn the wave of a sacred harmony. A Tibetan ikon painter plays his lay upon a bamboo flute before the unfinished image of Buddha-Maitreya. By adorning the image with all the symbols of blessed power, this man, with the long black braid, in his way, brings his utmost gift to Him Who is Expected. Thus shall we bring beauty to the people: Simply, beautifully, fearlessly!

Talai-Pho-Brang, 1924.

PRAISE TO THE ENEMIES

And so we shall discourse! You will impede and we shall build. You will delay the structure and we shall temper our skill. You will aim all your arrows and we shall uplift our shields. While you will compose subtle strategies, we shall already occupy a new site. And where we shall have but one way, you will have in persecution to try hundreds. Your trenches will but point out to us the mountain path. And when we direct our movements, you will have to compile a voluminous book of denials. But we shall be unimpeded by these com-pilations.

Truly, it is not pleasant for you to enumerate all that is done against your regulations. Your fingers will become numb as you count upon them all the cases of forbiddances and denials. Yet at the end of all actions, the strength will remain with us. Because we dispelled fear and acquired patience, and we can no longer be disappointed. And we will smile at each of your grimaces, your schemes and your silences. And this, not because we are specially anointed, but because we do not love the dictionaries of negation. And we enter each battle only on a constructive plan.

For the hundredth time we smilingly say: Thanks to you, enemies and persecutors. You have taught us resourcefulness and indefatigability. Thanks to you, we have found glorious mountains with inexhaustible beds of ore. Thanks to your fury, the hoofs of our horses are shod with pure silver, beyond the means of our persecutors. Thanks to you, our tents glow with a blue light.

You yearn to learn who we are in reality; where are our dwellings; who are our fellow-voyagers. Because you have invented so many slanders about us, that you yourselves are hopelessly entangled. Where is the limit?

At the same time, several keen people insist that it is not only useful but highly profitable for you to go our way, and that no one who has walked with us has lost anything, but has rather received new possibilities.

Would you know where is our dwelling place? We have many homes in many lands, and vigilant friends guard our dwellings. We will not divulge their names, nor shall we probe into the habitation of your friends. Nor shall we seek to convert them. Many are traveling with us and in all corners of the world, upon the heights, flame friendly beacon fires. Around them the benevolent traveler will always find a place. And verily, travelers hasten to them. For besides the printed word and the post, communications are dispatched by invisible forces, and with one sigh, joy, sorrow and help are transported through the world fleeter than the wind. And like a fiery wall, stand the battlements of friends.

This is such a significant time. You need not hope to attract to your cause many youths, for they also are the designated ones. In the most varied countries they also are thinking of one thing - and they easily find the key to the mystery.

This mystery leads youth to the glorious beacon fire, and our youth now is aware that the cruel every-day can be transformed into a festival of labor, love and achievement. They have the valiant consciousness that something glorious and radiant is ordained for them. And from that mighty fire, none can repulse them.

We have known those who after their hours of labor, come silently, asking us how to live. And their hands, reddened from toil, nervously twitch over the whole list of necessary, unuttered problems. To these hands one does not give a stone instead of the bread of knowledge.

We remember how in twilight they came, beseeching us not to depart. One could not tell these young friends that it was not away from them that we were departing, but for their sake we were going, in order to bring to them the treasure casket.

And now, you denying ones, you again ask how we can understand each other without disputes. Thus - a friend contributes that which is most needed; a friend does not waste time. Thus is the quarrel being transformed into a discussion. And the most primitive sense of rhythm and measure is being transformed into the discipline of freedom. And the comprehension of unity, which doubts not, but searches for illumination, transforms all life. And then, there is still some word which you can find only yourself, consciously unwavering and righteously striving.

Often you are angry and lose your temper, but you should be just the opposite. You slander and condemn and through this you fill the air with boomerangs which afterward snap your own forehead. "Poor Makar" complains at the cones which painfully strike him, but he has strewn them himself.

You do not object to becoming important and to surrounding yourself with presumption, forgetting that self-importance is the surest sign of vulgarity. Now you speak of science and yet new experiments appear suspicious to you.

Now you laugh about seclusion and you yourself do not realize the most practical usages of the laboratory of life. You yourself are seeking to escape as soon as possible from an over-smoky room.

You often hide yourself and express doubt, while doubt is the most insidious poison invented by vicious beings. Now you doubt and betray and do not wish to learn that both of these negations are the product of ignorance which is in no wise akin to children - on the contrary, it grows with years into a very ugly garden.

Now you are shocked if you are accused of prejudices, while your entire life is crowded with them. And you will not concede one of your customary habits, which are obscuring the most simple, practical understanding. You fear so much to become ridiculous, that you provoke smiles. And you are shocked at the call: Be new! be new! Not as on a stage, but in your own life.

You value property as highly as if you were preparing to take it with you to the grave. You do not like to hear the talk of death because it still exists for you, and you have given to cemeteries a great portion of the world. And you carefully outline your ritual of funeral processions, as though this procedure was worthy of the greatest attention. And you eschew the word attainment because for you it is linked with the cowl or with the red cross. According to your ideas, it is a strange and improper matter to be occupied in life with these ideas.

Nor let us even mention your deep reverence for financial matters. It is not only a necessity with you, but a cult is contained for you in the sham formulae of a contemporary world. You dream to gild your rusty shield. But while you will evoke the destroying Siva, we will turn toward creative Lakshmi.

Just now Saturn is silent and the Star of the Mother of the World surrounds the earth with its rays of future creations.

You accuse us of nebulous inconsistencies, but we are occupied with the most practical experiments. And how silently are our friends working, searching for the means of new experiments for good.

In irritation you named our discoveries "panther's leaps." You were ever ready to judge us utterly without knowledge of what we are doing. Although you pretend to condemn those who speak of that which they do not know, yet you yourself are acting so. Where is that justice for which you have sewn such clumsy theatrical togs for yourself? When, to your joy, you believe that we have disappeared, we will be again approaching by a new path. However, let us not quarrel; we must even praise you. Your activity is useful to us, and all your most cunning schemes give us the possibility of continuing the most instructive of chess-games.

Kashmir, 1925.

A LETTER

Large banners. A great many multicolored banners of various shapes: some oblong, some triangular, some square-shaped. Most of them are red, with huge golden, black and white Chinese inscriptions. From behind the banners, one hears the beating of gigantic drums. Here marches the army of the terrible Yang-t'u-tu!

The ruler of Turkestan is preparing to defend the people of Sinkiang from the Sining Amban. There are rumors that the old Sining Amban intends to take revenge for the murder of his brother, the old Ti-tai of Kashgar. By order of Yang-t'u-tu, the Ti-tai of Kashgar had been murdered in a most brutal manner by the Tao-tai of Khotan. And now the Dungans of Sinkiang are full of the thought of revenge. But, according to other rumors, Yang-t'u-tu has recruited ten thousand men in order to repel the possible attacks of Feng. Be this as it may, an army is gathering to march on Hami, or to be more exact, as much of the army as may reach Hami.

It is a strange army: ragged, limping, crooked-handed, mole-eyed, with all evidences of being opium smokers, and gamblers, and beggars. But it is no wonder, for these soldiers are recruited at the bazaars. They collect them everywhere they can. The gambling dens, and opium haunts supply a majority of the soldiers. Every one who cannot prove promptly that he owns property or cannot buy his freedom with the customary bribe - as if by a magic nod of Yang-t'u-tu, is transformed into a soldier. Of course, where "magic" is available, there is no use for the usual technical procedure. Why is it necessary to have long-continued target practise and military training, if without these, an extensive army can be made to appear from the ground? What does it matter, if even before reaching the town gates, this army begins - also as if by magic - to dwindle away? Walking beside the army one sees several boys, and each one of them carries two or three rifles. Of course these rifles are of different make and mechanism.

But where are the soldiers themselves? Of course they do not miss any opportunities and have already disappeared into the narrow alleys and into hidden corners of the clay court yards, having just had time to give their rifles to some casual, gaping passer-by. If a tenth part of the army reaches Hami, it is already an amazing thing. But for this circumstance even, the Yang-t'u-tu has his own considerations. Sometimes the army travels along on carts, and then one sees round the edge of the cart whole rows of sticks, on each of which hangs a soldier's cap! . . . Why must a soldier have hands and feet? A soldier has a head and the main part of this head is his cap apparently. If the soldier disappears, or even if he has never as yet materialized, there is still a wonderful remedy: the war department hangs out caps, each of which is supposed to be a soldier! And for these, the industrious Yang-t'u-tu receives the corresponding maintenance.

Besides, Yang-t'u-tu is aware that the army of Sining Amban is recruited in a similar fashion. Thus, habits of life equalize the forces of the opponents.

As I have already mentioned, Yang-t'u-tu is an experienced ruler. He knows how to transfer in due time to foreign banks, all his accumulated millions of *taels* and he decides the fate of his subjects by the aid of a cock fight... With the gods, as you know, Yang-t'u-tu is very harsh. He flogs them, and drowns them and cuts off their hands and feet. And then he replaces the guilty god by a local devil, whom he has just raised to this new dignity. The stern ruler of Sinkiang has managed to remain head of the province for sixteen years; he knew how to escape poison, demotion and destruction from war with his neighbors. A crude brass statue of Yang-t'u-tu has been erected, even during his lifetime. Of course, it was presented by the "grateful" subjects of Sinkiang, who received a special note from the local ambans. The officials say of Yang-t'u-tu: "he is cunning, our Yang-t'u-tu." Other officials say: "Our governor has a very small heart." And the people add heartily: "Anyhow, he will not live very long."

But strangely enough, in the street there appears a detachment of horsemen, quite unlike the ragged army that has just passed. They have not the huge goiters so characteristic of the inhabitants of Sinkiang. They are better dressed and one feels from their riding posture that they are horsemen from birth. They are Kalmuks, a detachment of the Toin-Lama, Khan of the Torguts.

The old Khan of the Torguts, owner of the Karashar lands, also fell under the domination of Yang-t'u-tu, the all-powerful, and in a moment of strange impulse, handed over the succession to the Chinese official who had been sent to him. The official hurried home to the capital of Sinkiang with these precious documents, but the Kalmuks discovered the strange behavior of their Khan. Every mountain pass is well known to the Kalmuk horsemen. And where a Chinese takes several days - the Karashar horsemen can overtake him in a day. The caravan of the Chinese envoy disappeared, and so also did the envoy himself with all letters and documents. For great is Tien Shan, the heavenly mountains, and not only a caravan, but a whole army can be buried within its passes. Thus the Kalmuk horsemen have sought to maintain their independence.

On returning home, the Elders decided that a Khan, who voluntarily gives away his power, must have lost his reason. So they administered to their Khan a soothing drink which soothed him forever.

After this unsuccessful Khan, there remained his young son. Hence, instead of the Khan, the reins were assumed by his uncle, the Toin-Lama - the same Toin-Lama in whom was incarnated the spirit of the Tibetan minister, Sangen-Lama. As a physical identification of this incarnation, the Toin-Lama had a characteristically deformed knee, exactly like the deceased Tibetan minister. Even now the Torguts are considered semi-independent. The Toin-Lama has trained a special detachment in all the maneuvers of the Siberian Cossacks. And yet the Lama turned out to be timorous, for when Yang-t'u-tu demanded that he should send him his complete detachment, this only security of the independence of the Tor-guts was sent at his demand. Yang-t'u-tu then also ordered that Toin-Lama himself should come over to live in the capital of Sinkiang and a special palace was built for the honorary prisoner. And again the demand of Yang-t'u-tu was carried out.

Yang-t'u-tu also once asked: "From where do all the displeasures of the ruler come?" His adherents replied: "From newspapers." Yang-t'u-tu's decision was ready as always: "Therefore prohibit all newspapers."

Yang-t'u-tu asks: "What causes unnecessary outer communications to be brought into the country, and what may clear the huts of their refuse?" Again there comes the reply: "Motorcars agitate the people with their speed and it is difficult to keep an eye on the boats." The remedy is self-evident: prohibit in all Sinkiang the use of motorcars and boats, excepting only the ruler himself." In spite of this, the postmaster of Sinkiang, an Italian named Cavallieri, by some miracle retained his car. He also supplies Peking and Shanghai newspapers to the officials of Yang-t'u-tu. But of course this is done quite privately.

How long will American and German firms continue to trade in guts and skins in Sinkiang? They have to be very careful indeed to avoid all the hidden rocks planted by this capricious ruler, who presents a strange sight, with his typical narrow Chinese gray beard, and his thunder-like coughing that drowns out all contradictions. He is ready for another world.

Destined for strange countries are these bales of wool, sewn into white skins and rolled up near the resting camels:

"Who is coming?"
"A caravan of the Belian Khan."
"Where are you going?"
"Directly to Tien-Tsin."
"How long will you be on your way?"
"Probably six months."

And the bells of the camels ring gaily, telling, in their inarticulate way, of far-off America.

What is this America? It is a far, far-away land, a land taken from a fairy tale, a land where anything is possible - where for sausages there are not enough guts from sheep of the Sarts, and where wool is wanted from all over the world; where people move and speak and write with the aid of machines; where people do not count the money on counting boards, but where machines themselves do all the counting.

Every Sart dreams of trading with America: silk, wool, sheep gut, dried fruit - all these which constitute his only riches, the Sart would like to offer to America, but again that same Yang-t'u-tu prevents him. The Sarts ask:

"Have you no pictures of America?" and struggling with each other, they snatch the pictures of New York from our hands. And it pains them that they cannot keep these pictures. It seems to them that in these gigantic skyscrapers there must live giants, which fly through the air like a flash on gigantic iron birds. The local population still recollects the old teaching that some time there will fly steel birds and that iron dragons will unite all countries. These men have also heard of the mysterious cities of saintly beings, who know everything. And again they ask:

"But can you give us a book about America? - a book that is written either in Turkish or in Arabian? Otherwise our mullah will not be able to read them. Let us keep the pictures of America!"

And not only is every photograph of the skyscrapers cherished, but even every colored label is kept and guarded as a sign from far-away America.

In the sands of Khotan, a long-bearded Moslem asks: "But tell me, could a Ford pass here, on the old Chinese road?" And in Kashgar people inquire: "Could not the area of old loess be lifted with a Ford?" And the Kal-muks question whether a Ford runs quicker than their horses. And the gray-bearded old-believer (starover) on the Altai dreams: "Oh, if we could but have a Ford here!"

Is it a man they refer to - is it a machine, is it a building, or is it an abstract concept? For Asia it is a moving power. Ford is the carrier of a new motion, of new possibilities, of a new life. His first name has long been lost. The depths of Asia have no information of the everyday life of this amazing person, but their conception of him has been blended with a conception of motive power, thus widening far beyond the scope of a definite idea. And so it has happened that in the minds of Asia, Ford can do everything.

And yet another American name has entered the minds of the peoples in the depths of Asia.

In a remote section of the Altai Mountains, in the most revered corner, where old sacred images are kept, our attention was drawn to the reproduction of a familiar face, cut from some magazine. Before we had time to draw nearer, and to recognize it as Hoover, the old-believer remarks: "This is he who feeds the people. Yes, there are such wonderful persons in the world, who feed not only their own people, but can even feed other nations." The old man himself had not received any message from the A.R.A., but this living legend has found its way across rivers and mountains, telling of the generous Giant who kindheartedly distributes sufficient food for the starving people of all the world.

And even in far-off Mongolia where one might think this legend could not penetrate, a forsaken yurta, a Mongol, again tells you that somewhere there lives a great man, who can feed whole starving nations - and with great difficulty he pronounces a name which resembles something between Hoover and Kuvera, the revered Buddhist deity of good luck and wealth. Even into these vast deserts some interested traveler has carried the uplifting legend about the great man, who works for the "Common Good."

The third outstanding cultural name - widely known in the spaces of Asia - is that of Senator Borah. A letter from him is considered as a good passport everywhere. Sometimes in Mongolia, or in the Altai, or in Chinese Turkestan you can hear a strange pronunciation of his name:

"Boria is a powerful man!"

In this way the people wisely value the great leaders of our times.

This is so precious to hear. So precious is it to know that human evolution by untold paths forces its way into the future.

And suddenly there arrived your letter from America, having successfully survived all the trials of the Chinese mail. Of course the letter had been opened and very clumsily closed again, but in it the Amban could see nothing terrible. The Amban did not consider it injurious that you, my friends, are beginning the construction of a new building. Of course it may have appeared rather strange to him that this building will be twenty-four stories high, whereas there is no necessity for the mighty yamen of the T'u-tu himself to be higher than one story. Of course he considers all your propositions about the school, lectures and books pretty dangerous, but he passed over them with a smile.

The people in America have a lot of money and they can occupy themselves with paintings. But the amban of to-day does not engage himself with such empty things and he does not even know a single name of any scientist or of any artist of contemporary China. And should you continue to question him more persistently, you would fall considerably in his opinion. Let him rather think that there are all sorts of queer persons in this world, busying themselves with most strange matters. "But these occupations are harmless as far as Yang-t'u-tu is concerned; why should we therefore destroy these queer fellows; let us return them their letters." Thus thinks the Amban.

Maybe with the help of some Sart or Turkish merchant, or through a Chinese interpreter, the Amban will also read this letter. And maybe he will not like what I have said about the Kalmuks and about the cock fights arranged by Yang-t'u-tu. But seeing that every Amban considers it his duty to hate Yang-t'u-tu, he may smile as he reads the letter, and may say: "Well, let them know in America about our old man - he has a small heart."

But now the Amban will be quite perplexed; we will speak a language entirely unknown to him.

My dear friends, at New Year, had you turned back or were you striving forward? A good year! Not a wish, but a command must be in this call! It must be good, for those who desire to work, who devote themselves to educational work.

December 17th, 1916, late at night the train left. It was unheated. Our relatives thought our departure was madness. Sviatoslav remembers exactly how we wrapped ourselves in all our blankets, at twenty-five degrees below zero. The dream of action! And the snow-covered rocks of Finland rose before us as the first messengers of the future Himalayan heights. E. I. was so impatient to go; she knew well the hardships of the way but nothing could stop her.

And you have now become so flexible, and all-armed to encounter obstacles and attacks, as though they were only inevitable stones and dust on the path. And before you are manifest the image of slander and distortion. You are becoming hardened and do not take to heart attacks in the press. You know that all this has its specific meaning. And the main reason - ignorance, that ignorance which permits entrance to darkness and calumny. In 1918 I had an amusing experience: I was apparently buried in Siberia; I was not even there at the time. Requiems were chanted and obituaries were written. Of course, during our remote journey, one may imagine how many false interpretations took place. I was shown a clipping of an interview with A. N. Benois. Even Benois was led astray and repeated the Parisian gossip and told of the anathema of the Pope. At the time when, according to the interview of Benois, I was in Lhassa, I was really passing Altai. Amusing!

The main thing concerns friends. I rejoice at your information about Zuloaga, Mestrovic, about Takeuchi, this unseen active friend! How does "Adamant" look in Japanese? Greetings to Stork for the idea of an international literary contest.

Friends, you are all so different, yet all striving. America, South America, India, China, Egypt, all unite and lose their casual frontiers. Your sudden paths to Asia, and my last sudden coming to America! All this in manifold episodes becomes indescribable but tensely unforgettable.

Remember the furious rains on Altai, when S., although valiantly acknowledging the necessity of the trip, all wet and plaintively silent, asked of space: "Will it end?" Or Nettie on the "sea of ice" in Chamounix. And the coming of Franc, among the dances of the American Indians in Santa Fe. And the falcon-like decision of L. in Monhegan. And O. valiantly deciding in Geneva. And S. M. with the coin of Elijah. Or Sv. marching on horseback through the mountain path of Sikhim with a book in his hands. Or the parting on the railroad station of Berlin and Tch. asking: "And thus it happened?" And Tat. and Georg. in Paris on the Rue de Messine, "could they wait?" Or W., who although he agreed to meet the unexpected, nevertheless, in India awaited the roar of the tiger. Or the tension of Sh. on the Lyons Railroad Station. And the Philosopher-warrior R. in Rome. And the anxiousness of Newb.: his apparatus spoiled at the crossing through Yarkent-Daria. And Av. who courageously walked the deck of the ship during the "mountainous" sea. And the caressing approach of B.

And you remember the evening of December 9th, 1924, and all that happened around the statue of St. Roque? So it evolved, incident upon incident; and so it blossomed. To all friends greetings! And you, build constantly! Build high towers!

Again we go away beyond mail communication, and wish to see all your work directed only into the future. Directed toward those masses among whom art penetrates with such difficulty. Toward universities, schools, the people's and workers' clubs, libraries, village communities, railroad stations, prisons, hospitals, orphan asylums. There the new consciousness is growing. There they await. And creation is growing together with labor. And all obstacles are only the birth of possibilities.

Speak to the people about creation in all work. Say that nothing should impede them, that each obstacle should be turned into a happy possibility. I used to say to pupils: "Imagine for a minute that you are Raphael and I am the Pope. I shall set up all kinds of conditions for your composition, and you will retain everything and by your free consciousness will create above all obstacles. If the consciousness lives freely in you, nothing will diminish it." And let all pupils create in all branches - in art, in ballet and in singing. Until suddenly they will sing their own song and give their own dance. By all measures let them sharpen the creative gifts.

In 1924 the article "Star of the Mother of the World" ended: "Not reclining on clouds, nor playing upon harps, not hymns of inertia, but constant and illumined labor is predestined. Not a magician, not a teacher beneath the tree; not the folds of the toga, but the workman's garment of the true toil of life will lead us to the resplendent gates, will lead in full readiness and inconquerability."

Since then two years have elapsed. You are fighting on the entire, varied educational front. The work calls you forward. Not desire, but assurance must be transmitted to your work; you will never cease; in other words, never grow old!

But do not think, my friends, that having begun the letter about China, I count myself among the enemies of China. You know well my admiration of the old Chinese art and philosophy, as well as of the wonderful Confucian chants, which not so long ago we heard in New York. But if, on the back of a passer-by, you see a scorpion or a tarantula, it is your duty to tell him. To-day the Chinese sea is so stirred, that in the formless foaming of the storm you cannot see the pillars of foundation; and instead of deep clear water everything is muddy. But I continue to believe that sincere demonstrations of all the outgrown forms and superstitions will bring only good.

May the Amban, if he likes, read these wishes of mine. No doubt he will also understand soon, that when we speak of art, science, and of beauty and culture, we touch the very best and most living, motive powers of humanity. I hope that this letter, even if not very soon, will reach you sometime and that we again will feel as if united, and distances will again seem non-existent.

Greetings to all Friends!

Ulan Bator Khoto, January, 1927.

URUSVATI

"*Vade, filii ad Montes India; et ad cavernas suas, et accipe ex cis lapides honoratos qui liquefiunt in acqua, quando commiscentur ei*" - "Go my son, to the Mountains of India and to their quarries and take thence our precious stones, which dissolve in water when they are mixed therewith."

So speaks the most excellent Hali, the Arabian, mentioned by Paracelsus. Let us go to the Mountains of India!

"*Sophiae cum Moria Certamen*," published in *Summum Bonum* discusses about the mountain and the treasures therein contained. And again old Paracelsus justly assures us: "*nihil est opertus quod nont revelabitur.*"

"*Lumen de Lumine*" outlines the special conditions of the path to the mysterious mountain: "To this mountain you shall go on a certain night, when it comes, most long and most dark and see that you prepare yourselves by prayer. Insist upon the way that leads to the Mountain but ask not of any man where lies the way. Only follow your Guide, who will offer himself to you and will meet you on the way. But you shall not know him. This Guide will bring you to the Mountain, when all things are silent. You need no sword nor any other bodily weapons. When you have discovered the Mountain the first miracle that will appear is a most vehement wind that will shake the Mountain and shatter to pieces the rocks. You shall be met also by lions and dragons and other terrible beasts; but fear not any of these. Be resolute and take heed that you return not, for your Guide will not suffer any evil to befall you. As for the treasure, it is not yet discovered but it is very near. After the wind, will come an earthquake that will overthrow those things which the wind hath left untouched and rend them. But be sure that you do not fall. After the earthquake, there shall follow a fire that will consume the earthly debris and unearth the treasure. But as yet you cannot see the treasure... Then, toward daybreak there shall come a great calm; and you shall see the morning star rise and the dawn will appear and you shall perceive the great treasure. The chief thing and the most perfect is a certain exalted tincture..."

This "story" was told by Thomas Vaughan, who gave up his life in an explosion during his research for humanity.

The same "story" will be told to you by a guide in the Himalayas, when he tells you how to find the black aconyte, how during the night you must go fearlessly to the mountains to search this phosphorescent flower.

It does not mean anything that in the whole world lives the legend about a miraculous flower. But this so-called "fantasy" is fulfilled by the reality of the Himalayas. A seller of aconyte shall tell you precisely about it, not knowing that he repeats a legend of world-wonder, to which so many stories are dedicated by many nations. For to transform a "fairy tale" into reality, you must go to the Himalayas.

And from another part of the world, the voice of Athanasius Nikitin Tveritin, a Moscovite of the Fifteenth Century, reaches us. He adds another aspect to the statement of Paracelsus, after his journey to India, when he exclaims: "And I, out of the midst of many troubles, went to India."

In the fairy-like, flower-like Yaroslavl, in the frescoes, in ornaments of the Sixteenth and Seventeenth centuries, was discovered the beauty of the flowers of the Orient. These exquisite frescoes of old temples sing of the precious gifts of India, of the power of stones and herbs.

"War has flooded the world with blood. Droughts and rains have violated the eternal order. Famine showed its face," and again from the highest mountain, from the mountain of "five treasures," in wind and in thunder, in sparks of lightning we hear the forgotten: "From many troubles, let us go to India."

In Vedic wisdom many medical herbs are prescribed and much wise council is given. Certainly these are veiled in symbols. But the ancient wisdom again rises and those sensing the greatness of the coming evolution are ready to serve humanity in the most practical way, in the reconstruction of health.

People ask where are the remedies to be found? And again from far comes the answer: In the Himalayas.

Crossing above the visible, the sage of Rig-Vedas chants the Hymn of Creation: "Neither death was there, nor immortality; nor the sheen of night, nor light of day. That *One* breathed breathlessly, by inner power; beyond It truly nothing existed."

In these lines of the Rig-Vedas, a Vedic Sage brushes aside all mythology and reaches the monism of an ultimate causative principle. This is a real "Hymn of Creation," as it was called. So that we are not surprised when we hear a lecture by Dr. V. R. Kokatnur, the Hindu chemist, in which he gives evidence that Cavendish and Priestly were not the first to discover hydrogen and oxygen, but that the sages of ancient India knew these great gases:

"It is known," he says, "that our almost perfect system of numerals was originated by the Hindus and introduced into Europe by the Arabs from whom it derives its name. The world also owes decimal notation to the Hindus, who taught it first to the Arabs. Algebra (Vijaganita) was already a developed science with the ancient Hindus. It was the Hindu mathematicians who developed trigonometry, Bhaskara's great work 'Lilavati' reveals a profound understanding of what is now called 'Higher Mathematics' and Brahmagupta shows even greater originality and scholarship."

The old country of Aryavarta only recently revealed to us the remnants of the most ancient culture of India. But we are not astonished because we know that even Pythagoras received the keys of wisdom from India. In this country in the environs of the Himalayas, eons ago a high intelligence had already descended to the bottoms of earth and ascending, touched the finest energies. From every side, from every summit, from every tree, are revealed, generously, various medicinal herbs. You recall the conjurations of the Atharva Vedas. "We wear Vishkandha's (rheumatics) antidote, the Amulet of Jangida (garlic), the Amulet of a thousand powers. Jangida, save us all around from pain and from inflammation, from rheumatism and tormenting pain."

During a single day's passage in the Himalayan slopes and valleys, one is overwhelmed: "Nature awaits here, full of gifts. Come and be cured! Charrura, Parura, Or-rura are the three important curative fruits against cough, cold and fever. Charrura is like a yellow cherry; parura like a green chestnut and orrura like a yellowish green crab-apple. All these are sharp to the taste and full of tannin. Here is the red bark of Aku Ombo, to cure wounds. Salve against fever is Sergi Pruba, like a dry giant bean. Chuta the dry bitter root, will cure swelling and heal the throat. Bassack is a brown powder against colds. The red-stemmed Tze produces magenta; bitter Purma is for incenses. A broth from the roots of Bese-kuro is effective against woman's ailments. The flowers of Dangero heal the stomach, much like the flowers of the red rhododendron, while the leaf of Dysro is a disinfectant against wounds. Memshing Pati is a sacred plant in Nepal where it is used for head ornaments at festivals. Endless are the useful plants, awaiting the best application and study." Elexir Damiana, Datura, Abroma, Agusta; Extracts of Arjuna, Asoka, Aswagandha, Ayapan, Chattim, Gokhura, Gulancha, Kalmegh, Kamala, Kan-tikery, Khetpapra, Kurchi, Punarvana; Syrup of Brahmi and Vasaka, Tincture of Myrobolan...

These are not mysterious invocations. These are simply the names of medicines, recently prepared out of the healing substances of India. I recall talks with Bhat-tacharya. I recall those who strove to fulfil their research of healing treasures, guarded near the Himalayas. This is not a fairy tale, not a "heavenly Fire Blossom," not the Fire Bird of a dream. This is earthly creative thought. This is earthly labor for the peaceful purification of humanity. The sick and the hungry cannot think of the glory of the finest energies.

Kalidasa says: "The mediocre dare not to begin a noble work from the moment they foresee obstacles.

"But for the daring ones no obstacles exist. All obstacles turn into brilliant possibilities for them. Aditi - the Primordial Light - will illumine their way.

"Devas and Rishis, the Fires and Flames, and the forty-nine Agnis of the ancient Aryas will offer their power to those aspiring, to those useful for humanity."

Urusvati the abode of research, the abode of science, is to be built in the Himalayas, within the boundaries of ancient Aryavarta. Again the human spirit, purified by the continuous currents of the Himalayas, will search in untiring labor. The healing herbs, medicinal research, wonderful magnetic and electric currents, the unrepeatable conditions of altitudes, unrepeatable glowing of planetary bodies with astrochemical rays, the radio-activity and all those unspeakable treasures, which are preserved only in the Himalayas...

Urusvati is a name, meaning the Morning Star. Is it not the morning of a glorious day of new labor and attainment - ever-healing, ever-searching, ever-attaining? In those places, where the great wisdom of the Rig-Vedas was crystallized, where passed the Mahatmas Themselves, here in the caves and on the summits has been accumulated the power of human thought!

Again, do not take this for an idealistic outburst. Take it in full reality. As real, as splendid, are the glowing summits of the Himalayas! Verily, only here, only on the Himalayas, exist the unique, unparalleled conditions of calm, for ascertaining curative results. The conditions for scientific study, undisturbed by the rush of modern cities, only exist here, where even planetary rays seem to be purer and more penetrating.

When you see the mineral colorings of mountains, when you study huge geysers, full of various mineral salts, when you see all types of hot springs, you understand the teeming character of this part of the world, which still untouched, has witnessed so many cosmic cataclysms. This is the place. This is the unique site of a many sided scientific research. Here you sense a festival of knowledge and beauty.

The great Indian biologist, Sir Jagadis Bose says: "The Golden Age is not in our past, but it lies in the Future." And he wisely advises that, with the danger of the present situation humanity is as on a sinking ship, and without discussion, should unite as for a common peril. It is his belief that we receive everything from somewhere and therefore we must give away freely with noblest intentions."

This wise scientist also knows the value of the great meaning of Teacher, and he who knows this can joyously face the Future.

With joy I notice the spreading of high intellectual and artistic forces in India. Highly gifted individuals now stand at the head of universities, institutions and schools and the names of Tagore, Bose, Raman and other men of science and art act as a living bridge between present-day India and the deep roots of its past culture. Thus, following the best milestones, we reach the highest paths.

The great Vivekananda, when asked by a devoted follower, what he ordained her to do in India, answered: "Love India!"

The great Teachings of the Vedas, the Covenants of Buddha, Apollonius of Tyana, Paracelsus, Thomas Vaughn, Ramakrishna, the numberless calls of the centuries and all nations, direct us to the Great Mountain of India, which guards the treasure.

Love India!

The Mountains of India guard the healing leaves and roots.

The Mountains of India have gathered powerful energies and have strained the best currents for the strengthening of body and spirit.

Love India!

"Lapis exilis dicitur origo mundi."

Ladak and Kashmir, Kangra and Lahoul, Kulu and Spiti are especially remarkable in their historical, geological and scientific respects. Here tracing their paths with achievement, have passed the Mahatmas and Rishis, the kings and heroes; here are mentioned the names of Na-garjuna, Padma Sambhava and Santa Rakhshita.

Here bloodshed occurred. Here were raised the cities and temples whose ruins still adorn the mountain ranges of the Himalayas.

The Himalayas, in their full might, cross these uplands; behind them, rises the Kailasa and still farther, Karakorum and the mountain kingdom crowned in the north by the Kuen Lun. Here also are the roads to the sacred Manasarowar Lake: here are the most ancient paths of the sacred pilgrimage. In this region is also the Lake of the Nagas, and the lake Ravalsar, the abode of Padma Sambhava. Here also are the caves of the Arhats and the great abode of Siva, the Amarnath Caves: here are hot springs; here are the 360 local deities, the number of which testifies how essential are these very sites of the accumulation of human thought through many ages.

But Kashmir is isolated, and so is Ladak. Naked rocks are massed together in Lahoul and Spiti. The summer heat there is excessive, and cruel is the winter frost.

Not safe is the eruptive soil of beautiful Kangra, and in neighboring Mandi there are also many ruins of past earthquakes. After the great earthquake of 1905, a Japanese geologist specially invited to investigate the condition of the soil, found that the earthquake belt passes through Kangra.

But between severe Spiti and Lahoul on one side, and the unsafe Kangra and Mandi on the other, north of Simla, along the river-bed Beas, lies the ancient valley of Kulu. This is the same Beas or Hypathos which was the boundary of Alexander the Great's aspirations. On this river the conqueror stopped. The same river Hypathos is also connected with the name of Apollonius of Tyana.

Through Amritsar the railway leads to the Pathankote terminal. An hour before one reaches this small place, there already appear on the northeastern horizon the snowy mountains. From Pathankote one can go by motor, along the winding road through Palampur Kangra, Mandi, where the rocks are decorated with sharp outlines of ancient ruins. A railway is now slowly being laid in this direction. At present it has reached Joggin-dar-Naggar. The survey has been carried up to Mandi. But the Silver Valley of Kulu does not yet want to exchange its free motor road for iron bars.

Through Kulu Valley passes the ancient road to Ladak and Tibet. And inhabitants of the valley, ages ago, valued the beneficent properties of this extraordinary place.

Chota and Bara Bhagal mountain ranges, parallel to the Himalayas, separate Kulu Valley from Kangra, serving beneficially in two most important respects. Apparently these mountain ranges protect Kulu from the earthquake belt, for in Kulu no earthquakes equal to those of neighboring Kangra are remembered. There have been shocks, but with no disastrous consequences. Likewise, the altitude, estimated by General Bruce as about twenty thousand feet, protects Kulu from excessive monsoons. Although in Dalhousie and Kangra, the monsoon approaches one hundred and twenty inches, in Kulu it reaches forty inches, providing all the advantages of a dry climate. And whereas in Kangra the heat reaches up to one hundred and ten degrees Fahrenheit, in Kulu no more than eighty degrees Fahrenheit are reported. Of course this data varies according to altitude, as on the terraces above the foaming Beas, one can find areas from five to ten thousand feet high. In the higher places there is naturally only one harvest but in the lower fields two harvests are the rule, and even lands slightly cultivated give unusual yield. Almost all kinds of European and American apples, pears, cherries, plums, nectarines, peaches and apricots, nuts and a large variety of berries and medicinal plants, provide the yield of this fertile valley. The Civil Engineer, Mr. Bernatzki, who came to this valley for a couple of days and has now remained for more than six years, says that he has tested two hundred and thirty-five kinds of plants in the Kulu Valley, and all the tests were convincingly successful. North of Kulu, in the eternal snows, shine the ranges of the Himalayas reminiscent, in their whiteness, of the special conditions surrounding these extraordinary sites.

It has been pointed out that electric and magnetic phenomena are especially pronounced on these heights. The latter provide exceptional possibilities for the study of special currents, and one may imagine what new researches could be made here by our great physicist Millikan to further his recent glorious discoveries.

It is remarkable how all the collected information augments the significance of these places, where fertility of soil combines with the unusual phenomena of height and with an historical heroic past.

Let us hear what is said of Kulu by other travelers, such as the explorer of the Himalayas and the leader of the Mount Everest expedition, General Bruce and Captain Enriquez, who toured the whole of Kulu and its surroundings; and A. H. Franke, the well-known explorer of these places; and the doctors A. R. and K. M. Heber; and let us remember H. L. H. Shuttleworth who enthusiastically wrote about Kulu in the *Geographical Magazine* and whose brother spoke on the antiquities of this valley in the University of Boston, calling Kulu the "Silver Valley."

General the Honorable C. G. Bruce writes the following, in his book *Kulu and Lahoul*:

"Our introduction to the true Kulu Valley the previous day had been very pleasant. The walk from Sultanpur to Katrain, though by no means equal in beauty to the higher marches of Kulu, is very characteristic, the broad and not too rapid Beas resembling a salmon river. The great groves of alder trees fringing the banks, the wide open slopes of the hillsides, also an unfamiliar hillfolk thronging the roads, with a fair sprinkling of Tibetan and Lahouli traders, were all full of interest to us.

"The Beas is spanned by a number of excellent bridges, so that we could have traveled along either bank. The view is as fine from one as the other.

"During some of our marches we passed two or three of the best known of the Kulu fruit-gardens, but were unable to see anything of them as yet, though we did later on. Given good means of transportation, the fruit industry of Kulu should thrive wonderfully. The few Europeans who have settled in the valley and have taken up fruit-farming produce excellent results. They raise the best of apples and pears, equal to any in the world, and this with probably the least amount of labor. When, however, one considers that all the fruit has to be sent about an hundred and fifty miles to the nearest railway it is evident what a handicap the trade suffers. For instance, several kinds of the fruit most prized in India, such as cherries, currants and peaches, suffer so much in transit that it is not worth while cultivating them for the market, only in small quantities for home consumption.

"Shortly before our arrival at Katrain, after passing Mr. Donald's fruit-farm at Dobi, we crossed the Phyrang River and had a really beautiful view up that valley. As is natural in early May, all the upper grazing grounds and minor points were still under snow, and the contrast between the splendid dark masses of the typical Kulu forest and white tops on a day full of color was a very pleasant and striking sight.

"One would think that there must be a great sameness in well-cut, well-wooded valleys backed by snowy mountains. Kashmir is full of them, so are all analogous regions, but, for all that, each has its own distinct character, and this particular view I should never take for one in Kashmir. It was completely new, a type of its own. Opposite Katrain, on the left bank of the river, we could see Naggar Castle, the residence of the Assistant-Commissioner of Kulu, besides several other buildings, evidently beautifully placed, and commanding, we felt sure, an outlook which at our lower level was barred from our view. It is wonderful to imagine any seat of Government having such a magnificent sight always before it.

"The coloring of the Kulu Valley is almost impossible to express in words. Artists should make it their own as they have so often done with regard to

Kashmir. But again I repeat the Kulu color is in a class alone, and this richness and brilliance gives a charm and character peculiar to itself.

"Having once tasted the flavor of Kulu, both in beauty and interest, I found it very hard to turn my back on it (pp. 16-17).

"The descent on the Kulu side was simply perfect... It was far enough on in September for the autumn tints to have touched the higher levels with gorgeous color, and the forest below in its dark tones only served better to throw up the rich green left by the rains. There were numbers of Tibetan encampments on the flats on the way down, always picturesque with their blue-topped tents. I have seldom enjoyed a march more than the five last miles into Rahla. Kulu was at its best... We had a fine view of the redoubtable peak 'M'... The valley to the south was perfect. The crops were just ripening and the mixture of the crimson of the amaranth fields gave the richest possible effect, a welcome note of color after the more neutral tones of Lahoul. I do not think I ever saw a mass of colors as on our walk down.

"The Kulu peasants all round may not be very good at working their country, but they certainly grow magnificent crops. The fields, too, are well watered. The soil, no doubt, is very fine and amply rewards the slightest attention, but what a living really hard-working Alpine peasants would make out of such a country! The people will not even travel if they can help it, and have no desire to better themselves in any way. They can get all they really require at a minimum of exertion. ... I am not blaming them in particular, if they have all they desire and are happy, as is apparently the fact. I am only regretting the more or less wasted possibilities of such a country...

"Whether by accident or from possessing a real sense of the beautiful, whoever built the average Kulu temple very seldom made a mistake in the selection of sites; they are nearly always well placed. After leaving the temple, a full two thousand feet of steep ascent leads at last to the main valley of the Hamta, and the path winds through beautiful forests and open glades, deep in grass and full of flowers, even as late as the time of our visit. The right bank of the valley is very precipitous and finely sculptured, and is the habitat of many tahr, a species of Himalayan wild goats... We passed over some splendid grazing grounds on our way down and beat a great deal of open birch jungle for pheasants... Besides rich undergrowth, there were many flowers, especially great groves of pink balsams eight feet high, with stems as thick as a man's wrist. The surroundings were splendid and the color very fine. Much oak, too, of a dusky coppery hue, which showed up most effectively against the autumn tints, for the hillsides above the forest were all colors, the grasses and shrubs all turning and adding every description of red and yellow and russet. ... It is always a pleasant ride or walk by the side of the Beas, passing continuously through great glades of fine alders - finer ones I have never seen...

"At the time of the great emigration, when all the flocks of sheep are driven over the Rohtang and Hamta Passes up to the blue grazing-grounds of Lahoul, and the Lingti plains and of Spiti, there must be about two hundred thousand sheep driven through Kulu, irrespective of local sheep owned by Kulu peasants. I have heard a considerably higher estimate, but am probably not far wrong in the round number I have given...

"The approach to Naggar from Katrain is charming. Here the main stream of the Beas is crossed by an excellent suspension bridge and the valley is broad and park like, and the alder groves splendid. A shady lane leads up to Naggar castle. In former times it was the royal center of Kulu, but the capital was moved to Sultanpur. Naggar is beautifully situated, a good height above the river and valley, over which it has a wide view. It is also of greater importance than Sultanpur. Naggar is said to have been the seat of the Rajahs of Kulu for over sixty reigns, the present castle having been built out of the ruins of the ancient place.

"It is a very fine old pile, constructed of age-darkened timbers and stone, but guiltless of mortar. Three stories in height it stands in an imposing manner, behind it is the oak temple and around it a gay flower garden. At this time of the year the color both of the garden beds and the surrounding country was simply brilliant, and not only the flowers and fields, but every roof of the peasants' houses glowed with the rich amber of Indian corn spread there to dry, and below the crimson of the amaranth swept the valley in broad touches, while the blue indigo of distant hillside and forest were lighted with the yellow of the turning trees and grass. Snowy peaks completed the picture.

"We were lucky enough to see both spring and autumn views, and although the snow on the hillsides in the earlier season gives a greater contrast and shows up the forest and valley, still we both agreed in preferring the autumn coloring. I have never seen anything so brilliant on so large a scale."

Captain C. M. Enriquez says the following in his book *The Realm of the Gods*:

"Naggar is a large village. The gardens are filled with roses, fruit trees and vegetables. The pears and apples of Kulu are famous. There are strawberries, artichokes, cabbages, asparagus, rhubarb and salads all growing up well. In the valley there are deodars, alders and fruit trees; and on the mountains, coming right down to the vale are deodars (*Pinus excelsa*) and blue pines (kial). Glorious snows completely encircle this favored spot. Many of the surrounding peaks are fourteen thousand feet high. Those up the valley, shutting out Lahoul, are considerably higher; and Ghepan's Peak is nearly twenty thousand. The last winter's snowfall had been the heaviest known for years, and even the Bubu Pass, which is only ten thousand feet, is not yet open for pony traffic. Naggar is five thousand, nine hundred feet above sea level.

"Such is Kulu, a land of great beauty, cool breezes and luscious fruit - an ideal holiday ground. Trout are breeding in its streams. There are chicore and munal innumerable on the hills. Four kinds of pheasants can be shot. There are dozens of black bear in the forests; and below the snows you can get tar, gurul and red bear. The red bear are not as plentiful as they were, but a good Kulu sportsman assured me that other kinds of game were now more plentiful than they used to be twenty years ago… For the artist Kulu offers unlimited scope, and the naturalist will be delighted with the butterflies and birds of paradise. Leading out from the main valley there are endless miles of wooded uplands to explore.

"There are few parts of Kashmir, which are more attractive than the upper portions of Kulu."

In A. H. Francke's *Antiquities of India and Tibet* we read the following:

"Let me now add a few notes on Mandi, collected from Tibetan historical works. There can exist no reasonable doubt as regards the identification of the Tibetan Zahor with Mandi; for on our visit to Ravalsar we met with numerous Tibetan pilgrims, who said that they were traveling to Zahor, thereby indicating the Mandi State, if not the town. In the biography of Padma Sambhava, and in other books referring to his time, Zahor is frequently mentioned as a place where this teacher (750 A.D.) resided. The famous Buddhist teacher Santa Rakhshita, who went to Tibet, was born in Zahor. Again in the days of Ral-pa-can (800 A.D.) we find the statement that during the reigns of his ancestors many religious books had been brought to Tibet from Gya (India or China), Li, Zahor and Kashmir. Zahor was then apparently a seat of Buddhist learning and it is even stated that under the same king, Zahor was conquered by the Tibetans. But under his successor, the apostate King Langdarma, many religious books were brought to Zahor, among other places, to save them from destruction.

"Among the Tibetans there still prevails a tradition regarding the existence of hidden books in Mandi, and this tradition in all probability refers to the books above mentioned. Mr. Howell, Assistant Commissioner of Kulu, told me that the present Thakur of Kolong, Lahoul, had once been told by a high lama from Nepal, where the books are still hidden. Unfortunately the Thakur had entirely forgotten the name of the place. My enquiries on the spot were of no avail, as none of the lamas and Tibetan laymen could or would tell where the books were concealed. I can suggest only one way of finding out the truth (or otherwise) of the tradition. A reward in money might be offered to the Thakurs of Kolong in order to induce them to make another attempt to find the old books."

And two doctors, A. R. and K. M. Heber in their book *In Himalayan Tibet*," refer to Kulu in the following way:

"Our further travels through Kulu and Mandi State are in better known regions, and need no description here, save that one cannot refrain from referring to the country there as one of the most beautiful handiworks of our Creator."

In such enthusiastic words the experienced explorers describe the beautiful Kulu Valley.

Silver Valley! Silver ore is brought. Antimony is brought. Many chemical processes have taken place underneath the fertile soil.

The great Arjuna laid a subterranean passage from Naggar to Manikaran - from the Silver Valley to the Fiery Spring.

In Bajaura there is an old temple, the origin of which is attributed to Buddhist times. It is said that the Blessed Rigden-jyepo, pursuing his enemies from the side of Ladak, captured and destroyed them at Bajaura. Thus this great name is connected with the Kulu Valley.

The village of Manali has received its name from the first law-giver - Manu. On the rocks of Lahoul are two images, a man and a woman, about nine feet high. A legend concerning these images states that they are the ancient inhabitants of this place. The same legend, as is well known, also surrounds the gigantic images of Afghan Bamian. Thus many great traditions are connected with the ancient valley of Kulu. And the Pandavas themselves, after the great war of the Mahabharata, regarding Nag-gar as the best site, settled there. On the high hill above the Thata temple can be seen ruins of the castle of these great warriors.

The Kulu Valley has its hero-protector - Narasimha, a Rajput Raja. A beautiful legend surrounds the name of Narasimha. The Raja had to flee from Rajputana. As a humble coolie the learned ruler hid in the Kulu Valley. Under the mantle of a simple worker he hid his identity but his great erudition did not permit him to remain unnoticed. The light of his justice and knowledge shone over his neighbors. The people guessed that no ordinary man had come among them and they of their own free will accepted Narasimha as their Raja. The ruins of the castle of Narasimha still stand, in Naggar and an image of the hero is erected under an old deodar. According to legends, Narasimha protects the Kulu Valley. And woe to him, who evokes the just anger of the hero Raja. As a majestic white-bearded seer he is said to visit his country by night and many people have seen him and have been blessed by the ruler.

Narasimha protects the rich harvests. He fills the valley with fragrant flowers, and at the will of the hero, the trees are covered with luscious fruits. Now he will protect Urusvati, our Himalayan Research Institute!

And above the image of Narasimha rises the white summit of the Guru Guri Dhar - the path of the Spiritual Teacher.

Naggar, 1929.

SON OF THE KING

That which human hands would divide, life itself unites. At a time when East and West are conventionally counter-opposed, life itself molds the foundations of one wisdom. Christianity and Buddhism would seem to be divided by many walls and yet the folk-wisdom does not recognize these divisions. With a pure benevolence, nations speak of Issa, the Best of Men. Widely varying nations revere the wisdom of Moses and in Christian Churches the name of Buddha is pronounced. One is surprised to see on the walls of the old Catholic Campo Santo in Piza, the beautiful Fresco by Nardo di Cione representing the Son of the King, the future Buddha, for the first time witnessing the ends of human existence - the corpses encountered on his journey. This is a Roman Catholic Church.

In the Greek Orthodox Church, in the old descriptions of the "Lives of the Saints," you have a detailed account of the life of Iosophat, the son of the King of India. You begin to understand that Iosaph, or Iosaphat, in distorted Arabian, is "Bodhisattva" wrongly pronounced.

You begin to study this lengthy narrative beyond the veil of Christian interpretation, and you perceive the fragments from the fundamental narrative of Buddha's life.

Without yielding to any personal conceptions, let us take a few literal passages from the old "Chetyi-Minei":

In the East there is a very large and broad country, called India, where dwell varied peoples. And the country outshines in riches and fertility all other countries and its boundaries reach up to Persia. This country was once enlightened by St. Thomas the apostle, but had not totally ceased to worship idols, because many were such inveterate heathens that they would not accept the teachings of salvation and continued to adhere to their alluring deviltries. In the course of time this heresy spread as do weeds, suffocating the good seeds, so that the number of heathens had become much greater than those of the faithful.

Then a King, whose name was Avenir, became ruler in this country and he was great and celebrated for his power and possessions. And a son was born to the King and he was called Iosaph. The child was extremely beautiful and this extraordinary beauty was a sign of the great beauty of his spirit. The King summoned a great number of Magis and astrologists and inquired of them what future awaited the child, when it came of age. To this they replied that he would be greater than all the preceding kings. But one of the diviners, the wisest of them all, and wise not through the stars but because of the divine knowledge within him, told the King:

"The child will not come of age in this kingdom, but in a kingdom far better and infinitely larger."

The King built a wonderful palace with a vast number of spacious rooms wherein Iosaph was to be educated.

When the child grew up and attained reason, the King retained mentors and servants who were young and of beautiful appearance, to attend to all his needs. And he gave strict commands that no stranger was ever to be admitted to see the prince. The King also commanded that no one was ever to talk to the prince of the sorrows of life; nor of death, old age, nor of illness and other griefs, which might overcast his pleasures. But every one was to speak to him only of beautiful and joyful things, in order to occupy his mind with enjoyments and pleasures and not to permit him time to think of the future.

Thus the prince, without leaving his beautiful palace, attained his youth and came to understand Indian and Egyptian wisdom; he grew wise and understanding, and his life was adorned with worthy principles. Then he began to ponder why his father kept him in such solitude and he asked one of his tutors about it. The latter, perceiving that the youth was perfect in mind and of great kindliness, told him what the astrologers had prophesied at his birth.

The King often visited his son whom he loved dearly. And once Iosaph spoke to his father: "Greatly do I desire to know, my father, of something which forever burdens my mind with grief and sorrow."

The father, feeling a pain at his heart, replied: "Tell me, dear child, what is the sorrow that torments you and I shall immediately try to transform it into joy."

So Iosaph asked: "What are the causes of my imprisonment here; why do you imprison me behind these walls and gates, depriving me of the outdoors and making me invisible to all?"

And the father replied: "I do not wish, my child, that you should see aught which may evoke sorrow in your heart and so rob you of happiness; I wish that you would live here all your life in ceaseless pleasures, surrounded with joy and happiness."

"Then know, father," responded the youth, "that this confinement brings neither joy nor pleasure, but such distress and despair that my very food and drink seem embittered. I want to see all that there is behind these gates, and therefore, if you do not wish me to die of grief allow me to go wherever I wish and let my soul enjoy the sight of that, which up to now I have not seen."

Hearing this, the King became downcast but realizing that should he continue to confine his son he would cause him still greater grief and sorrow, he said: "Let it be, my child, according to your desire."

And he at once ordered the best horses and arranged everything in full glory as befits princes. And he no longer forbade his son to leave the palace but allowed him to go wherever he desired. But he gave orders to all his followers, that they should allow nothing sad nor unworthy to approach the prince, and that they should show him only the very best and beautiful - that which would gladden his eye and heart. And along the road, he ordered choirs to sing and music to be played and all other manner of entertainments to regale the prince. Often the prince left his palace, riding in full regal splendor and glory. But once, through the oversight of his servants, he saw two men: one leprous and the other blind.

Then he asked his companions: "Who are they and why are they like that?"

And his companions, seeing that it was impossible to hide human ailments from him any longer, said: "Those are human sufferings, which usually befall people because of the frailty of nature and because of the feeble make-up of our bodies."

The youth asked: "Do such things happen to every one?"

And he was told: "Not to every one, but to those whose health has been destroyed through excess of worldly goods."

Then the youth asked: "If this does not happen as a rule to all people, then do those, to whom such mishaps befall, know in advance or do these things occur suddenly and unexpectedly?"

His companions replied: "Who of us can know the future?"

The prince ceased his questions but his heart became sad at sight of these happenings and the expression of his face changed. A few days later, he encountered an old man, feeble, his face full of wrinkles, with bent and frail limbs, entirely gray, toothless and almost unable to speak. Noticing him, the youth was overcome with horror and, ordering him to approach, he asked: "Who is this and why is he like that?"

"He is already very old, and because his strength is leaving him and because his body has become weak, he is in the unfortunate condition which you see."

Again the youth asked: "What will happen to him next, when he will live a great many more years?"

And they replied: "Nothing, but that death will take him."

The youth continued asking: "Will such happen to every one, or does it happen but to some of us?"

They replied: "If death does not overtake us in our younger years, then it is impossible, after many years, not to attain that state."

The youth asked: "At what age do people become like him, and if death awaits each one of us without exception, is there no possibility to escape it and to avoid this misery?"

And he was told: "At the age of eighty or one hundred, people weaken, become feeble and die, and it cannot be otherwise, for death is the natural due of man, and its approach is inevitable."

Seeing and hearing all this, the youth, sighing from the depths of his heart, said:

"If this is so, then our life is bitter and full of woe, and who can be gay and devoid of sorrow, when he is ever awaiting death, which is not only inevitable, but also, as you say, unexpected."

And he returned to his palace very, very sad, continually pondering over death and repeating to himself:

"If all are to die, I also must die, and I even do not know when... And after my death, who will remember me? And after long ages everything will pass into forgetfulness. ... Is there no other life after death and is there no other world?" ...

And he became very troubled by all these thoughts. However, he said nothing to his father, but asked his mentor whether he did not know of some one, who could explain all this to him and ease his mind for in thought he could find no solution.

His teacher said:

"I have told you before, that the wise hermits, who lived here and who pondered over all these questions, have either been killed by your father or have been exiled in his moments of anger. Now I know of no one within our boundaries."

The youth became deeply grieved at this, and his heart ached and life became a continuous torture; and thus all the sweetness and the beauty of this world became in his eyes but debris and dirt. And God, desiring that each one save himself and that reason should reach truth, with His usual love and His mercy to mankind, pointed the right way to the youth in the following manner:

At this time there lived a monk, wise, fully perfect in all virtues, by the name of Varlaam, a priest by rank. He lived in the desert of Senaridia. Inspired by Divine revelation, this wise man learned of the prince's plight, and, departing from the desert and changing his garments for those of a merchant, took ship and departed to the Indian Kingdom. Arriving in the city, where the prince lived in his palace, he stayed there many days acquainting himself with details about the prince and his near ones. Thus, finding out that the mentor was nearest to the prince, he went to the mentor and said:

"Know thou, my sir, that I am a merchant and that I have come from far-off lands. I have a precious stone, which has no equal anywhere and never had, and which up till now I have shown to no one, but I now speak to you about it, because I see that you are a clever and able man. Therefore take me to the prince and I will give him that stone, which is of such high price that no one can calculate it, for it exceeds all good and expensive things. The stone gives sight to the blind, hearing to the deaf, speech to the dumb, health to the ailing, and can cast out the devil from the obsessed, making rational the insane. He who possesses this stone can attain all the good he desires."

The mentor replied: "You seem an old man, yet you speak empty words and you overflow with self-praise: I have seen many precious stones and pearls and I have possessed many myself, but, I have never heard of nor seen a stone that possessed such powers. But let me see it and if your words are true I will immediately take you to the prince and you will be honored and you will receive the remuneration you merit."

Varlaam said: "You are correct in saying that you have neither seen nor heard of such stones, but, believe me, I have such a stone. I do not wish to praise myself, nor do I lie in my old age, but I speak the truth. But as regards your desire to see it, listen to what I have to tell you: my precious stone, besides the faculties and miracles mentioned, has also this property, that it can be seen only by those, who possess absolutely healthy eyes and a perfectly chaste body; if, however, some one unclean unexpectedly sees the stone, he at once loses his sight and reason. Knowing the art of healing I can tell that your eyes ache and I therefore fear to show you the stone, lest I be guilty of your blindness. But of the prince I have heard that he leads a pure life, that he has healthy and clear eyes, and I therefore would show him my treasure. So do not be indifferent and deprive your master of such an important possession."

The mentor replied: "If that be so, then do not show me the stone for I have defiled myself by many an unclean deed, and, as you say, I have an unhealthy vision. But I believe you and I will not be indifferent but will inform my master at once."

And the teacher went into the palace and related to the prince all in the order as it happened. And the prince having listened to this, felt a great joy in his heart and became uplifted in spirit. He ordered the merchant to visit him at once.

Varlaam entered the room of the prince and, bowing, greeted him with a wise and pleasant speech. The prince ordered him to be seated and as soon as the mentor had left, said to the old man:

"Show me the stone of which you spoke to my mentor and of which you said such great and wonderful things."

But Varlaam spoke thus to the prince:

"Everything that has been told to you about me, prince, is true and right, for it would not befit me to speak an untruth to your Highness. But before I have come to know your thoughts, I cannot open to you my great secret, because the Lord has said to me: 'A sower went forth to sow. And when he sowed, some seeds fell by the wayside, and the fowls came and devoured them; some fell upon stony places, where they had little earth; forthwith they sprung up, because they had no deepness of earth; and some fell among thorns; and the thorns sprung up and choked them; but others fell into good ground and brought forth fruit a hundredfold.' Thus if I will find in your heart good and fertile ground, I will not be hesitant but will sow the divine seed and will open to you the great mystery. But if the ground be stony or full of thorns, then better not to waste the saving seeds and better not to permit them to be devoured by birds and beasts, for it is strictly forbidden to throw jewels before them. But I hope to find in you the best soil for accepting the worthy seed and for beholding the precious stone and becoming enlightened by the dawn of light and yielding fruit an hundredfold. For because of you I have gone to many pains and I have sailed a long way, in order to show you what you have never seen and to teach you, what you have never heard."

Iosaph said to him in reply:

"I am possessed, O venerable sire, by an ardent desire to hear of new, worthy worlds, and within my heart there burns a fire, that impels me to gain knowledge of important and essential things. But until now I have not found such a man, who could explain that which is in my mind and designate to me the right path. But should I find such person never would I cast his words to the birds nor beasts, nor would my heart be of stone or full of thorns, but each word I would cultivate within my heart. And should you yourself know of something, please do not hide it from me, but teach me. For when I heard that you were from a distant land, my soul rejoiced and I became full of hope to receive from you that which I desired to know: this was why I asked you to enter immediately and why I received you with joy, as if you were long known to me or my peer."

So Varlaam explained the teaching in parables and allegories adorning his speech with many beautiful narratives and precepts. As wax, the heart of the prince softened and the more the old sage told him the more eager became the prince to listen to him. Finally the prince began to realize that the precious stone was the wonderful Light of the Spirit, which opens the eyes of the mind, and he believed without the slightest doubt everything which Varlaam taught him. And rising from his throne and going up to the old wise man, he embraced him and said:

"O, Thou most worthy of all men! This is, I believe, the precious stone, which you keep in secret and which you do not wish to show to every one, but only to the worthy, whose spiritual feelings are sound and healthy. For as soon as your words reached my ears, a sweet light entered my heart and the heavy cover of grief which so long burdened my soul dispersed into naught. So tell me, am I correct in my reason, and if you know anything further, please teach me!"

And Varlaam continued, telling him of the wise and of the evil death, of one resurrection, of an eternal life, of the beautiful consequences of good deeds and of the sufferings of sinners. And the words of Varlaam moved the prince deeply, so that his eyes filled with tears and he wept long. Varlaam also explained the emptiness and inconstancy of this world and told him about renunciation and about the solitary life of monks in the desert.

Like jewels in a shrine, Iosaph gathered all these words in his heart, and he began to love Varlaam so greatly that he wanted to be with him forever to listen to his teaching. He asked him of the solitary life, of their food and clothing, saying:

"Tell me, what do you and those with you, wear in the desert, and what is your food and where does it come from?"

Varlaam replied: "For food we gather the fruit of the trees and the roots that grow in the desert. If, however, a believer brings us bread, we accept it as God-sent; our clothing is of hair and of the skins of sheep and goats, worn and patched, and the same in summer and winter. The additional clothing that you see on me, has been borrowed from a worthy layman, so that none may know that I am a monk. Should I have come in my own clothing, they would not have permitted me to see you."

Iosaph asked Varlaam to show him his own garments and when Varlaam took off the merchant's garments, Iosaph saw a terrible sight: the body of the old man was quite dry and black from the rays of the sun, the skin hung on his bones. Around the loins and legs, down to the knee, was a ragged prickly hair-cloth and a mantle of the same hung on his shoulders. Iosaph was amazed at such hardship and at the great endurance of the aged man and he sighed and wept, asking the sage to take him with him into the lonely life.

Varlaam said: "Do not ask this now, for then the anger of your father may fall on us all. Better remain here, growing in the knowledge of the great truths. I will go back alone. Later on, when the Lord so wishes, you will come to me, for I believe that in this life, as well as in the future life, we will live together."

Iosaph replied in tears: "If such is the higher will, I will remain. Take with you plenty of gold to bring to your brethren in the desert, for food and clothing."

"The rich give to the poor," retorted Varlaam, "and not the poor to the rich. How is it that you want to give us, the rich, when you yourself are poor? Even the least of our brethren is incomparably richer than yourself. I hope that you also will soon acquire these true riches; but when you will become rich in this way, then you will turn miserly and incommunicative."

Iosaph did not understand him, and Varlaam explained his words to the effect, that he who renounces all earthly goods, acquires heavenly riches and the smallest heavenly gift is more valuable than all riches of this world. And he added:

"Gold is often the cause of sin, and therefore we do not keep it. But you wish, that I should bring to my brethren this snake, which they have already vanquished."

And for a long time, Varlaam visited the prince daily and taught him the wonderful path to the light.

One day Varlaam told him of his intention to leave, Iosaph could hardly bear the separation from his teacher and wept bitterly. As a last token he asked Varlaam to give him his mantle. The wise old man gave Iosaph the mantle and Iosaph valued it more than his royal purple robes.

Once Iosaph, praying long with tears in his eyes, wearied, fell asleep on the ground. In his dream he suddenly saw himself taken by some strangers through most wonderful lands into a large field covered with beautiful and fragrant flowers. Here he saw a large variety of gorgeous trees, bearing unknown and strange fruits, pleasant to look at and inviting to the taste; the leaves of the trees were swaying softly in the light breeze and a sublime aroma filled the air. Under the trees there were altars of pure gold, laid with precious stones and pearls, shining most brilliantly. He further noticed many couches bedecked with covers of untold beauty and luster.

In the center, a spring flowed, its clear and lovely waters caressing the eye. The strangers led Iosaph through these fields into a city, glowing in a most brilliant light. All the walls were of pure gold and of precious stones, hitherto unseen and the pillars and gates were of pearl in one piece. But who can describe the full beauty and glory of that city?! A light in abundant rays shone from the heights, and filled all the streets of the city, and winged and brilliant warriors walked in the streets and sang sweet songs, such as the ear of man has never heard. And Iosaph heard a voice:

"This is the resting place of the virtuous! Here you see the happiness of those who in their lifetime have pleased the Lord!"

The unknown men then intended to bring Iosaph back, but he, captured by the beauty and the glory of the city, said:

"I beg of you, please do not take from me this indescribable joy and permit me to dwell in some corner of this beautiful city!"

"Now you cannot remain here," he was told. "But for your many heroic deeds and aspirations, you shall in time enter this place, if only you will apply all your strength. For those who strive shall take possession of the kingdom of heaven."...

On the fortieth day after the death of King Avenir, Iosaph called together, in memory of his father, all the statesmen, counselors and commanders of the armies and told them his great secret and that he intended to leave this earthly kingdom and everything of the world, and wished to go into the desert and lead the life of a monk. All became saddened and wept because they loved him for his benevolence, humility and charity. And every one begged Iosaph not to leave them. But at night he addressed a decree to the entire council and to all the commanders. And leaving this decree in his bedroom, he departed secretly into the desert. In the morning the news of his flight spread and the people became deeply depressed and troubled. Many wept. Then all the inhabitants of the city decided to go and search for him and verily they found him near a dried stream, lifting his hands to heaven in prayer. The people surrounded him, fell on their knees before him and beseeched him with tears and sobs, to return to his palace. But he asked them not to cause him grief and to leave him free, for his decision was final. And he walked on into the wilderness. Then the people, weeping bitterly, had to turn home, but a few followed him at a distance until sunset, when the darkness set in and prevented them from following him further.

In the desert Iosaph led a life of hardship, for food was scarce, and even the grass was dry and the ground gave little fruit. But his spiritual achievements were great. And once again, in his sleep, he beheld a dream. The same strangers took him and led him again through the beautiful field, and he again saw the brilliant city. When they arrived at its gates, they were met by Divine Angels, who carried two wreaths of undescribable beauty, Iosaph asked: "Whose are these wreaths?" "Both are yours," replied the angels, "one for the saving of many souls and the other for departing the earthly kingdom and beginning the spiritual life."...

In such an original way the old book "Life of the Saints - Chetyi Minei" relates the life of the Buddha. Behind the ancient Slavonic ecclesiastic language, one perceives clearly the original narrative of the Life of the Blessed Buddha. And the vision of the prince, before his withdrawal into the desert, clearly corresponds to the enlightenment of the Buddha.

At the end of the narrative is added a prayer to the Indian prince which says: "And leaving his kingdom, he reached the desert... Pray for the saving of our souls." There is added still another prayer, stating that Iosaph "now has, as his home, the shining hills of Jerusalem," and asking that he may "pray for all those who have faith in Thee." Thus the followers of Christ pray and approach the Blessed Buddha.

In November, in all churches, the name of the saintly Indian prince, Iosaph, is mentioned, and the gray-bearded Old Believer on the Altai Mountain sings the ancient sacred verse devoted to the blessed Indian prince. It is deeply touching, on the heights of the Altai, to hear the words of the prince addressing himself to the desert:

"Oh, receive me and accept me, Thou silent desert!" - "How can I receive Thee, Prince, I have no palaces nor royal chambers to shelter Thee?" "But I need no palaces and royal chambers!"

Thus on the Altai heights sings the gray-bearded Old Believer. And on the mountain nearby a little shepherd, like ancient Lelor the blessed Krishna, weaving wreaths of marigold, ringingly proclaims another version dedicated to the same sacred memory:

Oh, my Beloved Master!
Why hast Thou left me so soon?
Thou hast left me orphaned!
Grieving through all my days.
Oh, thou desert, the beautiful!
Accept me in thy embrace.
Into thy chosen palace,
Peaceful and silent.
I flee, as if from a serpent,
From earthly fame and splendor,
From wealth and resplendent mansions.
My desert, beloved, accept me!
I shall reach thy meadows.
To rejoice at your wondrous flowers.
Here to dwell my approaching years.
Until the end of my days...

Altai, 1926.

SUBTERRANEAN DWELLERS

Once on our travels we reached a half-ruined village. There was a glimmer of light in only two houses. In a small room, an old man sat cleaning a utensil. He became our host for the night. I asked him the reason for his isolation. He answered, "Every one has departed. They have found more suitable sites for their dwellings. They were strong and enterprising. Something new attracted them. But I knew that nothing new exists on earth. And I did not wish to change the place of my death."

Thus the strongest ones depart. The decaying ones patiently await death. Is this not the story of all migrations, of all enterprises?

The subject of the great migrations is the most fascinating in the history of humanity. What spirit was it that thus moved whole nations and innumerable tribes? What cataclysm drove the hordes from their familiar steppes? What new happiness and privileges did they anticipate in the blue mist of the immense desert?

On rocks in Dardistan we saw ancient drawings. We also saw the same kind of drawings upon the rocks near the Brahmaputra, as well as on the rocks of Orkon in Mongolia, and in the tumuli of Minusinsk in Siberia. And finally we discerned the same creative psychology in the halristningars of Sweden and of Norway. And later we stopped in admiration before the mighty signs of the early Romanesque which we found, based on the same creative aspirations of the great migrators.

In every city, in every encampment of Asia, I tried to discover what memories were being cherished in the folk-memory. Through these guarded and preserved tales you can recognize the reality of the past. In every spark of folk-lore, there is a drop of the great Truth adorned or distorted. Not long ago we were too vain to appreciate these treasures of folk-lore. "What could these illiterate people know!" But afterwards we learned that even the great Rig-Vedas were written down only in the comparatively recent past, and perhaps for many centuries they were passed down by word of mouth. We thought that the flying carpet of fairy-tales belonged only to the children but we soon recognized that although each fantasy, in its own individual way, weaves a beautiful carpet ornamenting life, nevertheless this very carpet bears the footprints of great reality of the past.

Among the innumerable legends and fairy tales of various countries may be found the tales of lost tribes or subterranean dwellers. In wide and diverse directions, people are speaking of the identical facts. But in correlating them you can readily see that these are but chapters from the one story. At first it seems impossible that there should exist any scientific connection between these distorted whispers under the light of the desert bonfires. But afterwards you begin to grasp the peculiar coincidence in these manifold legends related by peoples who are even ignorant of each other's names.

You recognize the same relationship in the folk-lores of Tibet, Mongolia, China, Turkestan, Kashmir, Persia, Altai, Siberia, the Ural, Caucasia, the Russian steppes, Lithuania, Poland, Hungary, Germany, France; from the highest mountains to the deepest oceans. You will hear wonderfully elaborated tales in the Tourfan district. They tell you how a holy tribe was persecuted by a tyrant and how the people, not willing to submit to the cruelty, closed themselves in subterranean mountains. They even ask you if you want to see the entrance of the cave through which the saintly persecuted folk fled.

In Kuchar you will hear of King Po-chan, ruler of the Tokhars, and how, when the enemy approached, he disappeared with all the treasures of his kingdom, leaving only sand, stones and ruins behind him.

In Kashmir they speak of the lost tribe of Israel; some learned Rabbi may explain you that Israel is the name of those who are searching, and that it constitutes, not a nation, but the character of a people. In connection with these beliefs they show you in Srinagar, the tomb of Blessed Issa - Jesus. You may hear an elaborate story of how the Saviour was crucified but did not die and his followers carried the body from the sepulcher and disappeared. Issa is said to have recovered and spent the remainder of his life in Kashmir preaching the same gospel. It is said that from this subterranean tomb, one senses various fragrances. In Kashgar they will show you the tomb of the Virgin Mary where the Holy Mother of Issa fled after the cruel persecution of her son. Everywhere you have different stories of travels and movements of great meaning. As you continue with your caravan, this provides the greatest pleasure and the greatest education. From Tourfan there also comes the pleasing tale of how young people are sent for long trips as though on pilgrimages to acquire the best knowledge of other lands.

Each entrance to a cave suggests that some one has already entered there. Every creek - especially the subterranean creeks - draw one's fantasy to the underground passages. In many places of Central Asia, they speak of the Agharti, the subterranean people. In numerous beautiful legends they outline the same story of how the best people abandoned the treacherous earth and sought salvation in hidden countries where they acquired new forces and conquered powerful energies.

In the Altai Mountains, in the beautiful upland valley of Uimon, a hoary Old Believer (Starover) said to me: "I shall prove to you that the tale about the Chud, the subterranean people, is not a fantasy! I shall lead you to the entrance of the subterranean kingdom."

On the way through the valley surrounded by snowy mountains, my host told us many tales about the Chud. It is remarkable that "Chud" in Russian has the same origin as the word wonder. So, perhaps, we may consider the Chud a wonderful tribe. My bearded guide told how "once upon a time, in this fertile valley lived and flourished the powerful tribe of Chud. They knew how to prospect for minerals and how to reap the best harvest. Most peaceful and most industrious, was this tribe. But then came a White Tzar with innumerable hordes of cruel warriors. The peaceful, industrious Chud could not resist the assaults of the conquerors, and not wishing to lose their liberty, they remained as serfs of the White Tzar. Then, for the first time, a white birch began to grow in this region. And, according to the old prophecies, the Chud knew that it was the time for their departure. And the Chud, unwilling to remain subject to the White Tzar, departed under the earth. Only sometimes can you hear the holy people singing; now their bells ring out in the subterranean temples. But there shall come the glorious time of human purification, and in those days, the great Chud shall again appear in full glory."

Thus the Old Believer concluded. We approached some low stony hill. Proudly he showed me, "Here we are. Here is the entrance to the great subterranean kingdom! When the Chud entered the subterranean passage they closed the entrance with stones. Now we stand just beside this holy entrance."

We stood before a huge tomb encircled by great stones, so typical of the period of the great migrations. Such tombs, with the beautiful remains of Gothic relics, we saw in South Russian steppes, in foothills of the Northern Caucasus. Studying this hill, I remembered how during our crossing of the Karakorum pass, my sais, the Ladaki, asked me, "Do you know why there is such a peculiar upland here? Do you know that in the subterranean caves here many treasures are hidden and that in them lives a wonderful tribe which abhors the sins of earth?"

And again when we approached Khotan the hoofs of our horses sounded hollow as though we rode above caves or hollows. Our caravan people called our attention to this, saying, "Do you hear what hollow subterranean passages we are crossing? Through these passages, people who are familiar with them can reach far-off countries." When we saw entrances of caves, our caravaneers told us, "Long ago people lived there; now they have gone inside; they have found a subterranean passage to the subterranean kingdom. Only rarely do some of them appear again on earth. At our bazaar such people come with strange, very ancient money, but nobody could even remember a time when such money was in usage here." I asked them, if we could also see such people. And they answered, "Yes, if your thoughts are similarly high and in contact with these holy people, because only sinners are upon earth and the pure and courageous people pass on to something more beautiful."

Great is the belief in the Kingdom of the subterranean people. Through all Asia, through the spaces of all deserts, from the Pacific to the Urals, you can hear the same wondrous tale of the vanished holy people. And even far beyond the Ural Mountains, the echo of the same tale will reach you. Often you hear about subterranean tribes. Sometimes an invisible holy people is said to be living behind a mountain. Sometimes either poisonous or vitalizing gases are spread over the earth, to protect some one. Sometimes you hear how the sands of the great desert shift, and for a moment disclose treasures of the entrances of subterranean kingdoms. But none would dare to touch those treasures. You will hear how, in the rocks, in the most deserted mountain ranges, you can see openings which connect with these subterranean passes, and how beautiful princesses once upon a time occupied these natural castles.

From distances one might take these openings for eyries, because all which belongs to the subterranean peoples is concealed. Sometimes the Holy City is submerged, as in the folk-lore of Netherlands and Switzerland. And there is folk-lore that coincides with actual discoveries in the lakes and along the sea coasts. In Siberia, in Russia, Lithuania and Poland, you find many legends and fairy tales about giants who lived at times in these countries but afterwards, disliking the new customs, disappeared. In these legends, one may recognize the specific foundations of the ancient clans. The giants are brothers. Very often the sisters of the giants live on the other shores of the lakes or the other side of the mountains. Very often they do not like to move from the site but some special event drives them from their patrimonial dwelling. Birds and animals are always near these giants; as witnesses they follow them and announce their departure.

Among the stories of submerged cities, the story of Kerjenetz city in the Nijni Novgorod section possesses a superb beauty. This legend has such an influence on the people that even now, once yearly, numerous religious folk gather in holy procession around the lake, where the holy city was submerged. It is touching to see how vital are the legends, vital as the bonfires and torches of the procession itself, which resounds with holy songs about the city. Afterward, in complete silence, around the bonfires these people await and listen for the festal bells of the invisible churches.

This procession recalls the sacred festival on the Manasarowar Lake in the Himalayas. The Russian legend of Kerjenetz is attributed to the time of the Tartar yoke. It is related that when the victorious Mongol hordes approached, the ancient Russian city of Kerjenetz was unable to defend itself. Then all the holy people of this city came to the temple and prayed for salvation. Before the very eyes of the merciless conquerors, the city solemnly sank into the lake, which thenceforth was regarded as sacred. Although the legend speaks of the time of the Tartar yoke, you can distinguish that the essential bases of the legend is far more ancient and you can distinguish the traces of the typical effects of migration. This legend not only gave rise to many variants but even inspired many modern composers and artists. Every one may remember the beautiful opera of Rimsky-Korsakoff, "The City of Kitege."

The endless Kurgans of the southern steppes retain around them numerous stories about the appearance of the unknown warrior, nobody knows from whence. The Carpathian Mountains in Hungary have many similar stories of unknown tribes, giant-warriors and mysterious cities. If, without prejudice, you patiently point out on your map all the legends and stories of this nature you will be astonished at the result. When you collect all the fairy-tales of lost and subterranean tribes, will you not have before you a full map of the great migrations? An old Catholic missionary casually tells us that the site of Lhassa was sometimes called Gotha. In the Trans-Himalayas, at heights of fifteen thousand and sixteen thousand feet, we found several groups of menhirs. Of these menhirs in Tibet, nobody knows. Once after an entire day's trip through the barren hills and rocks of the Trans-Himalayas, we saw, at a distance, some black tents prepared for our camp. At the same time, we noticed, not far from the same direction, those long stones which are so meaningful for every archaeologist. Even from afar, could be distinguished the peculiar design of their construction.

"What kind of stones are these on the slopes?" we asked our Tibetan guide.

"Oh," he replied, "they are Doring - long stones; this is an ancient sacred place. It is very useful to put grease on the heads of the stones. Then the deities of this place help the travelers."

"Who laid these stones together?"

"Nobody knows. But this district from ancient times has been called Doring - long stones. The people say that unknown people passed here long ago."

Across the relief of the Trans-Himalayas we saw distinctly the long rows of vertical stones. These alleys finished with a circle with three high stones in the center. The direction of the entire figure was from west to east. After encamping, we hurriedly proceeded to the site. And with the full evidence before us we realized that here was a typical menhir, such as gave its glory to the stone field of Carnac. On the surrounding slopes, no objects were found. Not far from the menhir was a trace of a small river, temporarily dried. No excavation was permitted because of the stupid prejudice of the Tibetans who invented the story that Buddha forbade the touching of the soil. But no excavation was needed to recognize the typical Druidic construction so carefully transported from the shores of the ocean... "The strongest have passed this way and found the most suitable sites."

During the next four days we found four other groups of menhirs. Some of them had the same rather long alleys of stone; others consisted only of several long stones encircled by smaller stones. When we approached the high passes before the Brahmaputra, these constructions ceased. In connection with these old sanctuaries, we found several tombs, a square outlined by huge stones. Again a complete repetition of those in the Altai and Caucasus was revealed. Before me, from the same spot, is a characteristic fibula - the two-headed eagle. The same design is known to us from the graves of the northern Caucasus. Before me are Tibetan swords, exactly like those in the Gothic tombs. The women of the same district wear the head-dress, like the head-dress of the Slavonic peoples, the so-called Kofoshni. As you travel through the heights of Tibet with their unbearable cold and hurricanes; as you mark these savage Tibetans in decayed furs, devouring raw meat, you are deeply astonished when out of the fur hat peers apparently the face of a Spaniard, a Hungarian or southern Frenchman. Admittedly, they are somewhat distorted of feature, but they have no relation with the Mongolian or Chinese type. You can relate them only to Europeans. One may also imagine that the best and most courageous people have departed somewhere and now you have before you only the poor degenerate remnants.

Looking on the merciless glaciers of the Trans-Hima-layas, on this sterile soil, on barren rocks, where even animals are scarce, where even eagles are seen but rarely, you may conceive how people were impelled onward, and how, from the high mountains, they reached the expanses of the future deserts. But their spirits were unsatisfied. They longed for the mountains. Thus did the Altai Mountains give them the temporary illusion of a longed-for happiness. But the glaciers of the Altai were too close to them; only now are they beginning to recede, for scientists have estimated the recession of the glaciers to be about twenty-five feet during the last thirty years. Some new and more fertile dwelling site for the courageous travelers was to be found in the Northern Caucasus and in the Crimea. Once again, the mountains permitted them breathing space. But they no longer had to combat the glaciers. The long journey was rewarded. Why, then, not to try still further? The Carpathian Mountains were also inviting; so to the very shores of the ocean came the pilgrims. And they remembered all the sacred signs of their long journey. For this reason, we appreciated so much the menhirs and Stone Henge of Bretagne and the British Isles. We cannot give statements of finality because each finality is a conclusion, and conclusions mean death. In broad decisions, in broad expectations and search, we are happy to add more pearls to the string of searching.

When I was asked, "Why do you so rejoice over these menhirs?" I answered, "Because my map of fairy-tales was verified. When in one's hand you hold one end of an enchanted cord at Carnac, is it not a joy to find its beginning in the Trans-Himalayas?"

Somebody may argue, that perhaps the builders of the menhirs came into the Trans-Himalayas from somewhere, and that the Trans-Himalayas may thus have been their stopping place, but not their original abode. Of course, it may perhaps have been thus. Hence, the less-defined conclusions we build, and the less we expect, the better for the future.

"But are you sure that the people, about whom you are talking, are the so-called Goths?"

"It is immaterial to me, what they are called, whether they were forefathers of the Goths or their grandchildren. Were these deep links with Celts or Alans or Scythian tribes? These scrupulous calculations will have to be undertaken by some one else. But I rejoice at the fact, that on the heights of the Trans-Himalayas I have seen the embodiment of Carnac. I do not insist upon nomenclatures, because before my very eyes the superficial nomenclatures have changed so often, and often a so-called fact was easily juggled about for periods of approximately a thousand years. I shall not forget my amazement when, on excavating a kurgan which at the time had been definitely established as characteristic of a period not later than the Tenth Century, I found in the hands of the skeleton, a coin of the Fourteenth Century. Such are the fluctuations!"

The folk determine these problems much more simply: for them all which has disappeared, has departed underground.

When we are asking our centenarian grandfather about the covered wagon of his youth, we shall certainly hear many things in a fantastic manner. But there will always be some truths revealed. When we ask the people about their forefathers, they are still able to tell us, they may still sing to us some song of a great truth.

Old Tibetan legends since very ancient times have drawn attention to the menhirs and Dolmens of unknown origin. The memory of the Tibetan people thus records these Great Travelers:

"From far-away India there departed two princes and they turned their path northwards. On the way, one of the princes died and his brother honored his memory by erecting over him a resplendent abode of huge stones. And he himself continued his long way into the unknown lands."

Thus the memory of the people knows!

Tangoo, 1928.

LIGHT IN THE DESERT

Sound in the great desert. Rings out the conch shell. Do you hear it? The long, lingering, wistful call vibrates, quivers, melts in the chasms.

Is there perhaps a monastery or a hermit?

Here we have reached the most deserted spot. Not within six days from here is there one dwelling. Where, in these desolate mountains is there one lama, thus sounding his evocation?

But it is not a lama. We are in the mountains of Dun-bure, and from times beyond memory this signified: "The Call of the Conch Shell."

Far off, the mountain call fades away. Is it reechoing among the rocks? Is it the call of the Memnon of Asia? Is it the wind furling through the corridored crevices? Or is the mountain stream somewhere gurgling? Somewhere was born this enticing, lingering call. And he who named these mountains by their caressing title, "The Call of the Conch Shell," heard the summons of the sacred desert.

"White Chorten" is the name of our camp-site. Two mighty masses form great gates. Is not this one of the boundaries? White signs. White pillared drippings of the geysers. White stones. Known are these boundaries. Around us, from out the death mounds of avalanches, emerge the crags of rocks. It is evening.

Above us lies another mountain pass. One must examine this site. From here we heard the conch shell. A short ascent. Between two natural turrets, like cones, is an opening; and beyond, a small circular plain like a fortress, fortified on all sides by sharp rocks. There is abundant grass upon this square and under the rocks, silently gleams the ribbon of the rivulet. Here is the very place for a camp. One can hide long and securely within this natural castle.

"Look . . . Something moves there . . . People," whispers our fellow-traveler, and his eyes peer through the evening mist.

Through the curtain of fog it seems as if a spectacle of phantoms is passing. Or was it a sound that intrigued our imaginations? Were these perhaps swift antelopes that were noiselessly leaping by? Gazelles and antelopes are almost unnoticeable against the mellow rocks. Perhaps some one, preceding us, coveted this unapproachable site. But all is serene. In the dusk the grass seems not to rustle. The sounds and whispers slumber for the night. The fires flash out in the camp. For whom shall they serve as a guiding star?

* * *

Again fires. The shadows dance. The tents merge into the darkness. People seem to have multiplied. The men and camels seem numberless. Heads of camels and horses appear. The heat is ponderable. It is the time of rest. The arms are laid down and one forgets that this is the very site of the looting of caravans. Only one month ago a caravan bound for China was demolished here.

It is long since our men have seen trees. It is long since they felt the caress of the tall grass. Let the fires of peace glow. A rifle shot sharply pierces the silence! Our rest is broken.

"Put out the fires! Guards - form a file! Watch the tents! Two men with rifles, to the horses! Konchok is sent to reconnoitre. If there is peace, he will sing the song of Shambhala! If there is danger - a shot!"

Once again a leap, a quiver, passes through the camp and all becomes still. The row of rifle-men take their places in the tall grass. Between the trunks of the Kara-gach the tents disappear as though submerged. A whisper - "Perhaps the men of Ja-lama. His bands are still active. His head, impaled on a spear, was taken through all bazaars but his centurions wander the length of the Gobi. You - in the rear - listen! Is it the grass rustling?" Suddenly out of the darkness sounds the song of Shambhala. Konchok is singing. Somewhere, far off, the voice is heard. It means there is no danger. But the guards still remain at their posts and the fires are not lit. The song comes nearer. Out of the rustling grass appears the dim figure of Konchok and laughs:

"Stupid Chinese. He became frightened at our bonfires. And he fired a shot in order to frighten us. He thought we were robbers. And he himself is riding a white horse." A Chinese caravan was going from Kara-Khoto to Hami, with a hundred camels and but one rifle. The Chinese mistook our fires for the bonfires of Ja-lama and wished to frighten us. He himself was completely terrified. He constantly asked if we were peaceful people and pleaded that we stay away from his caravan by night. Then his caravan became noisy and merry little fires started to twinkle. Fire is the sign of confidence. Nevertheless, the watch increased. The password was given: "Shambhala" and the countersign: "Ruler, Rigden."

* * *

"Arantan" cries out lama Sange, as he reins in his horse. Between two hills in the morning mist leap the outlines of galloping horsemen with a spear and long rifles.

Now they are surely here! These are the same fifty horsemen of whom we were warned by the unknown well-wisher who came galloping to us from the mountains. Our road is intercepted. The attack will begin from the hill. Our forces are divided. The Torguts - our best shots - are far behind. Konchok and Tsering are with the camels. There is also Tashi and the other Konchok from Koko-nur. But behind us is a hill, a high one. If we succeed in reaching it, we gain a commanding position over the entire site. And there we can gather our forces. The enemy in groups approaches the next hill but we waste no time. We reach the hill. We are prepared. Osher and Dorje ride out to meet the enemy and wave a hatik. Osher calls out and his Mongolian address is heard far around.

He calls: "Beware of touching great people; if some one dares, he will feel the power of mighty arms which can demolish an entire city in ten minutes." The Panagis huddle together in a group. They listen to Osher and count our arms. Even our lama, Malonoff, has put a spade into his gun-case and threatens them. The counting of arms is in our favor. The Panagis do not dare an open battle. They lower their rifles. Only one long spear, as before, remains rising in mid-air.

"Can you sell this spear? I want to buy it." Our enemy smiles. "No, this spear is our friend. We cannot part with it." Afterwards I heard that this spear was a sign of war and that riders leave their yurtas only in case of hostile intentions. Our enemy, finally deciding to abandon hostilities, begins to relate some long story about a lost white horse which they had gone to search. This story about a lost white horse is already familiar to us. In other parts of Asia suspicious strangers would also begin a story about a lost horse, thus hiding their original intentions.

When we spread our tents, we saw how the herds were being driven home, from the mountains to the far-off yurtas. This also was a characteristic sign that a battle had been resolved upon.

Strange riders went to the mountains, in different directions. Did they ride to retrieve their hidden possessions or to summon new allies?

One must be ready for unexpected events and one's arms must always be at hand.

Towards evening, when the bonfires of peace were already lit, some of our "enemies" came to the camp. Their special interest concerned our firearms. With astonishment we learnt that this wild tribe knows such words as "mauser," "browning," "nogan," and were discussing very profoundly the quality of our rifles.

Again they went back and nobody knew what final decision they had taken. But they asked us, under various pretexts, to stay there one day more. Who knows! perhaps expecting some help on their side.

In spite of the peaceful fires of the camp we took measures against a night attack. In two points, defending the camp from two sides, dugouts were made in the soft sandy ground. The watch was increased and a post was assigned to every one, which he had to occupy in case of alarm.

Before the dawn we discovered the loss of a few camels. After long searches they were found in a very strange place, between the rocks. Perhaps some one hoped that we would depart, disappointed at being unable to find our animals.

The sun was already setting when we moved towards the pass, with guards flanking both sides of our caravan.

Again, strange armed riders rode past us. They dismounted from their horses and stood with their long rifles. Some of our men also dismounted and paraded before them with their rifles ready.

Passing a stony way we came to the pass, and suddenly we heard two rifle shots in the far distance. Later, on the very edge of the mountains we saw our vanguard with his rifle over his head. This was a sign of warning. We again took position and two of our men with field glasses approached the danger zone. Several minutes passed, they examined something and then we saw a signal - "no danger."

When we came near, our vanguards were still looking through the field glasses. One of them insisted that something had happened and that probably one of our Torguts and a horse were shot. But the other noticed that our mule detachment was proceeding without any obstacles and behind it was a black spot outlining several figures below the pass.

This must be something free from danger. Descending from the pass, we saw in the distance huge herds of wild yaks - several hundred heads - so typical of the mountains of Marco Polo. By now it was apparent to us that the black mass below was a huge yak, which had been shot and was being skinned by our Torguts.

But the danger of an attack had not completely vanished. Our Mongols insisted that the Panagis would not attack us near their yurtas, fearing that, in case of defeat, their yurtas would be set on fire. But that beyond the pass, in a far more isolated spot, there would be greater possibility of an attack. The Mongolian lama Sange was frightened to such an extent by these hypotheses, that he approached us with a white hatik in his hand and begged our leave that all Mongols depart and return at once to their homes. But we did not accept the hatik and this entirely unpleasant discussion remained hanging in the air.

Accidentally, another circumstance was already hurrying to our aid.

The local deities, in spite of September, had been spilling thunder for some time in the mountains and our Mongols whispered that the powerful god, Lo, was very angry at the Panagis for their evil motives. After the thunder and lightning, heavy snow began to fall, which was most unusual for that time of the year. The courage returned to our Mongols and they shouted: "You see the wrath of the gods! They are helping us! The Panagis never attack in snow, because we could persecute them, following their traces!"

But nevertheless our camp was a gloomy one. Through the blizzards the fires burned but dimly and the voices of the sentinels sounded faintly.

I recall another stop, also around bonfires, but other fires are seen in the distance. These are the camps of the Golloks. The entire night they shout: "ki-ho-ho!" and our horpas answer: "Hoyo hey!" By these distant calls the camps announce to each other that they are vigilant and ready to resist and fight. It means nothing, that at sunset the men were still visiting each other, for with the departure of the sun and the opposite luminary in sway, the mind may also change. And suddenly the fires of peace may be extinguished!

Again a snowfall. Huge sharp rocks surround the camp; gigantic shadows are throwing open their flat ridges. Around the fire sit some drooped figures. Even at a distance you see one of them lifting up his arms, and, against the red streams of fire, you see his ten fingers. He is ardently recounting something. He counts the innumerable army of Shambhala. He speaks about the unconquerable weapons of these legions; how the great conqueror, the ruler of Shambhala himself, leads them. How no one knows whence they come, but they destroy all that is unjust. And behind them follows the happiness and prosperity of the countries. Messengers of the ruler of Shambhala appear everywhere. And as an answer to this tale, on the opposite rock there appears a gigantic shadow! And some one, all golden in the rays of the fire, descends from the mountain. Everybody is ready for most exalted news. But he who comes is a yak driver. Nevertheless he brings good news; that the yaks for Sanju Pass are ready. Good news! But the charm of a fairytale is gone. With disappointment they throw new tar roots into the fire.

And the fire hisses and sinks again. On a guilded yellow stone, surrounded by the violet mountains with snowy white peaks, under the dome of the blue sky, they sit closely. And on the long stone something in shiny bright colors is stretched out. In a yellow high hat, a lama is relating something to an attentive listener, while with a stick, he points to something illustrating his story. This bright-colored picture is an image of Chang Shambhala.

In the middle there is the ruler, the Blessed Rigden-jyepo, and above him, Buddha. Many magnificent offerings and treasures are displayed before the Ruler, but His hand does not touch them and His eyes do not seek them. On the palm of His hand, stretched out in blessing, you can see the sign of high distinction. He is blessing the humanity of the future. He is on His Watchtower, helping the good and destroying the sinners. His thought is an eternal, victorious battle. He is the light destroying the darkness. The lower part of the picture shows the great battle under the guidance of the Ruler Himself. Hard is the fate of the enemies of Shambhala. A just wrath colors the purple blue clouds. The warriors of Rigden-jyepo, in splendid armor with swords and spears, are pursuing their terrified enemies. Many of them are already prostrated and their firearms, big hats and all their possessions are scattered upon the battlefield. Some of them are dying, destroyed by the just hand. Their leader is already smitten, and lies spread under the steed of the great warrior, the blessed Rigden. Behind the Ruler, on chariots, follow fearful cannons, which no walls can withstand. Some of the enemy, kneeling, beg for mercy, or attempt to escape their fate on the backs of elephants. But the sword of justice overtakes defamers. Darkness must be annihilated. The point of the lama's stick follows the course of the battle.

In the silence of the desert evening, seated around a bonfire, the sacred history of the Victory of the Light is related. Ten fingers are not accounted sufficient to indicate the number of legions of Shambhala. No hyperboles are adequate to describe the might of the King of the World.

Amidst the all-conquering frost, the bonfires appear meager and without warmth. The short period from eleven to one seems somewhat warmer, but after one o'clock the frost is augmented by a sharp wind and the heaviest fur coat becomes no warmer than light silk. For the doctor there is a wonderful possibility to observe the extraordinary conditions of altitude. The pulse of E. I. reaches 145, or as the doctor says becomes as that of a bird. Instead of 64, which is my normal pulse, I have a pulse of 130. The ears ring, as if all the cicadas of India were gathered together. We are attacked by snow blindness. Afterwards, it is followed by an extraordinary sensation: the eye sees everything double and both reflections are equally strong! Two caravans, two flocks of ravens, a double silhouette of the mountains.

Our doctor prophesies that with such frosts, the heart, already exhausted by the altitude, will begin to get weaker and during the coldest night a man may fall asleep forever.

The doctor writes another medical certificate: "Further detainment of the expedition will be considered as an organized attempt on the lives of the members of the expedition."

Early one morning, when the sun had just touched the highest summits, the doctor came in quite excited, but satisfied, exclaiming: "There you have the results of our situation! Even brandy is frozen! And so, all that lives may become frozen and quiet forever!" He was told: "Certainly, if we desire to freeze, we shall be frozen. But there is a remarkable thing, like psychic energy, which is warmer than fire and more nourishing than bread. The chief thing in cases like this, is to preserve our calm, because irritation deprives us of our best psychic weapon."

Naturally, I do not blame the doctor for his pessimism; the usual medicines, in such unusual situations, do not have good results. Moreover, the chief medicine of his supplies, strophanthin, is at its end. And of the other needed medicines - *Adonis vernalis* - he could produce only an empty bottle.

Fuel is almost impossible to get. For a bag of *argal* the inhabitants of the black tents demand large sums of money. And each one prefers some special coins. One requires old imperial Chinese *taels*; another insists on coins with a figure - a dollar from Sinkiang; the third wants money with the head of Hun-Chang and with seven letters, and still another desires this same coin with six letters. One person will only sell for silver Indian rupees. But nobody accepts American or Mexican dollars, nor the Tibetan copper sho, despite the imposing inscription upon it: "The government victorious in all directions."

But what gives their warmth to the modest bonfires? In spite of an indescribable cold, ten fingers are again uplifted. First they are lifted to count the frozen caravans and then to enumerate the numberless armies of sacred warriors, which shall descend from the Holy Mountain to erase all criminal elements. And during these stories of fiery battles, of victory, of righteousness over the dark forces, the bonfires begin to glow and the ten uplifted fingers apparently cease to feel the cold. Bonfires of the cold!

A black mass moves quickly up a very steep rock. Wild yak herds of no less than three hundred heads flee from the caravan. Our Mongolian shooters sit up, move their rifles and try to slow up and remain behind the caravan. But we know their tricks. Although they are Buddhists, and around their necks and even on their backs they have incense bags and small caskets containing sacred images, above all they are shooters, hunters, and great is their desire to send a sharp shot into the black mass of fleeing yaks. The hunters stop.

"Osher, Dorje and Manji, listen, you must not shoot! You have food in abundance!"

But does a hunter shoot for food? Far away on the flint-stone plains a black mass can be seen again. It is still larger, and even more dense. There is something awe-inspiring in such a large herd of wild yaks. This time the Mongols themselves advise us to take a side path and go around the herd, for they estimate the herd at a thousand yaks. And there may be very old and fierce ones among them.

But as regards hunting kyangs, the Mongols are unrestrainable. Fines were levied in the camp for every unnecessary shot, and also for wilful absence from the camp.

But what can one do when a hunter, despite this, disappears behind a neighboring hill and returns, some two hours later, with the still bloody skin of a kyang thrown over the rump of the horse and with pieces of meat, hastily cut from the carcass, hung all around the saddle? They are just like the Hunn horsemen carrying their meat under their saddles. All smeared with blood, the hunter smiles. Whether you punish him or not his passion is satisfied. And the other Buddhists also watch you disapprovingly for your prohibition to kill animals. They all simply delight at the thought of having fresh meat of yaks or kyangs roasting over their evening fires.

An antelope, pursued by a wolf, runs right into the caravan. The riflers, under restraint, look covetously. But, if people may be restrained, you cannot restrain a dog, and the poor antelope soon finds itself between two fires. However the wolf is also frightened in the neighborhood of the caravan, and turning aside takes off, jumping instead of leaping. But the antelope will escape the dogs. Even the mountain hen and small wild goats make fools of the Mongolian dogs, and lead them far away from their young ones.

And here are the bears! Dark brown with wide white collars. At night they come quite close to the camp and if it were not for the dogs, they would satisfy their curiosity calmly without any attempt at escape by daytime also. Now we move along the riverbed of the clear Buren-gol. Under the hoofs of the horses, blue copper-oxides shine like the best of turquoises. Above us is a steep rock and at the very edge of it a huge bear keeps pace with our caravan, watching us curiously. Who will touch him, and for what?

But certain species of animals have become real enemies of the caravan. Those are the marmots, the tabagans and the, shrewmice. The whole district is undermined by their innumerable burrows. Despite the greatest care, the horses often slip, and at once they are up to their knees in these underground cities. Not a day passes without a horse slipping into the treacherous excavations of these burrowers.

In the evening the Tibetan Konchok brings two mountain pheasants up to the bonfires. How he caught them barehanded, remains a riddle. One need hardly guess who it is that wants to kill and eat them, but there are also voices for their release. We again turn towards the Buddhist covenants and after some bargaining, we exchange the birds for a Chinese tael. And a minute later both prisoners gaily flit away in the direction of the mountains.

The fox hunts mountain partridges; a kite watches a hare and the dogs zealously chase marmots. The animal kingdom lives its own law. The last case regarding the animal kingdom concerned three hens. From Suchow we had taken with us a cock and two hens, and the latter dutifully presented us with eggs every day, notwithstanding the unpleasant stirring up they got during the daily voyage. However, when there was nothing more left with which to feed the fowl, we presented them to a Tibetan officer. The eye of a searcher noticed the absence of the hens and he immediately reported it to the governor. A very lengthy correspondence was started regarding whether we had eaten the three fowls. In fact there were even letters to Lhassa about it.

And again, by the light of the night bonfires, our shaggy Tibetans assembled and, blinking to each other, told the latest gossip from the neighboring dzong, as usual, deriding their Governor. And the same warming fire, which just before had been the scene of inspired narratives about Shambhala, now illumined the faces that were condemning the officials of Lhassa.

* * *

The lamas consecrate a suburgan in the name of Shambhala. In front of the image of Rigden-jyepo they pour water on a magic mirror; the water runs over the surface of the mirror, the figures become blurred and resemble one of the ancient stories of magic mirrors. A procession walks round the suburgan with burning incense and the head lama holds a thread, connected with the top of the suburgan, wherein various objects of special significance have been previously deposited. There is an image of Buddha, there is a silver ring with a most significant inscription, there are prophecies for the future and there are the precious objects: "Norbu-rinpoche." An old lama has come from the neighboring yurtas and he brought a small quantity of "treasures" - a piece of mountain crystal, a small turquoise stone, two or three small beads and a shiny piece of mica. The old lama had taken part in the building of the suburgan and he brought these treasures with the insistent request to place them into the opened shrine.

After a long service the white thread that connected the lama and the suburgan was cut and in the desert there remained the white suburgan, defended only by invisible powers. Many dangers threaten these shrines. When caravans stop for a rest, the camels spoil the edges of the base; curious deer jump upon the cornices and try the strength of the picturesque images and ornaments with their horns. But the greatest danger comes from the Dungan-Moslems.

The Mongols have a saying: "If a suburgan can resist the Dungans, then it is safe for ages." Round the bonfire, stories are told of the destruction of Buddhist sanctuaries by Dungans. It is said that the Dungans light bonfires in the old Buddhist caves, which are decorated with ancient murals, in order to burn and destroy these frescoes with smoke. The people, with terror in their eyes, tell how in the Labran province, Dungans demolished the statue of the Maitreya himself. Not only did they persecute the Buddhists, but also the Chinese followers of Confucius. The Mongols say, that though it is difficult with the Chinese, the Dungans are still worse - they are absolutely impossible. They are regarded as inhuman, cruel and bloodthirsty. One remembers all manner of atrocities that took place during the Dungan uprising. One sees ruins on every hill, and everywhere there are stones in formless heaps. In the mind of the people almost all these remnants are somehow associated with the name of Dungans. Here was a fort built by the Dungans; there were fortifications destroyed by the Dungans; here was a village burnt by the Dungans; and that gold mine became silent after the Dungans had passed through it; there again was a well which the Dungans had filled with sand in order to deprive the place of water.

A whole evening was devoted to these horrible stories.

And around the bonfire one could again see the ten raised fingers, and how they attested the cruelty of the Dungans.

The bells on the camels of the caravan are of different sizes and sound like a symphony. This is an essential melody of the desert. The heat during the day kills everything. Everything becomes still, dead. Everything creeps into the coolness of the shadow. The sun is the conqueror and is alone on the immense battlefield. Nothing can withstand it. Even the great river, even the Tarim himself, stops its flow. As claws in agony, are projected the burning stones, until the conqueror disappears behind the horizon, seeking new victories. Darkness does not dare to reappear. Only a bluish mist covers the expanse, without end and without beginning. To this bluish symphony, what kind of a melody may be fittingly added? The symphony of bells, soft as old brass and rhythmic as the movement of the ships of the desert. This alone can complete the symphony of the desert and as an antithesis to this mysterious procession of sounds, you have a song accompanied on the zither by the untiring hands of the baksha - the traveling singer. He is singing about Shabistan, about fairies, which come from the highest planes down to the earth, to inspire the giants and heroes and the beautiful sons of the kings.

He sings about Blessed Issa, the Prophet, who walked through these lands, and how he resurrected the giant, who became a benevolent king of this country. He sings about the holy people behind this very mountain and how a holy man could hear their sacred chants, although they were six months' distance away from him. In the stillness of the desert, this baksha joins the bells of our caravan. Some holiday is held in the next village, and he is going there to present his sacred art and to relate many stories about all sorts of wonderful things, which are not a fairy tale, but the real life of Asia.

The first camel of the caravan is adorned with colorful carpets and ribbons and a flag is placed high above his load. He is an esteemed camel, he is the first. He takes all the responsibility of filling the desert with his ringing and he steps proudly on. And his black eyes also seem to know many legends.

But instead of a baksha with holy songs, some rider overtakes us.

And high penetrating notes imperatively pierce the space.

This is a Chinese heroic song.

I doubt whether you can ever hear these heroic and sometimes Confucian chants in the European quarters of the harbor cities of China.

But in the desert the feeling of ancient China, of the Chinese conquerors of immense spaces even penetrates the heart of a contemporary amban. The rhythm of the camel bells is broken. The chimes of the horse of the amban are thundering. And the large red tassel is waving on the neck of a big Karashar horse, gray with stripes, like a zebra. And another tassel is hung on the breastplate of the horse. Under the saddle, there is a big Chinese sword. The points of the black velvet boots are curled upwards. The stirrups have gilded lions. Complicated is the adornment of the saddle. Several rugs soften the long ride. From Yarkend to Tunhuang, it is a two months' journey to follow the ancient Chinese road where jade and silk and silver and gold were transported by the same riders, with the same songs, with the same bells and the same swords. Noisily the amban with his retinue joins us. The camels are behind and the horses are inspired by this noise and by the piercing sounds of the chants. This is something similar to a passage of the hordes of the grandsons of Chingiz-Khan.

A small city. Another amban comes out of his yamen, surrounded by fenced walls, to greet our Chinese traveling companion. Both potentates with great ceremony greet each other. It is like something from an old Chinese painting. They are so glad to see each other and they hold each other's hands and enter the big red gates. Two black silhouettes in the sandy-pearl mist, guarded by two armed warriors, are painted on both sides of the clay wall.

Allah! Allah! Allah! - shout the Moslems, preparing for the Ramadan, when they fast during the day and can only eat at night time. And to avoid falling asleep they fill the air around the town with their shouts and songs.

But quite another shout is to be heard from the vicinity of a great tree. Two

Ladakis of our caravan are singing some prayers dedicated to Maitreya. So the songs of all religions are gathered round one bonfire.

On old stones, throughout the whole of Asia, are to be found peculiar crosses and names, written in Uighur, Chinese, Mongolian and other tongues. What a wonder! On a Mongolian coin is the same sign! In the same way the Nestorians have trespassed the desert. You remember how the great Thomas Vaughan cites a Chinese author of the early Christian era in Sia, on how the sands, as silk waves, have covered everything of the past. And only a pink line in the East crosses the silhouettes of the sand dunes.

Moving sands. Like miserly guardians they defend the treasures which sometimes appear on the surface. Nobody shall dare to take them because they are guarded by hidden forces and can be given out only at a predestined time. From the earth are spreading some poisonous essences. Do not lean over the ground, do not try to raise from the ground that which does not belong to you. Otherwise you will fall dead, as falls the robber.

An experienced rider sends a dog before him, because the dog will first feel the influences of these earthly essences. Even an animal will not dare to enter the forbidden zone. No bonfires will attract you in these hidden places. Only some vultures will fly high over the mysterious land. Are they not also guardians? And to whom belong the bones, which glimmer so whitely on the sands? Who was this intruder, who dishonored the predestined dates?

A huge black vulture rushes over the camp.

But what is this high above in the air? A shiny body flying from north to south. Field glasses are at hand. It is a huge body. One side glows in the sun. It is oval in shape. Then it somehow turns in another direction and disappears in the southwest, behind Ulandavan, the red pass in the Humboldt chain. The whole caravan excitedly discusses this apparition. An air balloon? An Ebolite? An unknown apparatus? Not a vision, because through several field glasses you cannot see visions. And then the lama whispers: "A good sign. A very good sign. We are protected. Rigden-jyepo himself is looking after us!" In the desert you can see wonderful things and you can smell fragrant perfumes. But they who live in the desert are never astonished.

Again around the bonfire ten fingers are raised and a story, convincing in its simplicity and reality, will uplift the human heart. Now the story is about the famous black stone. In beautiful descriptive symbols the old traveler will tell to the awed audience how from times immemorial from some other world fell down a miraculous stone - the Chintamani of the Hindus and Norbu-rinpoche of the Tibetans and Mongols. Now since these times, a part of the stone is traveling on earth, manifesting the new era and greatest world events. How some ruler possessed this stone and how the forces of darkness tried to steal the stone.

Your friend, listening to this legend, will whisper to you: "The stone is black, 'vile' and 'fetid' and it is called the origin of the world. And it springs up like germinating things. So dreamed Paracelsus." And another of your companions smiles: "*Lapis exilis*, the Wandering stone of the Meistersinger."

But the narrator of the fire continues his tale about miraculous powers of the stone, how, by all sorts of manifestations, this stone is indicating all kinds of events and the nature of existence.

"When the stone is hot, when the stone quivers, when the stone is cracking, when the stone changes its weight and color - by these changes the stone predicts to its possessor the whole future and gives him the ability to know his enemies and hostile dangers as well as happy events."

One of the listeners asks: "Is not this stone on the tower of the Rigden-jyepo, whose rays penetrate all oceans and mountains for the benefit of humanity?"

And the narrator continues: "The black stone is wandering on earth. We know that a Chinese Emperor and Tamerlane possessed this stone. And authoritative people say, that the Great Suleiman and Akbar had it in their possession and through this stone their might was augmented. 'Treasure of the World' this stone is called."

The bonfires are burning like old fires of sacrifice.

You are entering your tent. All is calm and usual. In the usual surroundings it is difficult to imagine something unreal and unrepeatable. You touch your bed - and suddenly there leaps up a flame. A silvery-blue flame. Entering through the gates of the practical you attempt to act in the usual way, trying to extinguish it. The flame does not burn your hand, it is slightly warm - warm and vital as life itself. Without noise or odor it moves, issuing long tongues. This is not a phosphorescence - this is a living substance. The fire coming from space by a happy combination of elements. An intangible moment passes. And the unceasing flame begins to droop as mysteriously as it was born. It is dark in the tent and not a trace is left of that phenomena which you felt and saw in full reality. And another time. In another place, also at night, out of your fingers the flame leapt up and rushed through all the objects touched by you, not harming them. Again you come in contact with some inexpressible combination of currents. This occurs only on heights. The bonfires did not yet grow brighter, when a shot resounded in the twilight. Who is shooting?

Tashi has killed a snake. What a strange snake! With a sort of beard, gray with black and gray shadings.

Around the fires long stories are told about snakes. One Mongol tells:

"If somebody does not fear the snakes, he should grab them by their tail and should shake them very strongly. And the snake will become as hard as a stick, until you will shake it again."

My companion was bending down to me:

"You remember the Biblical staff of Moses, how he manifested a miracle, when the staff was transformed into a snake. Maybe he used a cataleptic snake and with a powerful gesture returned her to life."

Many Biblical signs are to be remembered in the desert. Look at these huge pillars of sand, which suddenly appear and move for a long time as dense masses. This miraculous pillar, which moved before Moses, is so clearly visioned by him who knows the desert wanderings - and again you remember the burning and unburnable bush of Moses. After seeing the unceasing flame in your tent such a bush is for you no longer an impossible miracle, but a reality that lives only in the desert. When you hear how the great Mahatma traveled on horseback for the fulfilment of undelayable high missions you also do not wonder, because you know of the existence of the Mahatmas. You know their great wisdom. Many things which absolutely cannot find a place in the life of the West - here in the East are becoming simple.

There are still more Biblical echoes. On the very summit of a mountain several stones can be seen. Some ruins, probably.

"This is the throne of Suleiman," explains the leader of the caravan to you.

"But how does it happen that throughout Asia everywhere there are to be seen thrones of Solomon. We have seen them in Srinagar, near Kashgar; there are several in Persia."

But the caravaneer does not give up his favorite idea.

"Certainly there are many thrones of the Great King Suleiman. He was wise and powerful. He had an apparatus to fly all over many lands. Stupid people, they think that he used a flying carpet, but learned men know that the King possessed an apparatus. Truly it could not fly very high, still it could move in the air."

So again something of the way of the traveling is revealed, but the old flying carpet has been given up.

In the same way the stories of the conquests of Alexander the Great are mixed up. On one side the Great Conqueror is linked with Geser Khan, in another version he is the Emperor of India. But to Geser Khan is attributed quite an elaborate myth. It tells about the birthplace of the beloved hero. In a romantic way are described his wife Bruguma, his castle and his conquests, which were always for the benefit of humanity. Quite simply a Horpa will tell you about a palace of Geser Khan in the Kham province, where the swords of his innumerable warriors were used instead of beams. Singing and dancing in the honor of Geser Khan, Horpa offers to procure one of these inconquerable swords. Sands and stones are around, but still the idea of inconquerability is living.

In Europe when you hear about a city of a robber-conqueror you think that perhaps you have something of the old tales of Spain or Corsica. But here, in the desert, when you hear that your next stop shall be before the walls of the city of the famous Ja-lama, the bandit of Central Gobi, you are not a bit astonished. You only look over your arms and ask what kind of an attire is most suitable for this encounter: European, Mongolian or Sartian. During the night you hear dogs barking, and your men say calmly: "Those are the dogs of the men of Ja-lama. Ja-lama himself has already been killed by the Mongols, but his band has not scattered as yet. During the night, in the red flames of the bonfires you can again see the ten fingers. Some stories about the awe-inspiring Ja-lama and his cruel companions are being told. How he stopped big caravans, how he took many people as captives and how hundreds of these involuntary slaves worked upon the construction of the walls and towers of his city which gave life to the solitude of Central Gobi. It is told in what battles Ja-lama was victorious, what supernatural powers he possessed, how he could give most terrorizing orders and they were executed at once. How, following his orders, ears, noses and hands of the disobedient ones were cut off, and the living witnesses of his terrible powers were set to go free.

In our caravan there are two, who knew personally Ja-lama. One is a Tsaidamese, who was fortunate enough to escape from captivity. The other is a Mongolian lama, an experienced smuggler, who knows all secret paths in the desert, paths unknown to any one else, and hidden streams and wells. Was he not at one time the co-worker of Ja-lama? He smiles:

"Not always was Ja-lama a bad man. I have heard how generous he could be. Only you had to obey his great forces. He was a religious man. Yesterday you saw a big white suburgan on the hill. His prisoners were ordered to put these white stones together. And whoever was protected by him, could cross the desert quite safely."

Yes, yes, probably this lama had something to do with this late illustrious bandit. But why should a simple bandit build a whole city in the desert?

In the first rays of the sun we saw a tower and part of a wall behind the next sandy hill. A party of us, with carabins ready, went to explore the place, because our caravaneers insisted that some of the men of Ja-lama might be lurking behind that wall. We remained and looked through our field glasses, but after half an hour George appeared on the top of the tower and this was the sign that the citadel was empty. We went to inspect this city and found that only the spirit of a great warrior could have outlined such a building plan. Around the citadel we saw many traces of yurtas, because the name of the Ja-lama attracted many Mongols, who came to be under his protection. But later they scattered, having seen, in the Mongolian bazaars, the gray head of their former leader on a spear.

Probably Ja-lama dreamt to live long in this place, because the towers and walls were solid and his house was spacious and well defended by a whole system of walls. In an open field of battle the Mongols could not conquer him. But a Mongolian officer came to his place, apparently for peaceful negotiations. And the old vulture, who always penetrated into all sorts of ruses, was this time blind. He accepted this mission and the bold Mongol came, carrying a large white hatik in his hands, but behind the hatik a Browning was ready. Thus he approached the ruler of the desert and while transmitting to him the honorable offering, shot him straight through the heart. Really, everything must have been dependent on the strong hypnotic power of Ja-lama, for, strange to say, when the old leader fell dead, all his followers were at once in great commotion, so that quite a small detachment of Mongols could occupy the citadel without a battle. Behind the walls we could see two graves. Were they the graves of the victims of Ja-lama, or, laying to rest in one of them, was there the decapitated body of the leader himself?

I remember how in Urga I was told a long striking story about the speculations which arose regarding this head of Ja-lama. It was preserved in alcohol and so many wanted this peculiar relic, that after changing many hands the "relic" disappeared. Did it bring luck or sorrow to its possessor? Nobody knows the real psychology of Ja-lama, who was graduated in law in a Russian university and afterwards visited Tibet, being for some time in personal favor of the Dalai-Lama. One thing is evident, and that is that his story will complete the legend of Gobi and for many years it will be magnified and adorned with the flowers of fantasy of Asia. For long times to come the ten fingers will be in the air in front of bonfires. The flames of the bonfires are glowing.

But there are moments when the fires of the desert become extinct.

They are extinguished by water, whirlwind and fire.

Studying the uplands of Asia one is astonished at the quantity of accumulated loess. The changeability of the surface gives the biggest surprises. Often a relic of great antiquity appears washed up almost to the surface. At the same time an object of considerably recent times appears covered up with heavy accumulated layers. During the study of Asia, one has especially to consider surprises. Where are those gigantic streams which carried on their way such quantities of stone and sand, completely filling ravines and changing the profile of the entire district. Maybe all these are only catastrophes of long ago.

The sky is covered with clouds. In the neighboring mountains in the direction of Ulan-Davan, at night, a strange dull noise constantly fills the space. And not once, or twice, but for three whole nights, you awaken and hear this incomprehensible symphony of nature and you do not even know, is it friendly or hostile? But in these vibrations there is something attracting and compelling; you to listen attentively.

A gray day begins. Small rain. During the daily noises you do not discern this mysterious tremor of the night. People are busy with the customary tasks. Their thoughts are directed towards the usual perspectives of the near future. They are ready to sit at their usual dinner on the shore of a tiny stream, around which live peaceful marmots.

But the wonders of Asia are coming suddenly. Through a broad chasm, from the mountain tops a current rushes onward. Suddenly it overflows the high banks of the stream. It is no longer a stream, but a gigantic stormy river. It attacks a big area. Yellow, foaming waves full of sand catch the tents and whirl them away like the wings of butterflies. From the depths of the waves the stones are leaping to your very feet. It is time to think of saving oneself. Horses and camels, sensing danger, themselves rush up the mountain. From the distant Mongolian yurtas that stand in the valley, cries are heard. The current fills and demolishes strongly made yurtas. What can withstand this power? The tents are destroyed, many things are carried away. The current rushes through, transforming all into a slimy swamp. Twilight and a cold unfriendly night and as cold a morning.

The sun lights up a new site. The stream has settled already in new banks. Before us there lay lifeless, sloping hills, newly created by the power of the stream. Our things, during one night, became deeply imbedded in the new soil. Digging up some of them you imagine the formation of stratas of Asia. What surprises they present for an investigator, when really the prehistoric is mixed with the almost contemporary. The fires, extinguished by the stream, slowly begin to burn anew the dry branches and roots.

Not only water extinguishes the fires, but the great fire itself destroys these peaceful milestones.

The steppe is burning. Local people hurry to depart. And you rush away from these dangerous parts. Horses feel the danger equally strongly and tense their ears, harkening to the whirling, rumbling noise. The yellow wall, covered with black rings of smoke, is moving on. What an unheard-of noise and what leaps of flames.

Looking at the wall you recall how Mongolian Khans and other conquerors of Asia used to light up the steppes deciding thus the destiny of battles. But of course the fiery element sometimes turned against the creators of the fire themselves. Your fellow traveler measures the distance between the flames and you with calm Mongolian eyes and talks quietly, as of the most usual thing: "I think that we will succeed in departing in time. We have to reach that mountain" - and he points to a far-off hill.

The next morning you observe the burned steppe from the mountain top. All is black, all has changed. And again the layers of dust shall come and cover the black carpet. But you see smoke on the next mountain. What is it? A Mongol explains to you - there under the ground coal is burning and has burned for many months. Thus calmly speaks the Mongol of the destruction of his own treasures.

Likewise the whirlwind extinguishes the bonfires. After midday a gale begins. The Mongols cry out: "Let us stop, otherwise we will be carried away by the wind." Sand and stones fly in the air. You are trying to hide behind the boxes of the caravan. In the morning it appears that you stand on the very shore of a lake.

Various are the miracles of the desert.

And other fires, not the bonfires, are glowing in a far distance. They are yellow and red. From these mysterious sparks complicated structures are created. Look, there are cities in red sparks, some are rising as palaces and walls. Is that not a gigantic sacred bull glowing in red sparks? Are there not, in the far distance, several windows sparkling and inviting the travelers? From the darkness near you big black holes are emerging, like an old cemetery some ancient flat stones surround you. Under the hoofs of horses something strong and firm rings out like glass.

The Tsaidam guide says severely: "Walk, all of you. One after the other, without turning from the path. Caution!" But he does not explain the reason for caution and he does not want to go first. And the other Mongolian lama also does not wish to walk in front.

Some danger is lurking near. One hundred and twenty miles we walk steadily without a halt. There is no water for the horses. In the early dawn we see that we are going over a rather thin crust. One could see through the holes in it the black bottomless salt water. These are not the slabs of the cemetery but sharp precipitants of the salt. Maybe they can also become tombstones for those who carelessly fall into the gaping black pit. What metamorphoses took place in these regions? Flaming castles disappeared in the rays of light. But when this peculiar seeming cemetery ended, we saw again around us yellow rosy sands. Then came a story. Once upon a time a big city stood on this site. The inhabitants of the city were prosperous and lived at ease surrounded by great wealth. But even silver gets dark when not used. So the accumulated treasures have not been used in a proper way. And good principles of life were forgotten. But there is justice, even on our earth and all nefarious things are to be destroyed, when the great Patience is exhausted. With cries and screams, in fire, this city suddenly plunged down and the sea filled this gigantic cavern. A great deal of time passed. And again the sea was covered with salt, but this site still remains uninhabited. All places, where some injustice has been manifested, will remain uninhabited.

And the guide asks you with a mysterious look: "Perhaps during the night you have seen some strange lines in the darkness?" One of our fellow travelers whispers: "Is it not a story of Atlantis? Is not Poseidon revealed in this legend?" But the guide continues: "Some of the people of this city, the best ones, have been saved. An unknown shepherd came from the mountains and warned them of the coming disaster. And they went to the caves. If you want, you may go once to these caves. I will show you a stone door which is tightly closed. But we do not know how to unlock it."

"Probably you also know some directions, where are the sacred frontiers, which you dare never to cross?"

"Yes, only those who are called can enter these boundaries. There are some signs indicating these forbidden regions. But even without visible signs you can feel it, because every one who approaches, will feel a tremor in his whole body. A hunter was sufficiently strong to cross this boundary. He has seen there some miraculous wonderful things, but he was senseless and he tried to speak about the hidden matters, and therefore he became dumb. With sacred matters we must be very careful. Everything revealed before the destined date involves a great calamity."

In the distance some shiny white peaks are emerging. They are the Himalayas! Not so high they seem to be because we ourselves are on heights. But how white they are! They are not mountains, but realms of snow. That is the Everest - says the guide.

Nobody as yet ever ascended this sacred treasury of snows. Several times "pellings" tried to overpower this mountain. And some of them perished in the effort. And others had many hardships. This mountain is predestined for the Mother of the World. Its summit must be pure, unviolated and virgin. Only She, the Mighty, She can be there. The silence guarding the world.

The bonfires are glowing. Best thoughts are accumulating round the flames. In the far desert thousands of pigeons are living about the sacred massar old tombs. As holy messengers they are flying far around and inviting the travelers under the hospitable roof. Around the bonfires glimmer their white wings. The light in the desert.

Near the stream, over the very precipice, the silhouette of a horse becomes faintly visible in the mist. And something, so it seems, glitters strangely on the saddle. Perhaps this is a horse that has been lost by a caravan. Or maybe this horse has thrown off its rider whilst jumping over an abyss. Or perhaps this is a horse left behind because he was weak and without strength, and he now looks for his master.

So speaks the mind, but the heart remembers other things. The heart remembers how from the great Shambhala, from the beautiful mountain heights, at a destined hour, there will descend a lonely horse and on its saddle instead of the rider there will shine forth the jewel of the world: Norbu-rinpoche - Chintamani - the miraculous stone, preordained to save the world.

Has not the time come? Does not the lonely horse bring us the Jewel of the World.

Ganto, 1928.

GODS OF KULUTA

Sometimes it would seem that all the strange countries of Asia have already been described. We have admired the curious tribe of the Todas. We have been amazed at the sorcerers of the Malabar coast. We have already heard of the Nagas of Assam and of the extraordinary customs of the Veddas of Ceylon. The Veddas and Paharis of Northern India are always pointed out as most unique tribes.

Although many articles have already been published about the Northern Punjab, where an incomprehensible conglomerate of ancient hill tribes are massed together, yet the remote hillmen have been touched so little by civilization, that the inquisitive observer constantly finds interesting new material.

The mixture of ancient Rajputs, Singhs with Nepalese and Mongoloid hillmen has produced quite an individual type, which also produces a peculiar religion - a combination of Hinduism and Buddhism.

The sacred Kulu valley lies hidden on the border of Lahoul and Tibet, forming the most northern part of Punjab. Whether this was Aryavarsha or Aryavarta is difficult to say. But the most significant names and events have gathered in this beneficial valley. It is called the Silver Valley. Whether in winter, when the snowy cover sparkles, or in spring when all the fruit trees are covered with snowy-white blossoms, the valley equally well merits this name.

In this ancient place they have their three hundred sixty gods. Among them also is Gotama Rishi, dedicated to Buddhism, which is known to have been here for ages. There is also Akbar the Great, whose statue is in the Malana temple, and all teachers and heroes who by sword or spirit won great battles.

Deoban, their sacred forest, is entangled with century-old trees. Nothing may be destroyed in the silence of the protected grove. Even leopards, bears and jackals are quite safe in this abode of the god. People say that some of these protected trees are over a thousand years old and some even two thousand. Who has counted their age? Who knows their beginning? And their end is not near, so powerful are the unembraceable trunks and roots.

Equally ancient are the deodar trees round the Maha-devi temple in Manali. Heavy boulders, stones resembling huge monuments, are scattered all over the mountain-slopes of the Himalayas. Near the temple are seeming altars, built of stone. Here the gods are said to meet during the spring festivals. In the darkness inside the temple rises a rock, washed by a prehistoric stream. Was it here that Manu compiled the first commandments for the good of mankind?

On the mountain slope above every village can be seen a comb of ancient giant pine trees or deodars. These are all places sacred to the three hundred sixty gods of the glorious Kulu valley, or as the ancient people called it, "Kuluta."

These places were marked by the Indian pundits, by old Tibetans, and by the famous Chinese traveler of the seventh century, Hsuan-tsang.

In Kulu valley, even up till now, disputes are settled by the prophet priest. In the sanctuaries of temples are untold sanctities, which the human eye is not allowed to see. The guardian of a temple enters the sanctuary only rarely and always blindfolded, and carries out one of the sacred objects to an initiate, for a brief moment.

The people of the mountain nest, Malana, speak an incomprehensible language and nobody has as yet clearly defined this dialect. They live their own lives, and only rarely do their elected representatives descend into the valley to visit the temples of the god Jamlu. In high black cone caps, with long ear-pieces, and in homespun white garments these mountain hermits tread the snowy narrow paths.

During the New Year of India, the entire Kulu valley celebrates the festival. We were told that the goddess Tripura-Sundari had expressed the wish to visit us. The triumphal procession of the goddess, of her sister Bhu-tanta and the god Nag, arrived. In front of our house stood a long row of multi-colored banners. Further away was a multitude of drums, pipes and bent brass horns. Farther on, in finely ornamented costumes, dancing all the way, with bent sabers, came the priests, gurs, kadars and local festival dancers. On the broad terrace the procession halted. Every one of the three palanquins of the gods was covered with silver and golden masks. The music roared, songs were chanted, and they began a wild war-like sword-dance. Like Caucasian hillmen or sword-bearers of Kurdistan, the sons of the ancient militant valley madly but gracefully whirled round in dance.

Then an old Brahmin priest appeared. He took two sabers from the young dancers ... as if a miracle had happened, the bent old priest suddenly became full of life, and like a warrior leaped about in a wild sacred dance. The curved sabers flashed. With the back of the saber blade the old man inflicted on himself imaginary symbolical wounds. It seemed as if he would gash his throat. Then with an unexpected movement the bare steel was run between the open mouth . . . was this an old man, or a youth masked in a gray beard?

All this was unusual. But the most unusual was to come. The dancers calmed down. The musicians stepped aside. The palanquins of the goddess were borne upon the shoulders of the men, but the men who carried them did not touch the poles with their hands. On the contrary, the palanquins seemed to push them about, and, as if drunk, they staggered around, led by an unknown power. They began turning around with the palanquins on their shoulders. Suddenly the palanquin seemed to rush at a chosen person propping itself up with the end of the poles against his chest. He shuddered, became pale, and his entire body shook. ... In a transformed voice he shouted out prophecies. But the goddess also desired to speak through another. Again the palanquin moved around in a circle. And again some one was chosen and endowed. It was a pale youth with long black curls. Again the blunt look of the eyes, the chattering teeth, the trembling body and the commanding proclamation of prophecies. The New Year had been honored. The procession lined up again and returned by the steep hilly path to the temple, where drums were to thunder till long after midnight and where the dancers would again whirl round in sacred war dances.

It is good when the gods of Kulu are gracious.

What do the inhabitants of Kulu valley like most? Dancing and flowers. We visited another sword dance. Skilfully the sword blades whizzed through the air and around in a semi-circle danced a row of colorfully dressed men, arm in arm, singing drawling songs, accompanied by drum-beats and large kettle-drums. On rich stretchers, under an ornamented canopy, sat Krishna with a blue face and in gold brocaded garments. Next to him sat Radha, and in front was a small Kali, her face black, like a Nubian, with a long, red, outstretched tongue attached to it. The children who represented the gods sat up very seriously, with an understanding of their nomination. And round stood the crowd - a mixture of many nations: Paharis, Tibetans, Hindus, Ladakis and many other types of hillmen with strange faces. All this seemed to carry me back to the American Southwest Pueblos, where, during the festivals, we saw similar rows of people with their arms interwoven, who represented rain clouds, the harvest, and hunting - everything that harasses and delights the people who live in contact with nature.

During our travels, we heard much of every manner of god. We saw how the Chinese punish their gods, drown them in the river, cut off their hands and feet and deprive them of their dignity. The Samoyeds either anoint their gods with fat or flog them. In short, all sorts of things may happen even to gods. But, that in our times, a legal contract should be made with a god such as is done in Kulu still seems a novelty. In the Bible we read of covenants made with gods, but of course, this was without government revenue papers. But here in Kulu valley the gods are very close to life and they base all their decisions according to the up-to-date laws of the country. Here I have before me a contract between a private individual and the god Jamlu, concerning the water supply. Such written contracts with gods I have never before seen. Everything becomes modern and even gods sign contracts on revenue paper.

But not only do contracts with gods occur in Kulu, but even the fairy tale of the Coq d'Or. Before me is a deed of sale of an ancient fortress and there is a special clause that the previous owner retains his right to a quarter part of a golden cock, buried on these grounds. The tale of the Coq d'Or! . . .

The gur, priest of the gods, is the most revered person in all Kulu. He is all clad in white, in a homespun woolen mantle, with a small cap on his black and gray hair. His nose is aquiline and he has sparkling deep-set eyes. His legs are also covered with white.

The gur is seated on a rug, and having completed the burning of his incense, he gives every one of us a flower as a sign of the grace of the gods.

The gods are very satisfied, he informs us, We did not offend them. On the contrary we have even collected their images near our house, bringing them from an old ruined temple. There is the statue of Juga-Chohan on horseback, there is also the goddess Kali, the Rishi Kartik Swami Nansigang, Parbati and several images of Narsing, the protector of this place.

"Tell us, gur, have you seen Narasimha?" we ask him. "We heard that many people have seen the protector of these regions."

Before the gur had time to answer, a Hindu school teacher, who was present, replied:

"Certainly many of us have seen Narasimha. The old Rajah, who became the protector of this valley, wanders at night-time near his former castle and along the mountain paths. All your servants here have seen how on a moonlight night, a tall, majestic figure with a long staff has descended the mountain and disappeared under their very eyes. ... I have myself seen Narasimha twice. Once in this very house. The protector entered my room at night, and touching me, wanted to tell me something. But it was so sudden that I became frightened and the vision disappeared. Another night I returned by the mountain road from the castle homeward. And I met the protector himself, who said: 'Why walk so late when everybody already sleeps?' You can ask Capt. B. and the wife of the planter L. They both know of apparitions of Narasimha."

And the old gur, chewing his thin lips, said:

"I have seen Narasimha. And also the goddess. She came to me as a small child and blessed me for my initiation as gur. I was very young at the time. At the gates of the temple I imposed a fast on myself and sleeplessness for seventy-two hours. And in the morning after these hours had passed, an unknown little girl came to me. She was about seven years old, dressed in superb robes, as if for a festival, although it was an ordinary day. And she said to me: 'Your task is fulfilled. Go and act as you decided!'"

The gur has told us much about the great local Rishis: the gods in the valley live in prosperity. They have plenty of property and land. Without their sanction nobody is allowed to fell a tree. The gods visit each other as guests. Many people have seen the gods traveling. Sometimes they fly, sometimes they walk with great leaps propping themselves on sticks. Of course, besides that, several times every year they have triumphal processions with drumbeats and trumpets as accompaniment. In the store houses of the temples are hidden rich garments, pearls, gold and silver masks - all attributes of the gods.

The wife of the planter L. told us that indeed, staying once overnight at the Naggar castle, she was awakened by a noise in the neighboring room and on the threshold a white figure appeared of medium height, but she became terribly frightened and the figure disappeared, making such a loud noise that two English ladies, sleeping next door on the other side, became very much frightened. And with the same noise the figure moved along other parts of the castle. Mrs. L. also saw another interesting thing. On the maidan of Sultanpur she saw a dog running, pursued by a white transparent figure.

A Brahmin in a large yellow turban told us how the local gods help the inhabitants of Kulu valley.

"Some misfortune happened in the house of a man, and in terror he fled up into the mountains, seeking the help of the gods. Three days he spent on the rocks. Some one invisible brought him food and a voice said: 'You may return home.' And the man returned and found everything in order. Another man went into the mountains of Manikaran and secluded himself in meditation. An unknown yogi appeared before him and surrounded him with radiant light. From that day on all the inhabitants of the valley followed that man, paying him homage and trust. This was about fifty years ago. If you want to try to see a Rishi, go up into the mountains, to one of the mountain lakes. And in fasting and prayer stay there, and perhaps one of the protectors will appear before you."

Thus the people of Kulu regard their deities with familiarity. In this ancient place, as in Naggar, and in Manali, are gathered all the great names. The law-giver, the Manu himself, gave his name to Manali. The great Arjuna, in a miraculous way, laid a passage from Arjuna-gufa to Manikaran, where he went to the hot springs. After the great war, described in the Mahabharata, the Pandavas came to Naggar and high above the Thava temple they built their castle, the remnants of which are still being shown. Here also in Kulu valley lived Vyasa, the compiler of the Mahabharata. Here is Vyasakund the sacred place of fulfilment of all wishes. In Bajaura, near the river Beas, stands a temple connected with the name of Geser Khan. Coming from the side of Ladak, the great hero here overtook his enemies and defeated them. On the same river Beas, called in history Hypathos, near Mandi, Alexander the Great, once stopped. A hill is shown there connected with the conqueror's name. On the top of the hill are some ruins.

Here also in the neighborhood lies the famous lake Ravalsar, the place where the great teacher Padma Sambhava stayed. Thousands of pilgrims visit this remarkable place, coming from beyond the mountain ridges of Tibet, Sikhim, Ladak and Lahoul, where Buddhism prospers. From Kulu came the famous propagator of Buddhism, Santa Rakshita. It has been ascertained that Kulu and Mandi are the sacred lands Zahor, which so often are mentioned in ancient records. Here after the persecution of the impious King Landarma were hidden the most ancient books. Even the place of these hidden treasures is indicated approximately.

In Naggar is shown the cave of the famous spiritual teacher Pahari Babu, who converted the cruel Rajah into leading a pious life. It is a lovely, quiet place, hidden among dense deodars and pine trees. A small brook gurgles and birds call to each other. A Brahmin guards the sacred cave, which has now been adorned by a Temple. The chief deity of this temple is an image of - as the Brahmin calls Him - Taranata. He brings the image out of the temple, and one cannot fail to recognize in it Tathagata, the Gotama Buddha - the Teacher. In this way the Hinduism of the hill Paharis has become blended with its predecessor - Buddhism. In other temples also one can see, besides Shiva, Kali and Vishnu, images of Buddha, Maitreya and Avolokiteshvara. And all these memorial images are reflected in the gathering of the three hundred sixty Rishis, the protectors and holders of this blessed place.

One cannot omit to mention that under the name of Trilokanath - Lord of the Three Worlds - in upper Kulu, as also in Chamba State and Lahoul, Avolokiteshvara is worshiped. This is confirmed by the typical aspects of the images.

On the border of Lahoul, which is also an ancient former Tibetan principality, on the rocks, are inscribed images of a man and a woman up to nine feet high. It is said that this was the height of the ancient inhabitants. It is curious, that in Bamiam, in Afghanistan, where there are also huge images on the rocks, these are also connected with a legend of the height of ancient giants.

The earthquakes in Kangra have destroyed many of the temples, but the memory of the people preserves the names of heroes and teachers. Here also are erected monuments of a different character, reminding one of things which might well be forgotten. In Mandi and in Kulu you can see big stone stelae like ancient menhirs, with some time-worn images. In close groups stand these granite blocks, hiding some secret. What is this secret? What memory do they recall? These memorials refer to all the generations of local rajahs, and show the number of their wives, who were buried alive together with the body of their deceased sovereign. This is the cruel custom, against which Akbar had already fought; sometimes this unifier of India rushed personally on his steed to prevent the cruel fate of the innocent women.

These stones speak of the past. But to the north of Kulu rise the white peaks of the main Himalayan range. Beyond them lies the road to Lahoul and Ladak and the main white giant is called Guru-Guri Dhar - the Path of the Spiritual Teacher. This conception unites all Rishis into a great whole, leading the way to the Heights.

In this Silver Valley the Great Shepherd called to life all living beings by the silvery sounds of his flute. He calls toward joy. And the apple-trees, pear-trees, cherry-trees and plum-trees respond in their enthusiasm of blossoming. The willow-tree opens its fluffy blossoms, apricot-trees turn lilac, the vigilant nut-tree unfolds in rich yellow, and as a healing nectar flows the aromatic sap of the deodars.

Under the apple-tree, covered with rose-colored blossoms, the eternal Krishna, on his silver flute, plays his divine songs of regeneration.

Naggar, 1929

KING SOLOMON

Legends of the Orient - how unexpected they are! And what modern thought they reveal to us. How stirring it is to feel, in the myths of the remote places of Asia, a concept so related to our own aspirations and to our own enthusiasms. In some legends, they tell of strange diseases now appearing and every Western physician will share the interest in the still-undiscovered processes of the human organism. The legends speak of underground rivers and one's mind follows the modern systems of irrigation and rejuvenation of the deserts. They speak about the hidden treasures yielded to humanity by nature. And you smile, looking at Asia's rivulets of oil and admiring the iron and copper mountains. It is as a fairy tale.

To-day the front pages of all our newspapers are devoted to the daring attempts to conquer space and air. And in the sandy deserts your guide, rhythmically plodding along on his camel, tells you of the flying apparatus of King Solomon!

In these old symbols you do not feel only out-worn superstition. No, there is a thought of beauty and a feeling for evolution. The best images are collected by the people around these beautiful possibilities and in the name of evolution.

Up till now, in the people's conception, King Solomon soars on his miraculous flying device over the vast spaces of Asia. Many mountains in Asia are crowned either with ruins or stones bearing the imprint of his foot or of his knees, as evidence of his long-enduring prayers. These are the so-called thrones of Solomon. The Great King flew to these mountains, he reached all heights, he left behind him the cares of rulership and here refreshed his spirit. The Mountain of Solomon, the hidden treasures of Solomon, the wisdom of Solomon, the mysterious power of the ring of Solomon, the seal of Solomon, with its power to discriminate between Light and Darkness - to whom else has Asia paid so much admiration and so much respect?

The greatest mysteries and fables are attributed to the name of Solomon. The hoopoe, considered the most occult of birds, is also linked by legend to King Solomon. The hoopoes guarded King Solomon's rest at the time of his great work. Returning from his labors, the King asked his birds what they desired as a reward. They replied: "Give us, O King, your golden crown. It is so beautiful and we have seen nothing more wondrous than yourself when you don the crown." The King smiled and said:

"But, my dear ones, my crown is heavy. How could you wish to take such a burden?"

However, the birds continued to beseech him for his crown and the King ordered his goldsmith to make miniature crowns, exact copies of his own, and these were set upon the heads of the birds. Only a short while after the birds came again to the King with their little heads drooping under their golden crowns. And they appealed to the King:

"O King! Free us of these crowns. You were right, in your wise warning. What can we know, we little ones? Can we know that behind the glitter and charm, there lie such burdens? Free us, O King!"

The King replied: "Now you see where your desire to take a burden upon yourself has led you. Let it be as you wish! The golden crowns will be removed - but you must wear a remembrance of your senseless yearning for a crown. From now on, you will wear a crown of feathers. These will not overburden you, but will only be a crown of the secret kingdom, that you knew when serving my work."

And so it came to pass that the hoopoe, the most occult bird, knowing many secrets, still wears a crown of feathers. And whenever this bird follows a caravan or boat, people say:

"This will be a fine voyage - the bird of King Solomon knows!"

Other animals also served the King. A Moslem who came to Kashmir with his caravan across the Afghan border, told us that even ants helped the Great Suleiman to build the temple. Beginning with great Jinns, the spirits of the air and of the fire, down to ants, all labored upon the building. And in ceaseless prayer, King Solomon controlled without interruption, the work of the forces of nature for the creation of the wonderful Temple. When the strength of the King began to fade and he knew that his time to pass into another world was near, he commanded the Jinns to complete the building without him, but the tempestuous elemental spirits replied that on earth they would agree to submit themselves only to him, but that without him they were freed.

Then King Solomon, strengthening himself spiritually and leaning on his staff, remained in the Temple, summoning all his powers to the task. Although at that moment his spirit departed, the body remained motionless and erect so that the tempestuous Jinns might not fly away. And no living being nor any Jinn knew that the spirit of the King had already departed, nor did they dare approach the motionless Ruler. But each one strained himself to the utmost to finish the building. And the Temple was completed, but the Ruler remained immobile. Who would dare to disturb him in his aspirations! But the smallest co-worker of the King - the ant - began to gnaw at the staff of the King until the wood, having been eaten through, the body of the King fell and all saw that his Spirit had departed. But the Great Temple remained!

But King Solomon is not a celestial ruler alone. He goes down to the people and, as other rulers of the East, he changes his garments and mixes with the crowd in order to penetrate all the secrets of their life. His ring with the miraculous stone, in which is laid the foundation of the World, King Solomon left in safe-keeping with his wife, the Princess of Egypt. But cunning and artful was the Egyptian high priest, who, disguised as the King, took possession of the ring. And now the Ruler is condemned to many years of wandering, until Truth is restored.

Thus the people connect everything unique and extraordinary with King Solomon. He ascended the mountains, he descended under the earth, he met kings and he disappeared in the crowds of people.

In the old kingdom of the Uighurs, where now live the true-believing Moslems, the name of Solomon is linked with that of Alexander, or with the great Akbar. Sometimes one recognizes the same legends which adorned the King-Unifier of India:

"It seems that the same things are also told of Akbar, called the Great?"

The old gray-bearded Moslem in his green turban, who has fulfilled his pilgrimage of repentance to Mecca, bows his head low:

"Both Rulers were wise and great. When seeing two snowy mountains, how would you attempt to describe their differences? Both glitter under the rays of the sun. To approach them is equally difficult. Who would dare to ascribe to one Ruler what may be common to both? True, the Great Akbar did not leave the boundaries of India. He strengthened the land from within and we do not know what Jinns served him. Of King Solomon every one knows that he flew throughout the earth and that he learned the Truth in all lands and that he had even been on the far-off stars. But who can judge from below of two snowy summits? We even wear dark glasses to protect our weak eyes from their glitter."

Talai-Pho-Brang, 1928.

THE GREAT MOTHER

From the most ancient days, women have worn a wreath upon their heads. With this wreath they are said to have pronounced the most sacred incantations. Is it not the wreath of unity? And this blessed unity, is it not the highest responsibility and beautiful mission of womanhood? From women one may hear that we must seek disarmament not in warships and guns, but in our spirits. And from where can the young generation hear its first caress of unification? Only from mother. To both East and West, the image of the Great Mother - womanhood, is the bridge of ultimate unification.

Raj-Rajesvari - All-powerful Mother. To you, the Hindu of yesterday and to-day sings his song. To you, the women bring their golden flowers and at your feet they lay the fruits for benediction, carrying them back to their hearths. And glorifying your image, they immerse it in the waters, lest an impure breath should touch the Beauty of the World. To you, Mother, is dedicated the site on the Great White Mountain, which has never been surmounted. Because when the hour of extreme need strikes, there you will stand, and you will lift up your Hand for the salvation of the world. And encircled by all whirlwinds and all light, you will stand like a pillar of space, summoning all the forces of the far-off worlds!

* * *

Devastated are the ancient temples. The columns are cleft. And shells have pierced the stone walls.

At Goa the Portuguese ships landed long ago. Upon the high prows of the caravels, the images of the Madonna glittered with gold, and in her Great Name, cannon balls were fired into the ancient sanctuaries. By Portuguese cannon-balls the pillars of Elephanta were shattered! All for "La Virgin de los Conquistadores!"

In Sevilla, in the Alcazar, there is an old painting by Alexandro Fernandes, which bears this very title. In the upper part of the painting, in the radiance of the celestial light of clouds, stands the Holy Virgin with a benign smile, and under Her broad mantle is sheltered a host of conquerors. Below, there is a turbulent sea, covered by galleons, ready to sail far off to new soils. Perhaps these are the very ships which will destroy the sanctuary of Elephanta! And with a benign smile the compassionate Virgin regards the conquerors, as if She Herself rose with them to destroy alien acquisitions. This is no longer the threatening warning of Elijah the prophet, nor the Archangel Michael, the constant warrior. But She Herself, the Peaceful, is raised in the folk-consciousness for battle as if it befitted the Mother of the World to concern Herself with the deeds of human slaughter.

My friend is indignant. He says, "Look! This painting is certainly frank! In it is apparent the entire psychology of Europe. Look at the conceit! They make ready to lay siege to foreign treasure troves and to the Mother of God they ascribe protection for their deeds! Now compare how different is the mood of the East, where the benevolent Kwan Yin covers the children with her garment, defending them from danger and violence."

Another friend present defends the psychology of Europe, and also refers to certain paintings as true documents of the psychology of each era. He recalls how in paintings of Zurbaran or Holbein, the Holy Virgin covers all who come to Her with Her veil. Referring to the images of the East he recalls fearful horned *idams*, adorned with frightful attributes. He recalls the dance of Durga upon human bodies and upon necklaces made from skulls.

But the exponent of the East does not concede. He points out that in these images there is nothing of a personal element and that the seemingly frightful attributes are the symbols of the unbridled elements, and only by knowing their power may man understand that he can conquer them. The lover of the East pointed out how the elements of terror have been used everywhere, and that flames no less terrifying, nor horns less demoniac, were represented in the Hells of the frescoes of Orcana in Florence. All the horrors of the brush of Bosch or the austere Grunwald rival the elemental images of the East.

The devotee of the East cited the so-called Tourfan Madonna as being in his opinion an evolution of the Goddess Marichi, who after being a cruel devouress of children gradually evolved into their solicitous guardian, becoming the spiritual comrade of Kuvera, god of fortune and wealth. Recalling these benevolent evolutions and high aspirations, one may mention a custom still existing in the East. Lamas ascend a high mountain and, for the salvation of unknown travelers, scatter small images of horses which are carried far off by the winds. In this action lies a sense of benevolence and renunciation.

To this, the answer made to the lover of the East was that Procopius the Righteous, in self-renunciation, averted the stone-cloud from his native city and, on the high banks of the Dvina, always prayed for the unknown travelers. And it was also pointed out that in the West many saints like Procopius renounced their high worldly position for the good of the world.

In these deeds and in these orisons "for the unknown, for the unsung, for the unstoried" lies the same great principle of anonymity, and the realization of the transitoriness of incarnation which also is so attractive in the East.

The lover of the East stressed the fact that this principle of anonymity, or renunciation of one's temporary title, this inception of benevolent disinterested giving, has been carried to a much broader and higher level in the East. In this regard he reminded us that the art works of the East were almost never signed because the gift of the heart never needs its accompanying note. In response, however, his opponent recalled that all Byzantine, old Italian and old Netherland primitives, Russian ikons and other primitives were also unsigned, and that the beginning of personal signatures appeared much later.

The talk turned to the symbols of omnipotence and omniscience, and it was again evident that the identical symbols have passed through the most varied manifestations. The conversation continued, because life afforded inexhaustible examples. In answer to each indication from the East, an example from the West was brought forward. One recalled the white ceramic horses which, up to the present time, stand in circles in the fields of Southern India, and upon which, it is related, women in their astral bodies take their flights. In answer to this was placed forward the images of Valkyries and even the contemporary projection of astral bodies. It was then recalled touchingly how the women of India each day adorn the thresholds of their homes with some different design, the design of well-being and happiness; but at the same time it was remembered that the women of the West embroidered their many designs for the salvation of those dear to their hearts.

One recalled the great Krishna, benevolent shepherd, and involuntarily compared him with the ancient image of the Slav, Lel, a shepherd resembling in every way his Hindu prototype. One recalled the songs in honor of Krishna and the Gopis and compared them with the songs of Lel, and the choral dances of the Slavs. One recalled the Hindu woman on the Ganges and her torches of salvation for her family. And they were compared to the wreaths cast on the river during the celebration of the Trinity - a custom dear to all Aryan Slavs.

Remembering the conjurations and evocations of the sorcerers of the Malabar coast one could not overlook the very same rites of the Siberian Shamans, the Finnish witches, the clairvoyants of Scotland and the red-skinned sorcerers.

Neither the separation of oceans nor continents had affected the essence of the folk conception of the forces of nature. One recalled the necromancy of Tibet and compared it with the black mass of France and the Satanists of Crete...

By counter-opposing the facts, the exponents of East and West found themselves speaking about identical things: The seeming diversities became only various degrees of human consciousness! These two conversationalists looked at each other with astonishment - where was the East and where the West which one was so accustomed to contrast?

The third silent person present smiled, "And where is the boundary of East and West altogether? And is it not strange that Egypt, Algeria and Tunis, which are south of Europe in the general conception, are really considered as the Orient? And the Balkans and Greece, lying East of them are regarded as West?

I remembered then how walking on the San Francisco shore, with a professor of literature, we asked each other, "Where are we really - in the extreme West or the extreme East?" If China and Japan, in relation to the Near-East, Asia Minor, are considered as the Far-East, then, continuing the same line of argument - would not America, with her Incas, Mayans and Redskins, be considered as the Farthest East? What then can one do with Europe, which would then appear to be surrounded by "Easts" from both sides?

We recalled that during the time of the Russian Revolution, the Finns considered Siberia their own, giving as their reasons the tribal similarities. We recalled that Alaska almost touches Siberia, and the face of the Red Indians, compared with many Mongoloids, appears strikingly like an Asiatic face.

In this way it happened that for a moment all superstition and prejudices were laid aside by all adversaries, the exponent of the East spoke about the "Hundred-armed One" of the Orthodox Church, and the exponent of the West exalted and admired the images of the many-armed all-benevolent Kwan Yin. The exponent of the East spoke with reverence about the gold-embroidered garment of the Italian Madonna and felt the deep penetration of the paintings of Duccio and Fra Angelico, and the lover of the West gave reverence to the symbols of the many-eyed Omniscient Dukhar. They remembered the All-Compassionate. They remembered the multitudinous aspects of the All-Bestowing and All-Merciful. They remembered how correctly the psychology of the people had conceived the iconography of symbols and what an enormous knowledge lay hidden at present under the dead lines. There, where preconceptions disappear and prejudice is forgotten, appears a smile!

And as if freed of a great burden, they spoke of the Mother of the World. With affection they recalled the Italian cardinal, who was in the habit of advising worshipers, "Do not overburden Christ the Saviour with your request, for He is very busy; better address your prayers to the Holy Mother. She will pass your prayers on to whomever is necessary."

They remembered how a Catholic priest, a Hindu, an Egyptian and a Russian once set out to investigate the origin of the Sign of the Cross and how each searched for a meaning to suit his own purpose but how they all arrived at the same unifying meaning.

They remembered attempts that flashed through literature, intended to identify the words "Christ" and "Krishna," and again they remembered Iosaph and Buddha. And since at that moment the benevolent hand of the Mother of the World turned away all prejudices, the conversation could run in peaceful tones.

And instead of sharp contradiction, advocates of East and West turned to a creative reconstruction of images.

One of the speakers recalled the story of a pupil of Ramakrishna, who cited the great reverence given to the wife of Ramakrishna, who, according to Hindu custom, was called Mother. Another likened the meaning of the word Mother to the conception of "Materia matrix."

The images of the Mother of the World, of the Madonna, the Mother Kali, the Benevolent Dukhar, Ishtar, Kwan-Yin, Miriam, the White Tara, Raj-Rajesvari, Niuka - all these great Images, all these Great Self-Sacrificing Entities flowed together in the conversation as a benevolent Unity. And each of these in his own tongue, but comprehensible to all, pronounced that there should be not division but construction. All pronounced that the day of the Mother of the World had come, when Supreme Energies would approach our Earth, but that because of wrath and destruction, these energies, instead of the predestined creation, might result in disastrous catastrophes.

In the smile of Unity all became simple. The aureole of the Madonna, so odious to the prejudiced, became a scientific physical radiation - the aura, long since known to humanity.

The symbols of to-day, so poorly interpreted by rationalists, from being regarded as supernatural, suddenly became accessible to the research worker for investigation. And in this miracle of simplicity and understanding, there became distinct the breath of the evolution of Truth.

One of the speakers said: "Here we now speak of purely physical experiments, but did we not begin with the Mother of the World?"

Then the other took from a drawer of his writing desk a slip of paper and read it: "A Hindu of to-day, graduated from many universities, thus addresses the Great Mother, Raj-Rajesvari Herself:

"If I am right, then Mother, Thou art all - The ring, the way, the dark, the light, the void, And hunger, sorrow, poverty and pain - From dawn to dusk, from night to morn and life and death - if death there be - All things art Thou.

If Thou art they, then hunger, poverty and wealth are only transitory shapes of Thine. I do not suffer nor enjoy For Thou art All, and I am surely Thou. If Thou art He, to mortals manifest, Then pass me through Thy Light to Him - The Truth. The only Truth - to us so dimly known in Thee. Then lash this mortal body as Thou wilt, Or embed in golden comfort rich and soft - I'll feel it not, for with Thy Light I'll know For Thou art He and I am Thou - The Truth."

And the third one added: "At the same time, on the other end of the world, people sing:

"Let us glorify Thee, Mother of Light!"

And the old libraries of China and the ancient central-Asiatic centers guard, since most ancient days, many hymns to the same Mother of the World.

Throughout the entire East and in the entire West there lives the Image of the Mother of the World, and deeply significant salutations are dedicated to this High Entity.

The Great Features of the Face are often covered and under the folds of this veil, glowing with the squares of perfection, may one not see the One Great Unifying Aspect, common to Them All!

Peace be to the World!

JOY OF CREATION

Is not our epoch one of the most significant? Are not the most wonderful discoveries approaching for our daily use? And are we not becoming familiar with some of the most subtle energies? Is it not a happiness, not only to know about these energies but also to be able to utilize them actually in life? Before our very eyes, everything is being transformed. We know already how to divide our energies between individuals and the millions. And we know where and how to reach millions and how to exercise our energy with the individual.

The boundaries of spiritual life are broadening. And the physical frontiers are becoming flexible and vibrating. The idea of East and West - the idea of the twain which never shall meet - is to our mind already a fossilized idea. We are already ashamed to believe that superficial walls can exist and can divide the best impulses of humanity, this impulse of creative evolution. And now before our eyes is the so-called West and the so-called East. Piercingly they look at each other. They examine every movement of each other. They can be the closest friends and co-workers.

The West can easily understand the principal ideas of the East and cherish the eternal wisdom which is emanating from that part of the world, from where, as a fact, all religions and all creeds originated. And the great East is following the Western discoveries, and values the achievements of these creative minds. They desire the products of civilization. I avoid the questionable expression "mechanical" - because to my mind nothing is mechanical, when we know that matter and spirit is Energy, and we, as well as our Far-Eastern friends, are ready to accept the benediction of progressive evolution. But life through ignorance is full of misunderstandings. They are not enemies.

There are no enemies of evolution - there are misunderstandings; misunderstandings of family; misunderstandings of sex; misunderstandings of age; misunderstandings of countries; of continents, of worlds. And only through open-minded constructive thought can we solve them; when we are thinking not of ourselves but of the future generations. I repeat that the East can be a close friend, a most skilled co-worker, but this billion of people can also easily become an enemy through a simple misunderstanding. Is it not a beautiful task for our generation to solve the problem of misunderstanding, if we feel the oneness of the great Energy? The same single impulse of betterment, of upliftment, of creation, is the same for all humanity. With the same hand we may give our benediction and with the same hand we may commit murder. I do not believe in so-called varying conditions. One condition exists for all humanity - the mutual language of the heart, and with this language you destroy all misunderstandings because you are acting in full sincerity. You can proceed, you can surmount, because you know for what unifying purpose you are working. We speak so often about eternal peace, but from whence emanate the wars? From misunderstanding. And if we are so skillful in our discoveries, is it not also a most important discovery to determine how to solve the misunderstanding through the language of the heart? I am not speaking about anything metaphysical. After forty years of activity I affirm that everything is not ephemeral but if every energy can be discovered, measured and weighed, then in the same way our thought is also a tangible emanation. And the power of thought, without any metaphysical powers, can approach in the most friendly way each misunderstanding. Hence, from the highest, from the future, we can approach our reality. And our optimism is not the product of far-off dreams, but the result of studying dozens of countries and of approaching widely differing peoples, with quite varied psychologies. And after all, in spite of all variations, they are one. And the language of the heart, the language of love, is also one.

If the sign of malice is the minus, sharp as a piercing dart, then the sign of love is the plus, the eternal flaming cross which from immemorable time enlightened the consciousness and uplifted life.

Amidst the glaciers of the Himalayas, someone is coming from the summits. In his hands he carries a chalice. Whence has he come? And where shall he disappear in the cliffs, this silent, lonely pilgrim? Such are the unforgettable memories of the Himalayas. The carriers of the messages of Shambhala are recalling the links between the great traditions of the past and our aspirations of the future. He is the messenger of Rigden-jyepo, ruler of Shambhala, ruler of the future, ordainer of the coming achievements of humanity, who sends his messengers throughout the world.

From many nations have come these messengers. In devotion and reverence they bring the sacred message of the coming evolution.

What is the message? Throughout the world billions of hearts are beating. What shall link them together? In my article "Beauty the Conqueror" is the thought that the best way to approach an unfamiliar dwelling is in song. Not by night, not with covered face.

Unbound art, unprejudiced science, bring the smile of understanding. The great traditions of past and future, the high teaching which emanated from the eternal heights make it possible to approach the sacred spaces in cooperative understanding. Then hearts are opened and an immense blessed work is at hand.

Not war, not hatred, but the best constructive concepts shall bring to all the world the messengers of Rigden-jyepo, the ruler of Shambhala. The iron birds predestined by Buddha are already in flight, peacefully demolishing the conventional boundaries. In beautiful, scientific rays of Agni Yoga, evolution is knocking at the door. The messengers of Rigden-jyepo are speeding and blessed discoveries are bringing light and benediction to all mankind.

In twenty-five countries we have seen countless hearts who consider art, beauty, knowledge as the most unifying powers. Truly it is cause for the greatest enthusiasm to perceive how so many different peoples consider beauty and knowledge as the great motive power which set the stones for the coming progress.

Why have we the right to regard beauty and knowledge as real motive powers? For a moment imagine the history of humanity without the treasures of beauty and knowledge. For a moment erase from our memories the majestic images of Egypt and Assyria. Let us forget the beauty of the Gothic primitives, the enchantment of Buddhist glory and classic Greece. Let us disrobe the epics of heroes and rulers of the garb of beauty. How crude would the pages of history remain! Truly, not a single heroic achievement, not one constructive victory may be imagined without the sense of the beautiful. The form of life is the synthesis of evolution. Is it not inspiring to realize that the evolution of humanity culminates in beauty? A beautiful conception of life is growing in America and throughout the world. Humanity begins to realize that the *summa summarum* of art and knowledge is the noblest crest of the nations.

When we begin to think about something constructive, upbuilding, forward looking, not accidentally to our minds come both the lofty towers of North America and the majestic outlines of South America.

Not occasionally, on the sites of the most ancient culture, are growing the seeds of new peaceful conquests and erection. Pan-America stands as a balance of Asia. It is most instructive to learn how, on the places of the most ancient achievements, are growing the new flowers of human attainments. Even from the cold-blooded scientific point of view, we are already accustomed to speak about currents, rays and emanations. These emanations of culture fertilize the soil, and who knows, perhaps they provide the real enthusiasm of this constructive spirit.

As yet I have never been in South America. But in spirit I feel this physically unseen friendship and mutual understanding. From where does it come? Well, some have asked me if the root of our family comes from Spain, because a branch of our family is in Barcelona. Perhaps such pan-human feeling of advancing, searching and construction is deep in every human heart. Perhaps the sacred sense of adventures, in search of the great solutions, came into my being from the first years of consciousness, when as hunters, we traveled for days and days through the immense forests of Russia, certainly not with the idea of killing but with the comradeship of nature as our guiding star.

When we studied old structures of India, China and Tibet, our first comparison was with the remnants of the Mayan culture. And in my old article, "Joy of Art," I could not finish this conception with anything other than with some reference to the ancient Mayas. In this way, that which was most ancient and most beautiful came to mind.

Just now I look upon a ring from Asia, with an inscription of the coming Age of Maitreya. And I cannot forget how one lady, who has studied the remains of Yucatan, recognized the same inscription there, with the meaning of the Union of Fire. Now comes the solution in this formula: Our spiritual, unseen friendship and devotion - does it not come from the all-pervading element of fiery space? In these all-pervading beneficial flames our hearts are enlightened and through them we recognize our friends, sincerity and co-workers.

Is it not the Union of Fire which now illumines the builders of Pan-America? And Asia when she speaks of the Blessed Shambhala, about Agni Yoga, about the Teaching of Flame, knows that the holy spirit of flame can unite the human hearts in a resplendent evolution.

In March, 1914, I exhibited a series of paintings in which was previsioned the coming war; now I have been happy to bring for the Americas the visions of Asia - the Agni Yoga, the Teaching of Flame, the same conception outlined by the wisdom of the old Yucatan wise men, the Union of Fire.

Again some of the Great Truth comes to us and this Truth expresses the gathering of all the bearers of fire of the heart, to enlighten the world with peaceful and beautiful labor. The abstract conception of love can again be transmuted into benevolent action, because without constructive action love is dead. But in the New Era nothing is dead, everything lives, uplifted by enlightened labor and enthusiasm. When I hear beautiful songs of Spain and South America, they reveal for me the great East.

Where is East and West? After Asia you come to Greece and you feel the wisdom of the East; you reach Italy and the same wise romance penetrates you; Corsica, Spain - in all these places is something still of the Great East. And the banners of Ferdinand and Isabella are close to Moresque ornaments. You reach New Mexico and in the spaces of this beautiful country again sounds for you the anthem of the East; and you know that in Mexico, in Yucatan, in all castles of South America, the same note of great romance, of great vision, of great wisdom, shall be everywhere.

I do not diminish either west, nor south, nor north, nor east - because in practise these divisions are non-existent. And the entire world is divided only in our consciousness. But when, with this consciousness, the fire of space penetrates, then is created the Union of Fire, and the Fire of Enthusiasm is unconquerable.

With this holy banner, we can reach most beautiful lands and we can awaken ancient cultures for new achievements and for new splendors.

On one of the most ancient Druidic images of far-off Mongolia I have seen in the hands of a stony giant a flaming chalice. These beginners of the great migrations remembered also about the holy spirit of flame. And certainly this inextinguishable torch could bring them through all expanses of Asia, Europe and across all oceans. In the antiquities of Yucatan is inscribed the ancient commandment about fire. In the name of this unifying, great wise symbol, I greet you, my unseen friends of South America.

What a joy it is to see again the towers of New York! How often in the deserts of Asia and especially in Tibet we remembered the skyscrapers, the Indian Pueblos and the ancient cities of Italy and Spain! The many-storied Tibetan buildings evoke images of skyscrapers. The labyrinthian clay walls of the usual Asiatic home recall the Pueblos of New Mexico and Arizona. The monasteries, proudly clinging to the summits, resemble the old eagles' nests of Italy. When I saw once more, the towers of New York, I recalled the joyous exclamations which the photographs of these strongholds of human achievement evoked in Asia.

Never did we hear more enthusiastic admiration at the sight of postcards and photographs of New York than in the towns and nomad camps of Central Asia. The dwellers of clay-houses and yurtas tore these souvenirs out of each other's hands and exclaimed: "This is the land of Shambhala!"

What more can a son of Asia say than this, his most sacred conception, in which are united all his hopes and aspirations? In prayers, Asia awaits Shambhala - this new era of mankind; and therefore each comparison with Shambhala is indeed the highest praise.

The inhabitants of Asia added: "America is the chichab over all countries!" And chichab means protector.

How many reproductions of the towers of New York have remained in the desert! And they are kept in the sacred corners, where the most revered objects are collected.

In the remote yurtas of Asia's deserts, President Hoover is the giant Savior of starving peoples. Ford is considered as a symbol of motive power. The Mongols consider American Indians their lost relatives. All our latest discoveries are regarded by the East as signs of the era of Shambhala. Millikan's cosmic ray, Einstein's relativity, Teremin's music from the ether, are regarded in Asia as signs of the evolution of human consciousness, confirmed by Vedic and Buddhist traditions and the teachings of Shambhala. According to these ancient teachings, the forties of our century are regarded as the era of cosmic energies and expanded consciousness.

These touching memories rose before me, when I again saw the towers of New York. And among the old friends I noticed so many new strongholds, which rose during the last five years. Such unarrestable creation gives real joy. When thirty years ago I arranged the first exhibition of paintings of artists of the United States in Russia, I expressed the firm opinion that Art in this great country would expand widely as all its vigorous activities.

Eight years ago, summarizing the position of art in America, I wrote an article "Collectors," observing what colossal conquest of cultural principles had been achieved by America. In 1923, leaving for my long Central-Asiatic expedition, I could hear of the growth and art-movements in America, only from casual newspapers and clippings from magazines, or from letters, which rarely reached us. Of course it could be felt that the cultural-artistic and scientific work grew each year and that new co-workers and admirers entered. But returning to America and now stepping again into its cultural life, one must express sincere astonishment!

In the history of human achievement, America is an unique example of prodigious progress. Not bound by conventionalities and old forms, without prejudice, America built its life with the powerful hands of toil. Naturally, the question of material existence and life had first to be settled. Then attention was turned toward problems of technical necessity and social life.

Having built the foundation of civilization, America began to aspire toward the firm establishment of cultural principles. Knowledge and Beauty became imperative requirements in the life of the young country. In most unexpected ways, meriting great admiration, grew the conquest of Art and Science. The quality of production advances still higher, and this is always a sign of the growth of national creative genius. The wide industrial growth reaches the poesy of creation.

Business life becomes enriched with the true friends of the human spirit - books and creations of art. All the steps of culture lead, as they should, beyond national limitations. And another sign of true culture is the fact that what is gained is not kept for personal use alone. The treasures of achievement are open to society as a whole.

The most striving and vital forces of all nations have gathered in America, contributing to the gigantic growth of this country. By voluntary, faithful and sometimes even by anonymous hands, huge American institutions are built.

May the light, which has illumined human hearts, shine for all. These results of voluntary and conscious human aspirations are highly instructive. In them can be measured the specific value of the co-workers for the general good. It is also most interesting to note how American organizations and institutions are developed. One notices not limited specialization, but a broad outlook, unfrightened by prejudiced opinion. One can feel that there is liberality and true good will not hindered by chauvinism, nor by fossilized systems.

It is most valuable to confirm for oneself, how the artistic creativeness of America has expanded, and how in addition to the old known art patrons, many new and vigorous collectors welcome this creation.

There is a saying: "Flowers do not grow on ice." Artistic and scientific achievements, museums and schools, are necessary. But the essential thing is a broad response of the nation. It is necessary to have those loyal enthusiasts, who understand that striving toward culture is the highest duty and joy of humanity.

One notices that often colossal sums are paid for art works and for books. Is this folly on the part of the collectors or something which results from conviction? When humanity will become conscious that spiritual and creative genius are the highest achievements, and the milestones in the histories of nations, the prices of these works will become a special indicator. In our life, how can we compensate works of creative genius? With money? But only recently humanity had occasion to convince itself what a changing and precarious thing money is. Therefore the price for works of creative genius is very relative. If we hear that somewhere high prices are paid for products of culture, then we know that culture is valued there. And this fact will remain on the pages of history as the witness of the growth of this nation.

The people can value highly the results of labor of the creators of culture. The people can wish to have in their midst the best specimen of creative genius of bygone epochs. One must welcome every striving of thought in this direction. In life everything is relative; mistakes may occur, but it is the direction of thought which is valuable. At present, when old forms are changed so rapidly and vigorously into new, the direction of people's thoughts is extraordinarily precious.

America follows in its development the path of true progress. During the last few years America stands alone in the creation of new museums, schools, societies, agencies, lectures, theaters... One is amazed at the colossal resources of the country which absorbs this rich stream of creative power. Opportunity is also found both for the development of a national art, as well as for collecting the treasures of the whole world. There are multitudes of people who welcome artistic events and show response.

Reading the pages of history of the most cultural nations, we are glad to note when the people turned toward values of science and beauty. This always occurred at moments of the nation's ascendance. Now having returned from a long journey, it is admissible for me to express my joy at the artistic and scientific growth of America's consciousness. This is the very thing in which I had faith. When I was accused of excessive idealism I asserted that, on the contrary, my beliefs were real and practical. And I was right, because it is just the most practical people who show signs of high valuation of cultural achievements.

Creativeness is in its essence real and affirming. A creative nation cannot limit its activity to narrow civilized paths. The expanded consciousness leads to a synthesis of the whole life. The highest impulses and decisions become real and convincing.

America animates the consciousness by broad decisions; in her generosity she wants to have the best objects and wants to hear the best words and aspires to make of her children future creators. The statesmen of America and her finest leaders are at the same time collectors of most varied forms of creative genius.

There, where leading men, and where great men, devote the best part of their mind to creative products - there also the masses express the same aspirations and will think in the same direction of true evolution.

Unbound by prejudice or superstition, people want to have not only a convenient, but also a beautiful life. No small habits hang behind the back of the builder of life. And his success will be followed by new progress and even the very obstacles will become levers of energy.

I trust the Secretary of Labor, Mr. James Davis, will not mind if I quote a passage from his letter, sent to the Roerich Museum on March 24, 1929, on the occasion of the laying of the cornerstone:

"As we grow in material wealth it is all the more necessary to keep alive our knowledge and love of the beautiful things of the spirit and mind, otherwise we are in danger of gaining the world and losing our souls. It will gratify every high-minded American who has the destiny of his country at heart, to see enlisted in this preservation of culture and intellect a body of people and an organization as influential, vigorous and enthusiastic as yours.

"In whatever direction your endeavors reach out, I wish you a great and ever-growing success through the years. After all, while this is a time of danger to things of the spirit, that time has also its propitious aspect. Civilization attains its highest peaks only after it has amassed the material means with which to recompense the artist and the thinker. These ample means we have. The need is only for leaders to call forth this wealth and see that it is expended in cultural advancement. You and your associates are such leaders. May you build not only this building but a great new movement among us toward a love of the beautiful, and may both endure to serve our people and bring more light into their lives."

These are indeed remarkable lines from the mind of a statesman! There, where people think in such ways, there the land is on the path of happy achievements.

When you come from the mountains and deserts, where the best culture lies hidden in the shadow of centuries, the extraordinary growth of artistic and scientific work in America deeply amazes you and brings you great joy. The conquest of culture does not pass unnoticed. It creates that finesse of thought - the creative imagination and the ability to perceive the new wave of progress.

The era of happy attainments is predestined for America. As the rapid movement of a big ship attracts everything movable, so also is the irresistible development of America joined by the highest and the best.

New York, 1929.

GURU - THE TEACHER

Once in Finland I sat on the shores of Lake Ladoga with a farm lad. A middle-aged man passed us by and my small companion stood up and with great reverence took off his cap. I asked him after, "Who was this man?" And with special seriousness, the boy answered, "He is a teacher." I again asked, "Is it your teacher?" "No," answered the boy, "he is the teacher from the neighboring school." "Then, you know him personally," I persisted. "No," he answered, with astonishment... "Then why did you greet him with such reverence?" Still more seriously my little companion answered, "Because he is a teacher."

Almost a similar incident happened to me on the banks of the Rhine near Cologne. Again with joyous amazement I saw how some young man greeted a school-teacher. I recall the most uplifting memories of my teacher, Professor Kuinjy, the famous Russian artist. His life story could fill the most inspiring pages of a biography for the young generation. He was a simple shepherd boy in the Crimea. Only by incessant, ardent effort towards art, was he able to conquer all obstacles and finally become not only a highly esteemed artist and a man of great means, but also a real Guru for his pupils in the high Hindu conception.

Three times he tried to enter the Imperial Academy of Fine Arts and three times he was refused. The third time, twenty-nine competitors were admitted and not one of them left his name in the history of art. But only one, Kuinjy, was refused. - The council of the Academy was not of the Gurus, and certainly was short-sighted. But the young man was persistent and instead of uselessly trying, he painted a landscape and presented it to the Academy for Exhibition. And he received two honors without passing the examination. From early morning he worked. But at noon he climbed up to the terraced roof of his house in Petrograd where, with the shot marking each midday, thousands of birds completely surrounded him. And he fed them, speaking to them and studying them as a loving father. Sometimes, very rarely, he invited us, his disciples, to this famous roof. And we heard remarkable stories about the personalities of the birds, about their individual habits and the ways to approach them. At this moment, this short, stockily built man with his leonine head, became as gentle as Saint Francis. Once I saw him very downcast during the entire day. One of his beloved butterflies had broken its wing and he had invented some very skilful means to mend it, but his invention was too heavy and in this noble effort he was unsuccessful.

But with pupils and artists, he knew how to be firm. Very often he would repeat, "If you are an artist, even in prison you shall become one." Once a man came to his studio with some very fine sketches and studies. Kuinjy praised them. But the man said, "Well, I am unfortunate because I cannot afford to continue painting." "Why?" compassionately asked Kuinjy. And the man said that he had a family to support and he had a position from ten to six. Then Kuinjy asked him piercingly, "And from four to ten in the morning, what do you do?" "When?" asked the man. Kuinjy explained, "Certainly in the morning." "In the morning, I sleep," answered the man. Kuinjy then raised his voice and said, "Well, you shall outsleep your entire life. Don't you know that from four to nine is the best creative time? And it is not necessary to work on your art more than five hours daily." Then Kuinjy added, "When I worked as a retoucher in a photograph studio, I also had my position from ten to six. But from four to nine, I had quite enough time to become an artist."

Sometime, when the pupil dreamed about some special conditions for his work, Kuinjy laughed, "If you are so delicate that you have to be put in a glass case, then better perish as soon as possible, because our life does not need such an exotic plant." But when he saw that his disciple conquered circumstances and went victoriously through the ocean of earthly storms, his eyes sparkled and in full voice, he shouted, "Neither sun nor frost can destroy you. This is the way. If you have something to say, you will be able to manifest your message in spite of all conditions in the world."

I recall how once he came to my studio on the sixth floor, which at that time was without an elevator, and severely criticized my painting. Thus, he left practically nothing of my original conception, and in much uproar he went away. But in less than half an hour, I heard again his heavy steps, and he knocked on the door. Again he climbed the long steps in his heavy fur coat, and panting, said, "Well, I hope you shall not take everything I said seriously. Every one can have his point of view. I felt badly when I realized that perhaps you took too seriously all our discussion. Everything can be approached in different ways, and really, truth is infinite."

And sometime in the greatest secrecy, he entrusted one of his disciples to bring some money anonymously from him to some of the poorest students. And he entrusted this only when he was completely confident that this secret was not revealed. It happened once that in the academy, revolt against the Vice-President Count Tolstoy arose, and as no one could calm the anger of the students, the situation became very serious. Then finally at the general meeting came Kuinjy, and every one became silent. Then he said, "Well, I am no judge. I do not know if your cause be just or not, but I personally ask you to begin your work, because you have come here to become artists." The meeting was ended at once, and every one returned to the classrooms, because Kuinjy himself had asked. Such was the authority of the Guru.

From where his conception of real Guruship, in the refined eastern understanding arose, I do not know. Certainly in him it was a sincere self-expression, without any superficial intention. This was his style and in the sincerity of this style, he conquered not only as artist but also as a powerful vital type, who gave to his disciples the same broad inflexible power to reach their goal.

Long afterwards in India, I saw such figures of Gurus and I have seen the faithful disciples who without any servile obeisance, but rather with great enthusiasm of spirit, venerated their Gurus with that full sensitiveness of thought which is so characteristic of India.

I have heard a lovely story about a small Hindu who found his Teacher. He was asked; "Is it possible that the sun would grow dark to you if you would see it without the Teacher?"

The boy smiled, "The sun would remain as the sun but in the presence of the Teacher twelve suns would shine to me."

India's sun of wisdom shall shine because on the shores of a river there sits a boy who knows the Teacher.

In the same teachings of India it is said: "Blessed are you, India! Because you alone have guarded the concept of Teacher and disciple. The Guru can dispel the attack of sleep. The Guru can raise up the drooping spirit. Woe to him who has dared to lay claim falsely to some one as his Teacher and who lightly pronounces the word Teacher, while honoring himself! Verily flowers that spirit which understood the path of ascent; and he fails who drooped in duplicity of thought.

"One may ask a Hindu boy if he wishes to possess a Guru. No word is needed in reply. Because the boy's eyes will express desire, striving and devotion. The fire of Aryavarta will glow in his eyes. The stream of the Rig-Vedas will glow on the slopes of the mountains.

"Who can describe in words the entire procession of the Teachers? Either there is the realization of it, as a serpent of knowledge or lacking this, there is darkness, sleep, obsession. There is no need to terrify but one should tell all who have approached Yoga. "Your support is the Teacher. Your shield is devotion to the Teacher. Your destruction is indifference and duplicity."

"He who smiles alike on friends and foes of the Teacher is unworthy. He who does not betray the Teacher, even by reticence when speech is needed, may enter the step of the threshold."

Thus speaks Agni Yoga which foresees the splendid future of humanity if humanity will master its possessions.

Not only in India but in the whole East we have the same conception of the Teacher. Certainly in many Eastern countries, now the storm of the coming civilization roars. You can imagine how many misunderstood conceptions may harm this supreme feeling of the hierarchy of knowledge. So many symbols and beautiful signs are swept away through such superficial mechanization of life. And still, even in the most remote places you can distinguish this instinctive understanding of Guruship. How can one express in the customary words the dignity, the noble understanding, of accepting the chalice of knowledge?

The sense of conviction is the most hidden quality of high creation in art. The most skilful criticism cannot explain why we believe and cherish many of the Italian and Netherland Primitives, why so much in modernism cannot be explained and still convince. This quality'of inner rhythm, of inner contacts of color and line, this hidden law of dynamic proportions cannot be fully expressed by the conventional phrases; and still they exist and they govern our creations. Certainly there exists some inexpressible conceptions. I remember how in one philosophical society one of the most important contemporary poet-philosophers ceased to attend the meetings. And when he was asked the reason, he shrugged his shoulder, "Because they speak of the unspeakable." And still everything unspeakable and unconvincing in common conversation, becomes clear and convincing under the benevolent touch of the master. Every art creation is as a dynamo, charged with infinite uplifting energy, a real generator of enthusiasm. Certainly this is comparative. Some of the creations are charged with this primary energy for one hour, and some for eternity - this is relativity. But the most uplifting moment is when the Teacher and the disciples sometime even in a half-silent way are touching this fountain of the Beautiful. Every one knows how often, without a word, one rhythmic gesture covers the abyss of misunderstanding. And is it not the misunderstanding that we have to conquer? Verily, where can there be evil, especially in the vast field of Beauty? Certainly there can be ignorance and ugliness born of ignorance; there can be the offspring of ignorance, misunderstanding. In our day, of so much confusion and corruption, when the spirit is bound with heavy chains of conventionality, how we need to watch each beginning of misunderstanding, and how we must extinguish these ugly parasites which grow so rapidly and pervert the most beautiful garden into a jungle of refuse.

And who can heal this disease of ugliness? Only the Teacher. In what aspect can he act? As a Guru. Is it so difficult and so inapplicable for our day?

I am happy to speak to Teachers. All of you know better than any one else the inner meaning of the sacred conception of Guru and teacher. If we all know it, one may ask then, why speak of it? But we also know the strength of prayer; we know the meaning of incantation, we know the charm of chants; then, let us know what is the meaning of Guru, what is the meaning of a teacher of life and still in the best moments of our life we shall repeat this high conception. Because in repeating it, we are cementing the space with the best stones of the future.

Evolution, young generation, future heroes of a country, future martyrs of wisdom and beauty, we know our responsibility before you! With every affirmation of the Beautiful and of the highest, we are creating the quality of the future life. Is it possible to create this future life and some happiness for the coming generations, without joy and enthusiasm? And from where does this flame of enthusiasm, of incessant creative ecstasy come? Certainly it comes from the flowers of the field of beauty. If we shall take from life all expressions of beauty, we shall change the entire history of humanity.

The teachers of art - are they not the teachers of synthesis? In old teachings, art and beauty are explained as the highest conceptions. You recall the story from the Upanishads, when during the search for Brahma, Brahma was found in the smile of the beautiful Ima. Lakshmi, the Goddess of Happiness, is the most beautiful goddess. Ugliness really has nothing to do with happiness. In our service to art and to beauty, is it not the most gratifying and uplifting feeling, to know that we serve the real synthesis of the coming evolution? And in spreading the seeds of beauty we are creating the beautiful life. Where and how can we amalgamate all the strange formations of the conglomerate of contemporary life? Verily, verily, only the veil of beauty can cover and magically transform the grimace of misunderstanding into the enlightened bliss of real knowledge. Not only for Teachers but for the pupils, also, life is so complicated. How to find the balance between the healthy body and the ugliness of exaggerated sports? How to compromise the highest grace of the dance with the dullness and conventionality of some of the extreme modern dances? How to pacify the noble striving for music, with some of the disturbing jazz of to-day?

How to connect the highest spiritual factor with the lowest state of matter? Are these antitheses quite unapproachable, or can a true unifying basis be found, not alone in dreams and thought but here also on earth? Modern thought demands facts. The most calculating positivism, wants to draw heaven to earth. Let us recall what one of the most positive contemporary philosophers, Prof. Nicholas Lossky, in his remarkable studies, *"Matter and Life,"* says: "After all that has been stated, it is not difficult to give a conception of the most characteristic traits of the teaching of matter in the system of organic world perception. If matter originates in the highest existence - existence, which is also capable of creating forms of reality other than matter - then the laws of material nature are conditioned to a far greater extent than physicists admit. Naturally one doubts, that the formula of each law should permit a wide range of conditions, most of which are even still uncrystallized; thus the law is not always an exact one, in other words it is usually too broad.

"For instance, to expect that under all conditions, water will boil at one hundred degrees is to take the complexity of nature too little into account; in addition to the necessary temperature, a normal atmospheric pressure is needed, chemical purity of the water, etc. The physicist recognizes these incalculable additional conditions, but as he deals with matter alone he has become accustomed to think of all these conditions as being purely physical.

"Therefore in establishing the most common laws, such for instance as the law of the indestructibility of matter, when the question concerns the general nature of matter, the physicist presumes that there is no need to include the additional details into the formula of the law. Even further, to the mind of such a physicist, who tends towards materialism, any limitation of this law seems inconceivable. And truly, so long as we remain in the domain of material processes, the annihilation of matter through physical means, pressure or impetus, seems inadmissible and even inconceivable.

"But let us presume that matter is not the only form of existence in nature, and further, let us presume that matter is something evolving, subject to the action of the highest principles of the elements, then the place of matter in nature becomes far less durable than the mind of a materialist considers.

"Thus it is not difficult to conceive also conditions when the annihilation of a particle of matter is also possible."

Thus we see that even in the conception of the most positivistic scientist is clearly expressed the relativity of matter. In this relativity is an open window for the highest conceptions. Let them approach our earth! Let them saturate the coming evolution not only as an external transfiguration but also as the evolution of the innermost being. The facts are needed but the understanding of these facts should be without hypocrisy and superstition. In the field of teaching it is a special joy to expel not only ignorance but that ugly offshoot of ignorance, superstition, and the freedom of discipline enters where ugly superstition is destroyed. The self-denying study of the facts open to us the highest degree of matter. The cosmic ray is no longer a fairy tale but has entered the laboratory of the scientist, and the scientific mind knows how many more rays and forms of energy can enter our life and can be applied for the upliftment of every hearth. The benevolent transfiguration of life is on the threshold; even more, it knocks on our portals because so many things may be distributed at once without delay. How many social problems can be solved without hostility, but with only one condition, that they be solved in a beautiful way. Well, we can evoke the energies from the space; we can enlighten our life with powerful rays, but these rays shall be beautiful - as beautiful as is the conception of evolution.

Our responsibility before The Beautiful is great! If we feel it, we can demand the same responsibility to this highest principle from our pupils. If we know that this is a necessity, as during an ocean storm we can require from our companions the same attention to the keenest demand of the moment.

We are introducing, by all means, art into all manifestations of life. We are striving to show the quality of creative labor, but this quality can be recognized only when we know what is the ecstasy before the beautiful; and this ecstasy is not that of a transfixed image, but this is motion, this is all-vibrating Nirvana, not the falsely-conceived Nirvana of immobility - but the Nirvana of the noblest and most intensive activity. In all ancient teachings, we have heard about the nobility of action. How can they be noble, if they are not beautiful? You are the teachers of art; you are the emissaries of beauty; you know the responsibility before the coming generation, and in this is manifested your joy and your invincible power. Your actions are the noble actions.

And to you, my young unseen friends, we are sending our call. We know how difficult it is for you to begin the struggle for light and achievement. But the obstacles are only new possibilities to create beneficent energy. Without battle, there is no victory. And how can you avoid the venomous arrows of dark enmity? By approaching your enemy so closely that he shall lack space even to send an arrow. And after all, nothing enlightened may be achieved without travail. So, blessed be labor! And blessed be you, young friends, who are walking in victory! The Gurus of the past and future are with you.

Gurus, to you, my invocation and my reverence!

AZILOTH BOOKS

Aziloth Books publishes a wide range of titles ranging from hard-to-find esoteric books - *Parchment Books* - to classic works on fiction, politics and philosophy - *Cathedral Classics*. Our newest venture is *Aziloth Books Children's Classics*, with vibrant new covers and illustrations to complement some of the world's very best children's tales. All our imprints are offered to the reader at a competitive price and through as many mediums and outlets as possible.

We are committed to excellent book production and strive, whenever possible, to add value to our titles with original images, maps and author introductions. With the premium on space in most modern dwellings, we also endeavour - within the limits of good book design - to make our products as slender as possible, allowing more books to be fitted into a given bookshelf area.

We are a small, approachable company and would love to hear any of your comments and suggestions on our plans, products, or indeed on absolutely anything.

Aziloth Books, Rimey Law, Rookhope, Co. Durham, DL13 2BL, England.
t: 01388-517600 e: info@azilothbooks.com w: www.azilothbooks.com

PARCHMENT BOOKS enshrines the concept of the oneness of all true religious traditions - that "the light shines from many different lanterns". Our list below offers titles from both eastern and western spiritual traditions, including Christian, Judaic, Islamic, Daoist, Hindu and Buddhist mystical texts, as well as books on alchemy, hermeticism, paganism, etc..

By bringing together such spiritual texts, we hope to make esoteric and occult knowledge more readily available to those ready to receive it. We do not publish grimoires or any titles pertaining to the left hand path. Titles include:

The Prophet	Khalil Gibran
The Madman: His Parables and Poems	Khalil Gibran
Abandonment to Divine Providence	Jean-Pierre de Caussade
Corpus Hermeticum	G. R. S. Mead (trans.)
The Holy Rule of St Benedict	St. Benedict of Nursia
The Confession of St Patrick	St. Patrick
The Outline of Sanity	G. K. Chesterton
An Outline of Occult Science	Rudolf Steiner
The Dialogue Of St Catherine Of Siena	St. Catherine of Siena
Esoteric Christianity	Annie Besant
Thought-Forms*	Annie Besant
The Teachings of Zoroaster	Shapurji A. Kapadia
The Spiritual Exercises of St. Ignatius	St. Ignatius of Loyola
Daemonologie	King James of England
A Dweller on Two Planets	Phylos the Thibetan
The Imitation of Christ	Thomas à Kempis
The Interior Castle	St. Teresa of Avila
Songs of Innocence & Experience*	William Blake
The Marriage of Heaven & Hell*	William Blake
The Secret of the Rosary	St. Louis Marie de Montfort
From Ritual to Romance	Jessie L. Weston
The God of the Witches	Margaret Murray
Kundalini – an occult experience	George S. Arundale
The Kingdom of God is Within You	Leo Tolstoy
The Trial and Death of Socrates	Plato
A Textbook of Theosophy	Charles W. Leadbetter
Chuang Tzu: Daoist Teachings	Chuang Tzu
Practical Mysticism	Evelyn Underhill
Tao Te Ching (Lao Tzu's 'Book of the Way')	Tzu, Lao
The Most Holy Trinosophia	Le Comte de St.-Germain
Tertium Organum	P. D. Ouspensky
Totem and Taboo	Sigmund Freud
The Kebra Negast	E. A. Wallis Budge
Esoteric Buddhism	Alfred Percy Sinnett
Demian: the story of a youth	Hermann Hesse

* with colour illustrations

Obtainable at all good online and local bookstores.
View Aziloth Books' full list at: www.azilothbooks.com

CATHEDRAL CLASSICS hosts an array of classic literature, from erudite ancient tomes to avant-garde, twentieth-century masterpieces, all of which deserve a place in your home. All the world's great novelists are here, Jane Austen, Dickens, Conrad, Arthur Machen and Henry James, brushing shoulders with such disparate luminaries as Sun Tzu, Marcus Aurelius, Kipling, Friedrich Nietzsche, Machiavelli, and Omar Khayam. A small selection is detailed below:

Herland	Charlotte Perkins Gilman
With Her in Ourland	Charlotte Perkins Gilman
Frankenstein	Mary Shelley
The Time Machine; The Invisible Man	H. G. Wells
Three Men in a Boat	Jerome K Jerome
The Rubaiyat of Omar Khayyam	Omar Khayyam
A Study in Scarlet	Arthur Conan Doyle
The Sign of the Four	Arthur Conan Doyle
The Picture of Dorian Gray	Oscar Wilde
Flatland	Edwin A. Abbott
The Coming Race	Bulwer Lytton
The Adventures of Sherlock Holmes	Arthur Conan Doyle
The Great God Pan	Arthur Machen
Beyond Good and Evil	Friedrich Nietzsche
England, My England	D. H. Lawrence
The Castle of Otranto	Horace Walpole
Self-Reliance, & Other Essays (series1&2)	Ralph W. Emmerson
The Art of War	Sun Tzu
A Shepherd's Life	W. H. Hudson
The Double	Fyodor Dostoyevsky
To the Lighthouse; Mrs Dalloway	Virginia Woolf
The Sorrows of Young Werther	Johann W. Goethe
Leaves of Grass - 1855 edition	Walt Whitman
Analects	Confucius
Beowulf	Anonymous
Plain Tales From The Hills	Rudyard Kipling
The Subjection of Women	John Stuart Mill
Silas Marner	George Eliot
The Rights of Man	Thomas Paine
Progress and Poverty	Henry George
Captain Blood	Rafael Sabatini
Captains Courageous	Rudyard Kipling
The Meditations of Marcus Aurelius	Marcus Aurelius
The Social Contract	Jean Jacques Rousseau
War is a Racket	Smedley D. Butler
The Dead	James Joyce
The Old Wives' Tale	Arnold Bennett

Obtainable at all good online and local bookstores.
View Aziloth Books' full list at: www.azilothbooks.com

AZILOTH BOOKS — CHILDREN'S Classics

Aziloth Books is passionate about bringing the very best in children's classics fiction to the next generation of book-lovers. We believe in the transforming power of children's books to encourage a life-long love of reading, and publish only the best authors and illustrators. With its original design and outstanding quality, our highly successful list has something to suit every age and interest. Titles include:

The Railway Children	Edith Nesbit
Anne of Green Gables	Lucy Maud Montgomery
What Katy Did	Susan Coolidge
Puck of Pook's Hill	Rudyard Kipling
The Jungle Books	Rudyard Kipling
Just So Stories	Rudyard Kipling
Alice Through the Looking Glass	Charles Dodgson
*Alice's Adventures in Wonderland**	Charles Dodgson
Black Beauty	Anna Sewell
The War of the Worlds	H. G Wells
The Time Machine	H. G .Wells
The Sleeper Awakes	H. G. Wells
The Invisible Man	H. G. Wells
The Lost World	Sir Arthur Conan Doyle
*Gulliver's Travels**	Jonathan Swift
Catriona (David Balfour)	Robert Louis Stevenson
The Water Babies	Charles Kingsley
The First Men in the Moon	Jules Verne
The Secret Garden	Frances Hodgson Burnett
A Little Princess	Frances Hodgson Burnett
*Peter Pan**	J. M. Barrie
*The Song of Hiawatha**	Henry W. Longfellow
Tales from Shakespeare	Charles and Mary Lamb
The Wonderful Wizard of Oz	L. Frank Baum

*with colour illustrations

Obtainable at all good online and local bookstores.
View Aziloth Books' full list at: www.azilothbooks.com

www.ingramcontent.com/pod-product-compliance
Lightning Source LLC
LaVergne TN
LVHW051058080426
835508LV00019B/1944